D0098679

Books by DANIEL FORD

Three-Mile Island: Thirty Minutes to Meltdown
Energy Strategies (with Henry Kendall and Steven Nadis)
The Cult of the Atom

THE CULT OF THE ATOM

THE SECRET PAPERS OF THE ATOMIC ENERGY COMMISSION

DANIEL FORD

Simon and Schuster *New York*

Published by Simon and Schuster
A Division of Gulf & Western Corporation
Simon & Schuster Building
Rockefeller Center
1230 Avenue of the Americas
New York, New York 10020
SIMON AND SCHUSTER and colophon are trademarks of Simon & Schuster
Designed by Karolina Harris
Manufactured in the United States of America

10 9 8 7 6 5 4 3 2 1

Library of Congress Cataloging in Publication Data

Ford, Daniel F.
The cult of the atom.

Includes bibliographical references and index.
1. Atomic power—United States. 2. United States.
Atomic Energy Commission. I. Title.
TK9023.F67 1982 353.0087'22 82-10528
ISBN 0-671-25301-8

Portions of this book appeared originally in *The New Yorker.*

To Ann and Henry

Acknowledgments

THIS BOOK IS BASED on the tens of thousands of pages of U.S. Atomic Energy Commission internal documents I obtained using the Freedom of Information Act. My research, which began in 1971, has been carried out under the auspices of the Union of Concerned Scientists, and many people have contributed to it over the years.

The effort to gain access to sensitive A.E.C. files involved hundreds of Freedom of Information Act requests, as well as two major lawsuits. The lawyers who helped with this work were Thomas Arnold, Myron Cherry, George Deptula, Linda Donaldson, Mark Lynch, Anthony Roisman, and Ellyn Weiss.

In sifting through the voluminous A.E.C. archives and other source materials, I have been aided by John Abbotts, Rina Gentile, David Gottfried, Steven Sholly, and Lawrence Tye. Robert Pollard, a former A.E.C. safety engineer who joined the staff of the Union of Concerned Scientists in 1976, provided invaluable technical analysis of the safety problems disclosed in the government files. Henry Kendall of the Massachusetts Institute of Technology, the Chairman of U.C.S., with whom I first undertook the study of nuclear plant safety, contributed to the research on this book at every stage.

George Mazuzan, the historian at the Nuclear Regulatory Commission, offered helpful guidance to the source material, as did Richard Hewlett, the former chief historian of the A.E.C. and the Department of Energy. Joseph Felton of the N.R.C. records office processed my F.O.I.A. requests with impeccable courtesy.

The many scientists and officials interviewed for this book also deserve my grateful thanks, as do the friends and editors whose encouragement sustained me in the task of writing it.

CONTENTS

FOREWORD

THE UNITED STATES ATOMIC ENERGY COMMISSION, created by Congress in 1946, grew into a uniquely powerful, mission-oriented bureaucracy. One of its main goals, which it pursued with exceptional zeal, was the creation of a flourishing commercial nuclear power program.

By the late 1950s, the A.E.C. began to acquire frightening data about the potential hazards of nuclear technology. It decided, nevertheless, to push ahead with ambitious plans to make nuclear energy the dominant source of the nation's electric power by the end of the century. The A.E.C. proceeded to authorize the construction of larger and larger nuclear reactors all around the country, the dangers notwithstanding.

The A.E.C. gambled that its scientists would, in time, find deft solutions to all the complex safety difficulties. The answers were slow in coming, however. According to the A.E.C. secret files, government experts continued to find additional problems rather than the safety assurances the agency wanted. There were potential flaws in the plants being built, A.E.C. experts said, that could lead to "catastrophic" nuclear-radiation accidents—peacetime disasters that could dwarf any the nation had ever experienced.

Senior officials at the A.E.C. responded to the warnings from their own scientists by suppressing the alarming reports and pressuring the authors to keep quiet. Meanwhile, the agency continued to license mammoth nuclear power stations and to offer the public soothing reassurances about safety.

The nuclear-safety cover-up in the United States—the story of this book—can now be told in full as a result of information gathered from hundreds of Freedom of Information Act requests by the author and his colleagues at the Union of Concerned Scientists.

The nuclear power program, although championed ardently by the government, is now in a shambles—the victim of plant breakdowns, cost overruns, project cancellations, and rising public skepticism following the accident in 1979 at Three Mile Island. The secret papers of the A.E.C. expose the reasons for both the meteoric rise and catastrophic fall of the nuclear power program—the most ambitious, expensive, and risky industrial venture ever undertaken.

DANIEL FORD
Cambridge, Massachusetts
July 1982

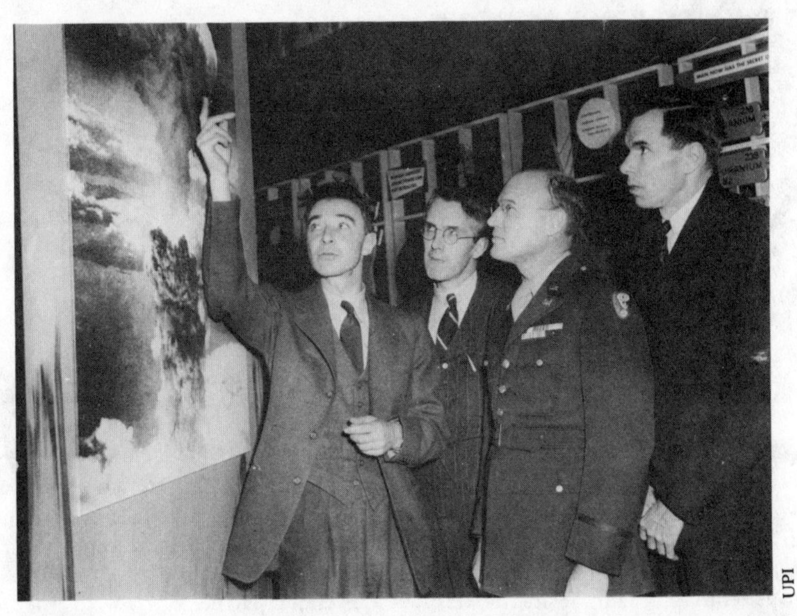

UPI

Leading scientists who served as A.E.C. advisers in the postwar years: physicist J. Robert Oppenheimer, left, and chemist Glenn T. Seaborg, right. Later, as A.E.C. chairman from 1961 to 1971, Seaborg became the number-one "salesman" for commercial nuclear power.

President Truman transfers control of the top-secret Manhattan Project to the new civilian Atomic Energy Commission in late 1946. The first A.E.C. chairman, David Lilienthal, is seated on the right.

UPI

UPI

Physicist Edward Teller, "father" of the H-bomb and chief safety adviser to the early A.E.C., worried about potentially "disastrous" nuclear-plant accidents. He concluded, however, that "the unavoidable danger . . . must not stand in the way of rapid development of nuclear power."

UPI

As a young A.E.C. lawyer, James T. Ramey wrote the unique government contracts that gave rise to the A.E.C.'s "friendly partnership" with the nuclear industry. Later, as a key congressional aide and then as an A.E.C. commissioner, he vigorously championed nuclear-plant construction.

Admiral Hyman Rickover pioneered the use of nuclear energy for submarine propulsion. His astonishing success opened the way for commercial nuclear power, but his insistence on quality control and meticulous attention to engineering details was often ignored by the civilian nuclear industry.

UPI

Lewis Strauss, a former Wall Street investment banker, served on the early A.E.C. and was named chairman of the agency by President Eisenhower. He prophesied that electric power from nuclear plants would become "too cheap to meter."

UPI

DANIEL FORD

The A.E.C. and the industry made broad promises to the public about the scope and success of their efforts to ensure nuclear-plant safety.

SAM SWEEZY

Professor Norman Rasmussen of M.I.T. headed the controversial "Reactor Safety Study" ordered by Schlesinger. He calculated that there was a greater danger to the public of being killed by falling meteorites than as a result of nuclear-plant accidents. The "arbitrariness" of some of his methods "boggles the mind," one independent review group later concluded. In 1979, the Nuclear Regulatory Commission repudiated Rasmussen's optimistic findings on nuclear-plant accident risks.

UPI

As criticism of A.E.C. safety claims increased in the early 1970s, A.E.C. Chairman James Schlesinger ordered a major "scientific" study to prove, once and for all, how unlikely serious accidents were. According to the A.E.C. plan for the study, "The report to be useful must have reasonable acceptance by people in the industry."

UPI

Joseph Hendrie, an A.E.C. official and later chairman of the N.R.C., rejected key recommendations from government safety experts because of the cost to the industry. He told staff safety reviewers, "Don't turn over new rocks."

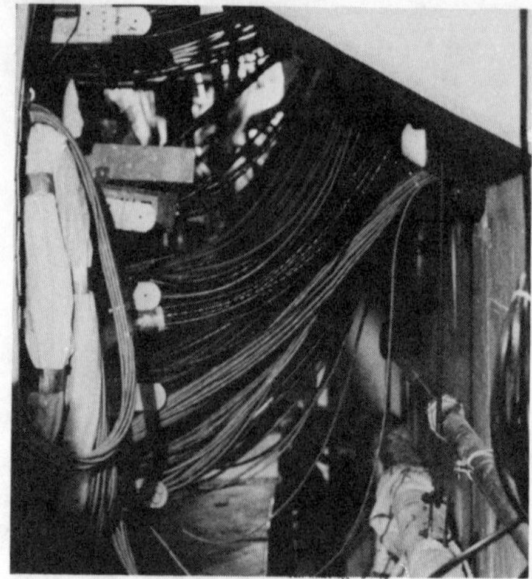

DANIEL FORD

The densely packed electrical cables at the Browns Ferry nuclear plant in Alabama caught fire on March 22, 1975, leaving the reactor perilously out of control for seven hours. A workman was using a lighted candle to check for air leaks in the wall at the right. Extensive warnings from A.E.C. experts about electrical-cable fires had been ignored.

Stephen Hanauer, a chief federal nuclear-safety adviser since 1965, has written hundreds of blunt internal memos on the government's neglect of major nuclear-safety problems. "Some day we all will wake up," he told his colleagues.

U.S. NUCLEAR REGULATORY COMMISSION

Members of the clean-up crew prepare to enter the reactor building at the accident-damaged Three Mile Island nuclear plant. The large new plant had been called "a scintillating success" that demonstrated nuclear power's "bright and shining" future.

UPI

PART ONE

HIGH PRIESTS

LATE ONE MONDAY NIGHT in January 1939, an excited young man walked the streets of Berkeley, California. Earlier that evening, at a seminar, he had heard astonishing news. In experiments just completed at the Kaiser Wilhelm Institute in Berlin, two chemists, Otto Hahn and Fritz Strassmann, had found evidence of "nuclear fission." The center of the uranium atom, its nucleus, they learned, could be split apart, literally broken in two. This was a very great surprise.

"It seems probable to me," Sir Isaac Newton wrote, "that God in the beginning formed matter in solid, massy, hard, impenetrable, moveable particles . . . so very hard as never to wear or break in pieces, no ordinary power being able to divide what God himself made one in the first creation."

Newton apparently was wrong. So, too, were the modern scientists who had dismissed the notion of atomic fission, though on less metaphysical grounds. In the early 1930s the Italian physicist Enrico Fermi had actually produced nuclear fission in his laboratory and hadn't recognized it. On the basis of theoretical calculations, Fermi had concluded that fission was impossible.

Some of the scientists at the weekly Berkeley seminar, which was given by the eminent physicist E. O. Lawrence, questioned the alleged discovery, but not the young chemist Glenn Seaborg. "I recall that at first the fission interpretation was greeted with some skepticism by a number of those present, but . . . I felt that this interpretation just had to be accepted," Seaborg said, many years later. "It is impossible to describe the excitement that this news produced in me . . . I walked the streets of Berkeley for hours turning over and over in my mind the import of that discovery."

The atomic nucleus is the storehouse for nature's most powerful forces, which would automatically be unleashed when the nucleus was opened up by fission. It seemed possible, therefore—as Albert Einstein wrote to President Franklin D. Roosevelt a few months later—that weapons of immense destructive power could be built from small amounts of uranium. It was also possible that a major new power source had been found. As he paced the streets of Berkeley, Seaborg's reflections were heightened by a strong, personal reaction to the news, "a combined state of exhilaration in appreciation of the beauty of the work [of Hahn and Strassmann] and of disgust at my inability to arrive at this interpretation despite my years of contemplation on the subject."

Glenn Theodore Seaborg had arrived on the Berkeley campus of the University of California in the fall of 1934. He was an extremely intelligent, ambitious, tall young man of twenty-two. He had been born in the little mining town of Ishpeming, on Michigan's upper peninsula, the son of Swedish immigrants, but his family had moved to southern California when he was a boy. In high school, an inspiring teacher introduced him to chemistry, which he then studied at U.C.L.A.—where he worked his way through school as a stevedore, apricot picker, and apprentice linotype machinist. By the time Seaborg entered graduate school at Berkeley, he had decided to pursue a career in chemistry. He was intent on finding a place for himself in the annals of science.

Seaborg received his Ph.D. in chemistry in 1937 and remained at Berkeley as a personal laboratory assistant to the great Berkeley chemist G. N. Lewis. His work was "completely outside the nuclear field," he recalls, but on his own he began to study the developments that were being made in that rapidly emerging science. According to one of his early associates, Seaborg had a good eye for where the "action" was, and it wasn't, at the time, in conventional chemistry. Seaborg devoured the papers that the world's leading nuclear scientists were producing—"I read and reread every article published on the subject"—and he enthusiastically discussed the latest developments with his Berkeley colleagues, often talking, he remembers, "in the postmidnight hours of the morning at the old Varsity Coffee Shop on the corner of Telegraph and Bancroft Avenues."

Of particular interest to the young scientist was the research of fellow Berkeley chemist Edwin McMillan. The universe has a fixed set of elements—such as hydrogen, oxygen, carbon, gold, and iron—out of which everything else is composed. The medieval alchemists had sought, unsuccessfully, to change one element into another, but McMillan was even more ambitious. He was trying to synthesize new elements that did not exist in nature. Since uranium was the heaviest known element, his approach was to bombard it with lighter particles to see if they would stick together with uranium to form something heavier. There were ninety-two known elements, and by the summer of 1940 McMillan had discovered "Element 93" and was looking for "Element 94."

"Since Ed McMillan and I lived only a few rooms apart at the Faculty Club, we saw each other quite often, and, as I recall, much of our conversation, whether in the laboratory, at meals, in the hallway, or even going in or out of the shower, had something to do with Element 93 and the search for Element 94," Seaborg said. War-related research was beginning, however, and McMillan left Berkeley to work on the development of radar at the Massachusetts Institute of Technology. Seaborg took over McMillan's research and continued the hunt for Element 94, for which McMillan already had derived some evidence. Within a few months, the work was completed.

On February 23, 1941, in an experiment that ran all night and well into the next morning, Seaborg and his co-workers got the "proof that what we had made was chemically different from all other known elements." The birth of a new element—which was named plutonium, after the planet Pluto—was a singular episode in the history of science. Burris Cunningham, who worked with Seaborg on the weighing of the new substance, has noted that "now, after all these years, it is difficult to recall the psychological impact of these events. Today alchemy is a thriving commonplace business. But at the time we, who had been brought up in an older tradition, saw it as a miracle and just a little bit difficult to believe in."

Plutonium was quickly proved to be more than a laboratory novelty. Five weeks later, on March 28, 1941, Seaborg and his collaborators showed that plutonium could be fissioned, a finding that gave immense practical value to the new element. Fissionable uranium is in very short supply, since the particular isotope of uranium which can be fissioned, known as U-235, is very rare. (Less than one percent of natural uranium is of this type, the remainder consisting of nonfissionable U-238.) Plutonium, on the other hand, could be produced in large quantities. (Plutonium is made, after all, when the abundant U-238 is enlarged and turned into Pu–239.) Plutonium, theoretically, could provide the fuel to sustain industrial society for tens of thousands of years.

The implications of plutonium were not lost on the young Glenn Seaborg, who shared the 1951 Nobel Prize in Chemistry for the discovery with Edwin McMillan. He recognized—indeed, became obsessed by—the historic significance of what he had done. "He had a tremendous sense of his own importance and a tremendous sense that he had come on the scene as sort of a scientific savior of the world," says John Gofman, one of Seaborg's graduate students at the time who was the codiscoverer with him, in 1943, of U-233. Seaborg ultimately "hung up his lab coat and devoted the rest of his career to promoting the use of plutonium," Gofman said in an interview, adding that he found this slightly puzzling "since McMillan was the real discoverer of plutonium." (Seaborg himself has gone to great lengths to document his part in the discovery. In recent years, he has interviewed his old laboratory assistants, collected their notebooks and other documents relating to the plutonium project at Berkeley, and written a "diary"—ex post facto—that recounts his own role in each day's work at the laboratory from August 1940 through April 1942.)

Richard Hewlett, the chief historian of the U.S. Atomic Energy Commission, and the author of its official history, also knew Seaborg well. "Seaborg was the granddaddy of plutonium, and it was always extremely important to him that he discovered a new element that would be the salvation of mankind," Hewlett said. "It's probably not too extreme to put it that way. It's all sort of naïve in a way, but he believed it. Plutonium to him was very sacred. It made him a hero in the world of science. He saw the whole world revolving around this technology, and here he was in the center of it all."

The future of civilization, as Seaborg saw it, was in the hands of the nuclear scientists who formed the elite team that would "build a new world through nuclear technology." Never mind that plutonium was used in the bomb dropped on Nagasaki, or that it would be one of the principal raw materials out of which vast arsenals of nuclear weapons would be made by the United States and the Soviet Union over the postwar decades. "Seaborg was never really interested in the military program and never gave it much attention," Hewlett observed. (In June 1945, Seaborg had been one of the Manhattan Project scientists who signed a secret report to the Secretary of War urging that the power of the atomic bomb be demonstrated to the Japanese by dropping it on a barren island rather than on a city.)

Seaborg focused his attention instead on a visionary dream of atomic-powered plenty. According to his prospectus on its possible applications, nuclear energy was a magician's potion that could free industrial society permanently from all practical bounds. Millions of homes could be heated and lighted by a single large nuclear reactor. Factories could be powered forever by the cheap and inexhaustible electricity generated by nuclear fission. The deserts could be made to bloom, sea water could be made potable, mountains could be moved, rivers diverted—all as a result, he prophesied, of "planetary engineering" made possible by the miraculous new element that he had discovered. There could be vast farming and manufacturing centers, or "agro-industrial complexes," built around giant nuclear electric-generating stations—"each nuclear power plant surrounded by its own little Eden," as he described it. There would be nuclear-powered earth-to-moon shuttles, nuclear-powered artificial hearts, plutonium-heated swimsuits for SCUBA divers, and much more. "Where science fiction goes, can the atom be far behind?" Seaborg asked. "My only fear is that I may be underestimating the possibilities."

The prediction of a coming utopia, made possible by nuclear energy, was received approvingly in the 1950s and 60s. The scientific effort of the United States during World War II had been notably productive. Its dramatic successes led to postwar hopes of what a continuing partnership between science, industry and government might accomplish. Like the gold fever of the 1850s, another spontaneous season of collective excitement occurred, based on predictions, which grew into popular fantasies, about the coming marvels of "advanced technology." Leading scientists, turned into celebrities by the national news media, were looked upon as the high priests of a state religion that promised social progress by means of made-to-order technological advances.

"Scientists," according to the scientist-writer C. P. Snow, one of their prophets, "are the most important occupational group in the world today." "Their work shapes the life of every human presently inhabiting the planet," *Time* noted in 1961, and it lauded the "Age of Science." Seaborg and other leaders of this secular religion, dismissing the "naysayers" and expressing the confidence, in his words, that "history will redeem this new generation of optimists," promised a broad spectrum of innovations for engineering a new civilization. Pills would control fertility, miracle grains would feed humanity, wonder drugs would control disease, human toil would be eliminated as automatons took over the workplace and the home, outer space would be made accessible, and an era of ease and plenty would be achieved.

Nuclear energy held a prestigious place among the popular technological panaceas, and pioneering scientists, industrialists and government officials joined together in an idealistic campaign to create a large nuclear power program. The billions of dollars in potential revenues from commercial exploitation of "the peaceful atom" provided a further incentive. Others promoting the program rivaled—sometimes even exceeded—Seaborg's exuberant claims about the "countless benefits" of atomic energy.

Alvin Weinberg, the theoretical physicist who patented the first design for a water-cooled nuclear reactor, smiled broadly in a recent interview and said that one could debate whether Glenn Seaborg or he had been the more optimistic. "At one point I was *the* most optimistic," Weinberg said. "And why was I optimistic? Because about twenty or twenty-five years ago I read this book by Charles Darwin (that's the grand-nephew, I guess, of the biologist). He's a physicist. He wrote a book called *The Next Million Years,* and he said that life on this planet would be essentially intolerable unless man developed an inexhaustible energy source other than the sun. It was about this time that I remembered some conversations that I had with Phil Morrison"—one of the Manhattan Project's leading theoretical physicists—"and Phil was the first to have pointed out that there's more energy in the uranium in the rocks than was needed to extract it. Therefore, you had in the uranium in the rocks, in principle, an inexhaustible energy source—enough to keep you going for hundreds of millions of years. I got very, very excited about that, because here was an embodiment of a way to save mankind. I guess I acquired a little bit of the same spirit as the Ayatollah has at the moment."

Glenn Seaborg and other proponents of nuclear energy worked with uncommon zeal to establish a large nuclear-power program, under the auspices of the U.S. Atomic Energy Commission, which Congress established in 1946. Seaborg served as an A.E.C. adviser in the late 1940s, as a presidential science adviser in the 50s and, finally, as chairman of the A.E.C. from 1961 until 1971, heading the agency longer than anyone else. In articles, interviews and official reports, in testimony before Congress and in speeches throughout the country, in travels that took him as the "atomic diplomat" to some sixty countries, he made the case for nuclear energy. No longer doing scientific work himself, he became, according to A.E.C. historian Hewlett, "an entrepreneur of science" who promoted the special fuel he had discovered as a tonic cure for society's energy needs.

By Seaborg's own description, he was the nuclear program's number one "salesman," but in truth he was more. Under the terms of the Atomic Energy Act, as adopted by Congress in 1946 and amended in 1954, the A.E.C. became one of the most powerful federal agencies ever created. Chairman Seaborg and the four other commissioners who worked with him acquired extremely broad authority over every aspect of nuclear energy. Among other things, they had the mandate to make all the rules and regulations governing the commercial nuclear power program and could decide where and how—and whether—proposed nuclear plants would be built. As the chief executive of this agency, Seaborg authorized and nominally supervised the most ambitious construction program in the United States since the building of the railroads in the nineteenth century. During his tenure, the A.E.C. issued construction permits for more than sixty-nine nuclear plants, the first installment on the thousand plants the A.E.C. hoped to have in operation by the end of the century.

Empowered and directed by Congress to promote nuclear energy—a specific assignment set forth in the Atomic Energy Act of 1954—the A.E.C. was also explicitly called upon, by the same law, to regulate the emerging nuclear industry. Thus, the agency was to play the incompatible roles of coach and umpire, of partisan as well as judge, and was supposed somehow to be the champion and the disciplinarian of the industry. This dual mandate led to a continuing, unacknowledged, conflict within the agency. The enthusiasm of Seaborg, who was rushing to create a nuclear-powered world, was not easily reconciled with the practical safety precautions that the A.E.C.'s own experts believed were necessary.

As A.E.C. chairman, Seaborg was left to resolve the dilemma that arose when his own vision was threatened by A.E.C. scientists who warned him repeatedly about safety problems that might lead to catastrophic accidents. A.E.C. internal files, which the agency withheld from Congress, the courts, and the public, document the safety controversy within the A.E.C., and show how Seaborg and his fellow commissioners resolved it. To study these private A.E.C. records, which contain the unpublished history of the nuclear power program, is to understand how the program grew into an unprecedented national enterprise—and why, ultimately, the whole undertaking got into serious trouble.

THE FAMILIAR EARLY HISTORY of the nuclear power program is one of breathtaking technical accomplishments by the scientific geniuses of modern times. Working as part of the supersecret "Manhattan Project," the nation's leading scientists raced to create an atomic bomb, and, as they did so, leaped from one fundamental discovery to the next. They quickly grasped why the uranium nucleus fissioned, and how the process could be exploited for military, and possibly civilian, purposes.

Atoms, according to the ancient Greeks, are the building blocks of nature, and according to the model developed by Danish physicist Niels Bohr, early in this century, they are constructed like miniature solar systems. At the center of the atom, like the sun, is the nucleus, surrounded by orbiting particles called electrons. The nucleus is a heavy clump composed of protons and neutrons, which are very dense particles. The more protons and neutrons it contains, the heavier the atom. Hydrogen, the lightest element, has only one proton in its nucleus. On the other hand, U-235 has a much larger nucleus of 92 protons and 143 neutrons. The nuclear force, which is what holds the nucleus together, is the strongest force in nature.

Scientists quickly developed an explanation for why the nucleus of U-235 fissioned: it was so large that the forces that held it together were barely able to do so. It was already slightly unstable and could be thoroughly destabilized if it absorbed another neutron. This extra neutron would cause the U-235 nucleus to oscillate wildly, and within about a millionth of a millionth of a second it would split itself apart with a great release of energy.

As soon as the possibility of fission was appreciated, another aspect of this phenomenon was quickly investigated. According to researchers like Fermi, who came to the United States in 1939, the fissioning of U-235 might be a contagious process. Every uranium atom that fissioned, in addition to releasing energy, also released some of its neutrons. One fission, therefore, might cause more fissions as these extra neutrons collided with other uranium atoms. There might be a "chain reaction"—the rapid-fire fissioning of one uranium atom after another—that could unleash enormous amounts of energy. Theoretical calculations quickly suggested that this was so. (Fermi had learned by this time what was wrong with his earlier calculations that had predicted the impossibility of fission.) Still, it remained for him to demonstrate, in a practical way, that chain reactions could actually be achieved.

By December 1942, the world's first nuclear reactor had been secretly constructed at the University of Chicago. The device, intended to produce a controlled chain reaction, consisted of a "pile" of graphite blocks in which uranium was embedded. It was assembled in a squash court under the west stands of Stagg Field, the university's football stadium. To limit the reaction, control rods were inserted into the pile. Since neutrons brought about fission, the control rods were made of material that would absorb neutrons, like a blotter, and thus regulate the rate at which fissioning took place. As a safety device, a special emergency control rod was suspended over the pile. It was held by a rope so that safety officers—"the suicide squad," they were called—could cut it in an emergency and drop the rod into the reactor. An ax was provided for this purpose. (The emergency shutdown of reactor, which on today's models is accomplished by elaborate automated equipment, is still referred to as a *SCRAM*—short for "safety control rod ax man.") Many other precautions were taken. Fermi had made elaborate calculations on how the reactor would perform, but no one was really sure.

At 3:25 P.M. on December 3, 1941, with Fermi and some of the country's leading nuclear scientists in attendance, physicist George Weil withdrew the main control rod the final fraction of an inch. The sensitive instruments monitoring the pile reported that a self-sustaining nuclear chain reaction had begun, exactly as Fermi had predicted. The reactor was allowed to run for twenty-eight minutes, producing as it did only a few watts of heat—a meager output but enough to prove that the energy inside the uranium nucleus could be tapped in a practical way.

Physicist Eugene Wigner had brought a bottle of Chianti to the experiment, and the assembled crew of researchers drank the wine out of paper cups, leaving their autographs on the bottle. (Glenn Seaborg missed the historic experiment; he was outside the room, working on another project.) No news headlines reported the results of this secret experiment, but a simple coded message was sent from the laboratory to Harvard President James Bryant Conant, the distinguished chemist who headed the wartime scientific effort in the United States. "The Italian Navigator has landed in the New World," it said.

THE FEVERISH WARTIME A-bomb effort precluded any diversion of resources for a major study of the peacetime uses of nuclear energy. Toward the end of the war, however, a Manhattan Project task force was appointed to develop a policy on postwar nuclear research. The committee, headed by Dean R. C. Tolman of the California Institute of Technology, was not enthusiastic about commercial nuclear power plants. "The development of fission piles solely for the production of power for ordinary commercial use does not appear economically sound nor advisable from the point of view of preserving national resources [i.e., the limited supplies of fissionable materials]," it concluded.

When the war ended, such restrained assessments were quickly pushed aside in the general euphoria about what *Newsweek* called "the miraculous powers of atomic-fission energy." Instead of reflecting on the horrors visited upon Hiroshima and Nagasaki or on whether the bombs should have been used in the first place, news reports helped to alleviate the nation's feelings of repulsion and guilt by focusing public attention on the more congenial aspects of "the new force." Thus, barely two weeks after Hiroshima, having canvassed experts in the field, *Newsweek* reported that, "even the most conservative scientists and industrialists were willing to outline a civilization which would make the comic-strip prophecies of Buck Rogers look obsolete."

Robert M. Hutchins, Chancellor of the University of Chicago, which had hosted so much Manhattan Project research, predicted that "Heat will be so plentiful that it will even be used to melt snow as it falls. . . . A very few individuals working a few hours a day at very easy tasks in the central atomic power plant will provide all the heat, light, and power required by the community and these utilities will be so cheap that their cost can hardly be reckoned."

David E. Lilienthal, head of the Tennessee Valley Authority and President Truman's nominee to head the new Atomic Energy Commission, wrote of the "almost limitless beneficial applications of atomic energy."

George Gamow, the physicist and writer, in a 1946 book *Atomic Energy in Cosmic and Human Life,* described how

> the newly discovered possibility of liberating the hidden energy of uranium atoms promises us an almost unbelievable technical progress in the years to come. We may speak confidently about the miraculous "K-ration" fuel, a small package of which will be enough to fly a huge passenger airliner across the ocean. We may also prepare ourselves for a trip to the moon and to various planets of our solar system in a comfortable rocketship driven by atomic power.

David Dietz, science editor for the Scripps-Howard newspapers, compiled what was perhaps the most elaborate description of the coming atomic utopia in his *Atomic Energy in the Coming Era,* published in late 1945.

> All forms of transportation will be freed at once from the limits now put upon them by the weight of present fuels. The privately-owned airplane now suitable only for cross-country hopping, will be equal to a flight across the Atlantic. There should be no difficulty in building passenger and cargo airplanes of any desired size. Planes carrying several thousand passengers, with as much cabin space as a luxury liner, will make non-stop flights from New York to India or Australia.

> Instead of filling the gasoline tank of your automobile two or three times a week, you will travel for a year on a pellet of atomic energy the size of a vitamin pill . . . The day is gone when nations will fight for oil. . . . Larger pellets will be used to turn the wheels of industry and when they do that they will turn the Era of Atomic Energy into the Age of Plenty.
>
> The world will go permanently off the gold standard once the era of Atomic Energy is in full swing . . . With the aid of atomic energy the scientists will be able to build a factory to manufacture gold.
>
> No baseball game will be called off on account of rain in the Era of Atomic Energy. No airplane will by-pass an airport because of fog. No city will experience a winter traffic jam because of heavy snow. Summer resorts will be able to guarantee the weather and artificial suns will make it as easy to grow corn and potatoes indoors as on the farm.

There were doubts expressed about some of this. A number of economists wondered whether nuclear energy would really be competitive with conventional fuels. They also questioned the practical significance of nuclear energy, even if it turned out to be very cheap. "Would people start driving their cars more or use much more heat in their homes if the cost of power were suddenly lower?" they asked. The proponents treated such objections the way boosters usually do. They ignored them. After the success of the war effort, American ebullience was not to be given up simply because some academic economists were quibbling.

POPULAR ENTHUSIASM NOTWITHSTANDING, there was small immediate prospect for the wondrous potential of atomic energy. Although Congress and the Administration wanted, as President Truman said, to "make a blessing" of atomic energy, the Cold War, as well as bureaucratic, technical and economic obstacles, stood in the way. Testimony before Congress on the potential civilian applications of nuclear energy was inconclusive, and there was much disagreement on the likely timetable for achieving usable power from atomic reactors. There was no disagreement, however, about the ominous military implications of nuclear fission. When it passed the Atomic Energy Act of 1946, Congress addressed itself almost exclusively to these grim issues. The legislation was designed principally to protect "atomic secrets," in order to preserve the United States monopoly on nuclear weapons and nuclear technology, and to establish an "Atomic Energy Commission" that would provide civilian control over nuclear weapons. The Act mentions the peaceful uses of atomic energy in passing.

The Atomic Energy Commission, which was given total control over all aspects of atomic energy, opened its doors for business in August 1946. The A.E.C. was soon overwhelmed by its responsibilities for nuclear-weapons development. Its problems were acute. The agency had inherited from the Manhattan Project a vast empire of laboratories and manufacturing facilities that employed some forty-four thousand people and had almost no central management. (For security reasons, these installations had been scattered throughout the country, many in remote locations where "atomic cities," complete with schools and fire departments, had been run by the Manhattan Project.) Leading scientists had left the Manhattan Project at war's end, and the A.E.C.'s laboratories were in disarray. The uranium mine in the Belgian Congo that supplied the raw material for the American nuclear-weapons program was being rapidly exhausted. The reactors built during the war for manufacturing plutonium were falling apart. The spare parts needed to assemble nuclear weapons were not available.

The chairman of the new agency, David Lilienthal, had to report to a shocked President Truman on April 3, 1947, that, contrary to world belief, the United States had *no* stockpile of nuclear weapons ready for use. "There was nothing in the cupboard," Carroll Wilson, the first general manager of the A.E.C., said in a recent interview. As the Cold War proceeded, and especially after the Soviet Union exploded its own atomic bomb in September 1949, the A.E.C. was absorbed in a frantic nuclear-weapons buildup and had little time or resources to devote to the peacetime development of atomic energy. "The power thing was pie in the sky, really," Wilson said. "We knew we had to do something with it, but we just had one hell of a lot of absolutely overwhelming problems. All of the other priorities were higher than nuclear power."

A.E.C. scientists, moreover, told the Commission of a broad array of practical problems that needed to be solved before power-producing reactors could become a reality. Lilienthal was flabbergasted by the pessimism of a draft report on the prospects for civilian nuclear power that was prepared in July 1947 by J. Robert Oppenheimer. Oppenheimer was the leading Manhattan Project physicist, and he was then heading the A.E.C.'s General Advisory Committee, a prestigious group that largely determined A.E.C. policy during its first few years. Arguing that "a realistic evaluation of atomic power" was necessary to counter popular misconceptions, the report stated that "it does not appear hopeful to use natural uranium directly as an adequate source of fuel for atomic power," and that to develop plutonium reactors capable of producing enough fuel for the power industry would take decades.

"Had quite a blow today," Lilienthal wrote in his diary. "The General Advisory Committee drafted a statement that, as written, not only discouraged hope of atomic power in any substantial way for decades, but put it in such a way as to question whether it would ever be of consequence." Revising this draft a few months later, the full advisory committee, which included A.E.C. adviser Glenn Seaborg, tried to be more optimistic, but the best that it could say was that it did "not see how it would be possible under the most favorable circumstances to have any considerable portion of the present power supply of the world replaced by nuclear fuel before the expiration of twenty years."

The General Advisory Committee saw numerous technical and economic problems that beclouded the future use of nuclear energy, but they had other concerns as well. Physicist Eugene Wigner, who had pioneered some of the early reactor work at Oak Ridge, felt that there was a notable lack of first-rate scientists and engineers in the A.E.C.'s postwar reactor development effort. Enrico Fermi, who had led the early work in nuclear reactors, felt that the reactor program had lost much of its appeal. He regarded the A.E.C.'s highly structured and bureaucratic research effort as cautious and uninspired. After the exciting breakthroughs of the Manhattan Project, the remaining work that needed to be done to develop power reactors appeared relatively mundane—selecting and testing materials, studying the properties of different types of coolants, designing the pumps and valves and instruments that would be used. Nobel prizes are not given to people who do plumbing, even if it is for a nuclear reactor's cooling system, and scientists of the highest caliber automatically dismissed most of the tasks needed for reactor development as hack work that was not for them.

"We despair of progress in the reactor program," Oppenheimer said in 1948, summarizing the views of the General Advisory Committee. But the members of this elite group were not about to give up their own personal scientific careers to do the work themselves. Advisory Committee member Glenn Seaborg was typical of the Manhattan Project scientists. After the war he went directly back to Berkeley to head the research team that was continuing the work that had made him famous: discovering new elements. The A.E.C.'s work on reactor development would never get more than token attention from leading nuclear scientists.

Although its principal technical advisers expressed firm views on the subject, the A.E.C. was hesitant to speak with candor to the public about the uncertain—and possibly doubtful—prospects for commercial nuclear power. The Commission had been under attack in Congress, and Lilienthal himself had undergone a bruising Senate confirmation hearing, during which he was rebuked by conservative Republicans who were critical of his former role as head of Roosevelt's "socialistic" Tennessee Valley Authority. Given the A.E.C.'s weak political base, he and the other commissioners feared the backlash of deflating the public's expectations for nuclear energy. He particularly did not want to give the advocates of a return to military control a concession that "might well have finished off the rather fragile life of civilian direction of this project," he wrote in his diary.

Commissioner Lewis L. Strauss also argued that a highly pessimistic official statement about the A.E.C.'s ability to deliver on the promise of nuclear energy would undercut the agency's case when it tried to win its annual budgetary appropriations from Congress. Further complicating the A.E.C.'s political quandary was the concern that if it didn't try to curb runaway hopes about the imminence of nuclear power it would be embarrassed by its failure to produce the miracles that were expected of it.

Ultimately, the Commission straddled the political and public-relations problems it faced by making whatever statement about the prospects for nuclear power seemed most expedient at the moment. Thus, although the General Advisory Committee had talked in its November 1947 report in terms of decades, A.E.C. Commissioner Robert Bacher declared in a January 1948 speech before the Oak Ridge Rotary Club that economical nuclear power might be available in perhaps as little as five years.

Chairman Lilienthal, on the other hand, thought it necessary to delicately soft-pedal expectations, and he said, a few months after that, that "atomic power is not just around the corner, nor around two corners." His own candor had limits, however. He tried very hard to create the public impression that A.E.C. research on nuclear weapons would help to produce peacetime atomic power, an argument he advanced to justify A.E.C.'s vast expenditures on weapons development. "As to the military uses of nuclear energy, this must always be remembered: atomic-energy research and development—whether for the uses of war and destruction or for beneficent and creative purposes—is virtually an identical processs: two sides of the same coin," he said. His claim was absurd, technically, since nuclear reactors and nuclear bombs, as he perfectly well knew, worked on very different principles; research to develop the one, accordingly, had little or no benefit in terms of advancing the other. Although the A.E.C. was a bastion of the nation's scientific prowess, its spokesmen were not always governed by the usual standards of scientific objectivity.

By the early 1950s, no A.E.C. statements, however they attempted to finesse the issue, could conceal the basic fact about the era of atomic power: it was not arriving very quickly. The A.E.C. remained preoccupied with weapons development, and private industry was reluctant to put up the large sums that were needed to explore the technical possibilities for commercial nuclear power. "You can find a great many more buyers for the Brooklyn Bridge than businessmen interested in doing something about atomic power," *Business Week* commented. The years passed, Carroll Wilson observed, and all that the government had been able to organize was "a small, shallow reactor development effort."

The euphoria of the early postwar years gave way to gloom about the prospects of an atomic future. "As yet no deserts have burst into bloom, no polar icecaps have melted away," *Newsweek*'s science column noted at the end of 1950. "The brave new world of cheap and abundant atomic power seems far more remote than it did just after the war." The impatient congressmen on the Joint Committee on Atomic Energy regularly and bitterly attacked the A.E.C. for the lack of progress. Composed of nine members of the House of Representatives and nine members of the Senate, the Joint Committee was established in 1946 to be the congressional "watchdog" over nuclear energy. Surveying the reasons for the slow progress in reactor development, the committee's staff reported, in 1952, that "those interviewed perceived a tendency on the part of both those in private industry and in government to hold back in the hope that someone else will assume the responsibility in each problem area, that someone else will make the investment in the pilot or prototype plant, and someone else will force the policy issues which must be decided before the atomic power industry can go forward aggressively."

Dr. Kenneth Pitzer, who had been the A.E.C.'s Director of Research, resigned that year, and he publicly criticized the "excessive red tape" and "unnecessary caution" that were delaying the reactor program. The task of advancing the nuclear program, he said, had to be given to "men with real daring and enthusiasm."

DESPITE THE SLOW and disappointing progress in reactor development, one small office in the A.E.C. was quietly making giant strides toward the goal of usable power from nuclear fission. This was the Naval Reactors Branch that was working, together with the Navy's Bureau of Ships, to build the first nuclear-powered submarine.

The conventional subs used during World War II had dual propulsion systems: electric batteries, which they used when submerged, and diesel engines that could be used only on the surface (because they needed an air intake and exhaust). The diesels were used to charge the batteries, which meant that the subs had to resurface frequently. The faster the sub traveled when submerged, moreover, the quicker the batteries would run down, which made the subs very slow. Nuclear propulsion was attractive because the sub could stay submerged for long periods—possibly months—and would have enough power to operate at high speeds for pursuit and maneuvering.

Still, nuclear submarines were not a high priority of either the A.E.C. or the Navy. The A.E.C. had its own reactor-development program, and the strongly traditional Navy, which favored surface ships, had a disdain for submarines, nuclear or otherwise. Nuclear submarine development was carried out largely as the personal project of a remarkable Navy captain, Hyman G. Rickover. An Annapolis graduate, and an engineer, Rickover outmaneuvered the two cumbersome bureaucracies for which he worked—he had a dual appointment with both the A.E.C. and the Navy—and single-handedly administered one of the most successful technological development efforts in modern history.

In June 1946, with a delegation of other Naval officers, Rickover went to Oak Ridge, Tennessee, to the Manhattan Project's Clinton Laboratory, which had become one of the principal postwar research-and-training centers in nuclear technology. (Its name was later changed to the Oak Ridge National Laboratory.) After a few months there, Rickover and his team had quickly absorbed the available technical information on potential reactor systems and had begun, with shrewd technical judgment and uncanny bureaucratic skill, to organize a tightly scheduled program to build a nuclear-powered submarine. By 1948, the program was under way, and Captain Rickover was able to predict, in 1950, that the first American shipboard reactor would be built by the end of 1953.

From physicist Alvin Weinberg, the leader of the Clinton Laboratory scientists, Rickover picked up the idea of a "pressurized-water reactor"—a water-cooled reactor that would operate under high pressure. The principles of a "PWR," as it was called, were simple, and it could be built compactly to fit into the hull of a submarine. The reactor would be a steel tank that housed a small "core" of uranium fuel. The uranium chain reaction produced heat, and that heat would be used to boil water. The resulting steam would drive a turbine that was directly connected to the propeller shaft of the sub. The energy released by nuclear fission would thereby be harnessed as a power source for the sub's propulsion. Rickover knew that engineering all of this would be complicated, but he felt that it could be done—if he could overcome the inertia of the A.E.C. and the Navy.

The key to success, in Rickover's mind, was the focusing of the submarine-reactor development project on engineering practicalities rather than on abstract scientific research. A.E.C. laboratories, he felt, were captivated by fascinating technical novelties, regardless of their practical significance. They would irresistibly pursue every new technical issue the way dogs sniff down rabbit trails. He wanted an engineering effort that would not be distracted by side issues but would systematically produce the nuts and bolts and pumps and wiring for a pressurized-water reactor that would work.

Accordingly, Rickover wanted to keep his project out of the hands of the Commission's scientists and to bring in industrial engineers who would work under his precise direction and control, an idea that Glenn Seaborg, who was then an A.E.C. adviser, enthusiastically supported. Rickover went directly to the large corporations that supplied the power systems for naval vessels—which were, incidentally, the same companies that supplied the boilers and turbine generators for the electric utility industry—and arranged to get the technical support for his effort. The government-subsidized research they would carry out would give them, at public expense, an opportunity to get in on the ground floor of a possible commercial nuclear power industry, and it would get him, on his own terms, the hardware he wanted.

Rickover set up his most important working relationship with the Westinghouse Electric Corporation. The company was eager to explore the possibilities for commercial nuclear power and agreed to set up a laboratory for Rickover at the old Bettis Airport, thirteen miles southeast of Pittsburgh. An unprecedented contract was negotiated with Westinghouse by a young A.E.C. lawyer, James T. Ramey.

To start from scratch and invent a whole new branch of technology, it was difficult to specify at the outset all of the work that Westinghouse might be asked to perform. Ramey suggested, therefore, that the contract *not* include a detailed list of obligations on the part of Westinghouse, but that it be drawn up simply as a broad, general pact between the A.E.C. and the company. According to the contract he wrote, the Commission and Westinghouse vowed to work together "in a spirit of partnership and friendly cooperation with maximum of effort and common sense in achieving their common objective." In addition, of course, the A.E.C. agreed to foot the bill for the work at Bettis.

The cooperative arrangement between the A.E.C. and Westinghouse was subsequently extended to the other companies that entered the nuclear industry. So closely did the A.E.C. and the industry work together in "partnership and friendly cooperation," former Senator Abraham Ribicoff once observed, that it became "difficult . . . to determine in the organization scheme of the A.E.C. where the Commission ends and the industry begins."

Ramey's contract with Westinghouse, however loose and informal it appeared on paper, became the tool that Rickover used to exercise absolute control over Bettis. Aggressively, painstakingly and, at times, even ruthlessly, he set about establishing his personal management of the work that he felt was needed to develop the nuclear submarine—and to do it on schedule and within budget. Within his own office, for example, he directed the secretaries to give him a pink carbon copy of everything they typed for his staff—even copies of rough drafts and incomplete reports. He personally reviewed the "pinks" every day and handed them back to his staff—annotating them with questions, corrections and admonitions designed to keep the project under his control. He wanted to know, down to the last detail, what was happening, and he had representatives at Bettis and at other facilities who would report to him on the day-to-day activities they were observing. At any sign of serious trouble he would personally go to his laboratories—sometimes unannounced—to straighten things out. He was not content to know that a given problem had been solved, moreover, but wanted to know what the root cause of it was, so he could take steps to prevent recurrence.

When it came to the actual building of the first submarine reactor, Rickover wanted precise-scale prototype models tested at the A.E.C.'s remote reactor-testing station in Idaho. He demanded exhaustive checks of the reliability of key components. He wanted every last detail to be worked out. How would the equipment be arranged in the tight confines of the sub? Would maintenance technicians be able to reach all of the equipment they might need to work on? What kind of malfunctions could arise when the reactor was operating? How would such contingencies be handled? To all these questions, Rickover insisted on firm answers.

By January 1954, he had them, and he had the U.S.S. *Nautilus,* the first nuclear submarine. Its pressurized-water nuclear reactor worked perfectly, and its development had produced a set of technical handbooks that laid the foundation for a workable technology to generate power through nuclear fission. The general despair about the prospects for nuclear energy, which had prevailed only a few years earlier, suddenly dissipated.

"THE UNITED STATES knows that peaceful power from atomic energy is no dream of the future. That capability, already proved, is here—now, today," President Eisenhower declared, before the U.N. General Assembly, on December 8, 1953. He spoke with euphoria about "atomic power for peace." Instead of enlarging the existing stockpiles of weapons, the President urged that nuclear materials be used "to provide abundant electrical energy in the power-starved areas of the world." He would ask Congress for new laws to make such a program possible. "The United States pledges . . . before the world its determination to help solve the fearful atomic dilemma—to devote its entire heart and mind to find the way by which the miraculous inventiveness of man shall not be dedicated to his death, but consecrated to his life."

Reacting speedily to the President's call, the Congressional Joint Committee on Atomic Energy began drafting new laws to promote peacetime nuclear power. The Atomic Energy Act of 1946 had expressly forbidden private ownership of nuclear materials and had established an absolute government monopoly over nuclear energy. President Truman had considered atomic energy "too important a development to be made the subject of profit-seeking," but the business-oriented Eisenhower Administration wanted the restrictions eased so that private industry could enter the nuclear-energy business. The President nominated Lewis Strauss, a former Wall Street investment banker who had served on the Commission from 1946 until 1950, to be the new chairman of the A.E.C. Unleashing "the genius and enterprise of American business," Strauss announced, was the key to atomic-power development, a proposition that led to a bitter ideological fight with congressional Democrats. They attacked the proposals to open up atomic power to private developers as a "giveaway" to industry that would replace the government monopoly over nuclear energy with a private one. Leading Democrats on the Joint Committee wanted the A.E.C., instead, to build and operate power reactors and sell the electricity to the public.

The full committee, chaired by Republican Representative Sterling Cole, sided with the Administration, and so did the Republican-controlled Congress, which passed a new Atomic Energy Act on August 30, 1954. Among its principal provisions was the instruction to the A.E.C. to issue licenses to private companies to build and operate commercial nuclear-power stations. A corollary assignment directed the agency to adopt whatever regulations it deemed necessary "to protect the health and safety of the public."

"There are about thirty-one references in the law to the 'health and safety of the public,' " Harold Green, a former A.E.C. attorney and authority on atomic energy law, said in a recent interview. "I counted them once. But there is not a single reference in the legislative history"—the four thousand pages of reports, testimony and debates before Congress relating to the law—"as to what those health and safety considerations really were. Nobody really ever thought that safety was a problem. They assumed that if you just wrote the requirement that it be done properly, it would be done properly."

The members and staff of the Joint Committee on Atomic Energy had become familiar with basic technical aspects of atomic energy. They certainly knew at least some of the potential risks. The previous year, for example, the Joint Committee had heard a description of the effects of possible accidents from physicist Edward Teller. He was the leading nuclear-weapons expert, and he also headed the A.E.C.'s Reactor Safeguards Committee, a select group established in 1947 to review the hazards of all proposed reactors. "Up to the present time, we have been extremely fortunate in that accidents in nuclear reactors have not caused any fatalities. With expanding applications of nuclear reactions and nuclear power, it cannot be expected that this unbroken record will be maintained," he told the congressmen, in an appearance before the Committee in September 1953.

The "public hazard" arising from reactor accidents, Teller explained, "is due to the fact that nuclear plants contain radioactive poisons. In a nuclear accident, these poisons may be liberated into the atmosphere or into the water supply. In fact, the radioactive poisons produced in a powerful nuclear reactor will retain a dangerous concentration even after they have been carried downwind to a distance of ten miles. Some danger might possibly persist to distances as great as one hundred miles . . . The various committees dealing with reactor safety have come to the conclusion that none of the powerful reactors built or suggested up to the present time are absolutely safe. Though the possibility of an accident seems small, a release of [radioactive materials from a reactor] in a city or densely populated area would lead to disastrous results."

The Joint Committee did not probe the safety issues raised by Teller as it considered the proposed Atomic Energy Act of 1954. Neither he nor any other representative of the Reactor Safeguards Committee appeared before it, and the members did not ask anyone else in the scientific community to comment on the potential for catastrophic accidents. A few well-known scientists, such as James B. Conant, had expressed reservations about the desirability of a large nuclear program—the long-term hazards associated with the radioactive waste was one problem they cited—but they were not called, and the issues that concerned them were not considered. The committee delegated responsibility for safety to the A.E.C., and it did not inquire into what kind of regulatory program would be needed to cope with the unique hazards of nuclear reactors.

There were precautions that could have been written into the 1954 Act that might have helped reduce the risk of damaging nuclear accidents. The committee, admittedly, did not have the expert knowledge to develop highly technical safety guidelines, but there were some steps—requiring the siting of reactors in remote areas, for example—that it could have asked for. In his briefing to committee members in 1953, Teller mentioned past A.E.C. practice of requiring substantial "exclusion distances" around the experimental reactors it was building, areas from which the public would be banned. The larger the reactor, the greater the required separation between it and any neighboring populations. The committee did not pause to consider whether such practice should be required for the commercial reactor program it was about to authorize.

Nor did Teller urge the congressmen to do so. To the contrary, he advised them that "rigid enforcement of such exclusion distances might hamper future development of reactors to an unreasonable extent," and he offered the general observation that "no legislation will be able to stop future accidents and avoid completely occasional loss of life. It is my opinion that the unavoidable danger which will remain after all reasonable controls have been employed must not stand in the way of rapid development of nuclear power."

The Joint Committee concurred with Professor Teller and focused its deliberations on the Atomic Energy Act of 1954 on how best to get a large nuclear program started. The only real topics of debate involved commercial matters—such as the granting of patent rights, contracting procedures, ownership of nuclear materials, and the question of public versus private ownership of nuclear power stations. The Committee saw the issuance of licenses to build commercial nuclear power plants as a commonplace task that the A.E.C. would fulfill in the ordinary course of business; it would issue them the way the State Department routinely issued passports to travelers. The authors of the Atomic Energy Act of 1954 had copied their provisions for reactor licensing almost word for word from the Federal Communications Act of 1934, which had established procedures for the federal licensing of radio stations. They had added a vague requirement that nuclear-plant licensees must "observe such safety standards . . . as the [Atomic Energy] Commission by rule may establish."

Joint Committee Chairman Sterling Cole explained the very general language of the Act by remarking that it was premature to "lay down the ground rules for the regulation" of a "nonexistent atomic power industry." The legislation, he said, was simply, "aimed at hastening the technological development of atomic power." At some point—perhaps in "five or ten or fifteen years from now"—Congress would draft more specific rules for the nuclear power industry. It never did so.

The only major piece of additional atomic-energy legislation Congress considered focused on a concern that was repeatedly emphasized by prospective manufacturers and operators of nuclear power plants: their liability in the event of a serious accident.

"[W]e cannot exclude the possibility that a great enough fool aided by a great enough conspiracy of circumstances could bring about an accident exceeding available insurance," Charles Weaver, vice-president of Westinghouse, testified before the Joint Committee in 1956. If they had to accept the risk of bankrupting liabilities in the event of an accident, industry representatives told the Committee, they would abandon the nuclear power business.

In order to define the extent of potential liability, the Joint Committee asked the A.E.C. in 1956 to do a study of the consequences of a major reactor accident. The Commission's Brookhaven National Laboratory, on Long Island, reported to the committee in March 1957. The document prepared by A.E.C. scientists, entitled "Theoretical Possibilities and Consequences of

Major Accidents in Large Nuclear Power Plants," became known, by its A.E.C. publication number, as "WASH-740."

The Brookhaven scientists considered the hypothetical case of a power reactor located about thirty miles upwind of a large city. The assumption was that it had suffered an accident that had released a major fraction of the radioactive material it contained into the air, which was then carried across the countryside by the wind. In the "worst case," A.E.C. scientists estimated that thirty-four hundred people would die and another forty-three thousand would be injured, and seven billion dollars in property damage would result. The authors insisted that such accidents were improbable, and that the report, in order to determine the upper limit on possible liability, was pessimistic deliberately. "The study must be regarded only as a rough estimation of the consequences of unlikely though conceivable combinations of failure and error and weather conditions; it is not in any sense a prediction of any future condition."

The findings of WASH-740 reinforced industry's concern about potential lawsuits. Lobbyists for the electric-utility companies and their equipment suppliers pressed Congress for legislation to protect them against massive damage claims. Eager to remove all roadblocks to nuclear development, Congress obliged them. It passed the Price-Anderson Act of 1957, whose complex provisions made legal history; they effectively repealed every citizen's common-law right to sue for damages caused by some one else's negligence. In the event of injuries from an "extraordinary nuclear occurence," no one could bring a claim against those responsible for building and operating the ill-fated plant. The companies responsible would be absolved of all liability, no matter what carelessness or recklessness on their part caused the accident.

The Price-Anderson Act did provide that the public would get some compensation in the event of a nuclear accident. The victims would apply for money from a $560-million fund that the A.E.C. and private insurers would establish. However, if damages exceeded that amount, no extra money was provided. The $560 million would be apportioned to the victims, with no obligation on the part of the industry to assume the remaining liability.

The fund established by the Price-Anderson Act was a token gesture. The amount to be put into it had been recommended by Senator Clinton Anderson, who suggested that five hundred million dollars would be large enough to indicate that something substantial would be done for the victims, but not so large as to "frighten the country and the Congress to death" by revealing the magnitude of the potential risk.

The Joint Committee was concerned that discussion of the liability issue would raise a public controversy. It had skipped over the subject when the 1954 Act was being considered. When the liability question was taken up in 1956 and 1957, the matter received scant public attention, however, and Congress worked out the details of the new law with industry lobbyists. The Price-Anderson Act was passed on a voice vote in the House of Representatives, after perfunctory debate, and passed by the Senate without debate. This completed the legal foundation for the new industry.

AT THIS POINT, the A.E.C. confidently set to work to create a commercial nuclear power industry. Chairman Strauss declared his "faith in the atomic future," which had the additional backing of a "Higher Intelligence [who] decided man was ready to receive" the knowledge of the "atom's magnitude." "My faith tells me that the Creator did not intend man to evolve through the ages to this stage of civilization only now to devise something that would destroy life on this earth," he added.

In January 1955, guided by what Strauss called "Divine Providence," the Commission announced its "Power Reactor Demonstration Program," which one member of the Joint Committee on Atomic Energy later described as an attempt "to force-feed atomic development" with tax dollars. Intended to "open the way for American industry to develop, fabricate, construct and operate experimental reactors," the program entailed various subsidies that the A.E.C. would give to any company that wanted to enter the nuclear power business. The Commission offered free nuclear fuel for up to seven years and government payments to the companies for performing research and development on reactor design, and also agreed to carry out research and development in A.E.C. laboratories to aid in the design of proposed reactors. The companies would put up the capital to build the plants.

There were a number of possible designs for commercial reactors, and the A.E.C. wanted to encourage private industry to explore all reasonable alternatives. Some reactors, like the one used on the nuclear submarine *Nautilus,* might use ordinary water to cool their nuclear fuel. In others, various kinds of gases, liquid metals, or other substances might be employed to remove the heat produced by nuclear fission. (This heat would then be used, as in conventional power plants, to create steam to drive a turbine generator.) It was also necessary in many designs to slow down—"moderate"—the speed of the neutrons which brought about the chain reaction, since they did so more efficiently at slower speeds. Accordingly, the A.E.C. wanted industry to study the kinds of "neutron moderators" that might be used. So many possible types of reactors were proposed that, it was jokingly said, the A.E.C. had considered everything except a beer-cooled, sawdust-moderated reactor.

In practice, the Commission had a decided preference for one particular kind of system: the pressurized-water reactor that Rickover had developed for the *Nautilus.* While encouraging general exploration of other types, the agency considered commercial use of the PWR to be the fast route to a large nuclear power industry. Even before it announced the broader Power Reactor Demonstration Program, the Commission had sought "industrial partners" who would, in a joint project with the Commission, build a commercial plant based on the system pioneered by Rickover, and it asked Rickover himself to take charge of the task of building such a plant. The Duquesne Electric Power Company of Pittsburgh agreed to participate in the venture and offered the A.E.C. a site on the Ohio River, at Shippingport, Pennsylvania, for the plant. Rickover and the Westinghouse team at Bettis designed and built the Shippingport Nuclear Power Station together.

Technically, A.E.C. scientists doubted that there was much of a future in the kind of PWR technology that was to be employed at Shippingport. Alvin Weinberg, one of the inventors of the PWR concept, believed it an appropriate kind of reactor for a submarine—where compactness was a key requirement—but plainly inappropriate technology for commercial power production. After all, it used rare U-235 as a fuel, which was not available in sufficient quantity to support a large nuclear industry. The A.E.C., however, was eager to take the PWR technology, the most developed one it had, and use it to build a showpiece for the atomic future.

On Labor Day, 1954, President Eisenhower appeared on television, from Denver, Colorado, to announce the beginning of construction at Shippingport. The A.E.C. had a keen appreciation of the techniques needed to promote nuclear power to the public, and it wanted to use the Shippingport project as a demonstration that atomic power was finally a reality. The President lauded the effort and then waved a "magic wand" that started an unmanned bulldozer in Shippingport, where it broke ground for the new plant by remote control.

Progress at Shippingport and at other experimental reactors was recorded in dozens of films that the A.E.C. produced and distributed throughout the country to churches, schools, and business and civic groups. Glenn Seaborg noted, in 1970, that more than 40 million people had attended screenings of A.E.C. films in the previous ten years; another 158 million had watched them on television. (Like reactor development, the A.E.C.'s public-relations work was carried out in close collaboration with the "partners" in the nuclear industry—the A.E.C. and an industry lobbying group, the Atomic Industrial Forum—jointly producing promotional films and pamphlets on the nuclear program.) The films—with such titles as "Power Unlimited," "Power and Promise," "Nuclear Energy Goes Rural," "Atomic Venture," "The New Power"—dramatized the benefits of atomic energy but contained no hint of the potential for the kind of "disastrous" accident that Teller, its chief safety adviser, had privately described.

The scientists in the A.E.C. films did not discuss the risks and, indeed, hardly ever said anything. They were shown in scenarios—handling nuclear materials by remote control, pressing buttons to turn on equipment, or sitting behind drafting tables working on the blueprints for the atomic future—while A.E.C. announcers described how "the sure hand of science brings power unlimited from the magic of the atom."

"Many safeguards are provided," the announcer in the A.E.C. film "Atomic Power Today: Service with Safety" explained, noting that the safety apparatus was installed in "duplicate and triplicate" on every nuclear plant. "All of this is like designing an unsinkable ship, and then wrapping a life preserver around it." The A.E.C. showed its own licensing process to be one of meticulous reviews carried out by cadres of safety experts, such as those who served on its Reactor Safeguards Committee (whose name was changed, in 1953, to Advisory Committee on Reactor Safeguards.) The A.E.C. had received numerous reports from this committee, and some of these raised serious questions about the adequacy of the safety measures of certain nuclear plants. "A discussion of unknowns in reactor safety could be lengthy indeed," the chairman of the committee, C. Rogers McCullough, wrote in 1957. Although the films alluded to the existence of this committee and its qualifications, the "unknowns" which concerned it were not discussed.

Nor were these safety problems disclosed to the public in other ways. The A.E.C. had chosen at this time to keep secret all the reports by the committee. The Commission assured the public that "all reasonable steps" were taken to "minimize the probability" of serious accidents. Officially, there were no doubts about the safety of the commercial nuclear reactors that it was promoting.

A public-relations effort in behalf of nuclear power was not merely an incidental activity of the Commission. It was a fundamental part of what A.E.C. officials, at the highest level, saw as the agency's mission. Chairman Strauss was mindful of the results of opinion surveys that showed that postwar enthusiasm for nuclear power had faded and that public support for the peaceful uses of atomic energy was relatively weak. The Commission knew that it would have to work systematically to win public support for a large nuclear industry, and to lessen public fear of the hazards. Strauss concluded that the national press—and science writers, in particular—provided the A.E.C.'s "critical contact with the public," as he termed it, and that the media would have to serve as the conduit for the A.E.C.'s atomic power boosterism.

In a speech before the National Association of Science Writers in September 1954, Strauss set out the themes that the A.E.C. wanted the media to present to the public. Electric power from the atom, he said, could be available, according to the A.E.C.'s experts, in "from five to fifteen years, depending on the vigor of the development effort." "Our time scale can fold like an accordion," he added. "Transmutation of the elements—unlimited power . . . these and a host of other results all in fifteen short years. It is not too much to expect that our children will enjoy in their homes electrical energy too cheap to meter, will know of great periodic regional famines in the world only as matters of history, will travel effortlessly over the seas and under them and through the air with a minimum of danger and at great speeds, and will experience a life span far longer than ours . . . This is the forecast for an age of peace."

Strauss invited the science writers to "work together" with the A.E.C. and its scientists to educate the public about the atom and its promise. From the laudatory articles on nuclear energy that appeared over the next two decades—and the rarity of any critical coverage of the potential hazards—it is evident that the national media responded to the Chairman's invitation as he had intended. With unquestioning support from the media, and unqualified endorsement by Congress and the Administration, the advocates of a large nuclear power program proceeded, unchallenged, with their ambitious enterprise.

THERE WAS ONLY ONE major obstacle that Strauss believed might stand in the way of commercial nuclear power: the A.E.C. itself. According to the Atomic Energy Act of 1954, the agency had to adopt regulations governing the industry. Strauss feared that burdensome safety rules might "straitjacket" the industry and impede its progress. Willard Libby, a physicist and fellow A.E.C. commissioner, and a consistent backer of the Chairman, shared the concern that the industry "will be killed aborning by unnecessary regulation."

Others associated with A.E.C.'s reactor-development effort, such as former research chief Kenneth Pitzer, criticized the A.E.C. for being "ridiculously cautious" when it came to safety. Pitzer was opposed, for example, to the use of a remote Idaho desert as a reactor-testing station; he wanted experimental reactors built in more convenient locations and believed that the building of the Idaho facility had caused a major delay in the reactor-development program.

The A.E.C.'s Reactor Safeguards Committee, which had recommended the various precautions adopted by the agency, such as the use of the Idaho testing station, regularly nettled A.E.C. scientists. "The Committee was about as popular—and also as necessary—as a traffic cop," Edward Teller, its chairman from 1947 until 1953, observed. "Some of my friends, anxious for reactor progress, referred to the group as the 'Committee for Reactor Prevention,' and I was kidded about being assigned to the A.E.C.'s 'Brake Department.' " Teller himself, however, was quite willing—as he stated in his September 1953 briefing of the Joint Committee—to ease the earlier "safety measures which have necessarily retarded development" in order to help advance plans for a commercial reactor program.

By 1955, with the Power Reactor Demonstration Program under way, and with the intense pressure from Congress for results, the official attitude toward safety was aptly summarized by Alfonso Tammaro, the Assistant A.E.C. General Manager for Research and Industrial Development. Given the additional assignment of managing a new "Reactor Hazard Evaluation Staff," Tammaro told the commissioners, in a closed Commission meeting, that he needed that assignment "like I need a hole in the head. I have enough to do."

The problem of fulfilling its regulatory mandate, without inhibiting the growth of the industry, was deftly solved by the A.E.C.'s legal staff. Led by Harold Price, who would serve for the next seventeen years as the agency's chief of regulation, the Commission's attorneys prepared a set of "basic regulations for the civilian atomic industry"; these were issued in 1955 and 1956. There was little danger that these regulations would interfere with what the industry wanted to do, for the basic notion behind them was to let the industry regulate itself. "The A.E.C.'s objective in the formulation of the regulations was to minimize government control of competitive enterprise," Chairman Strauss stated in April 1955, when the first set of regulations was issued. Kenneth Nichols, the General Manager of the A.E.C. at this time, remarked in a meeting with the Commission that the governing principle behind A.E.C. regulations "was to get into the licensee's business as little as possible."

In a few sensitive areas—such as security and the protection of classified documents—the regulations were explicit. (They specified the kind of safe and padlock that should be used to protect classified data, provided that guards responsible for this material "be armed with side arms of not less than .38 caliber," and discussed in detail the exact kind of envelope that should be used in shipping "Restricted Data.") But on the many technical questions about safety, the regulations, purposely, said practically nothing.

The regulatory scheme adopted by the A.E.C. was, in effect, a version of the early Ramey contract with Westinghouse for its work on the nuclear submarine. Instead of promulgating detailed safety instructions and supervising industry's compliance, the A.E.C. avoided conventional regulatory paradigms in order to work with the industry "in a spirit of partnership and friendly cooperation." The A.E.C. simply asked the companies that joined the commercial nuclear program to work, with good sense and good faith, toward a common goal, which it vaguely specified as "reasonable assurance that the health and safety of the public will not be endangered." A self-regulating industry was left to decide how best to do this. If the industry was to move ahead quickly, A.E.C. officials reasoned, the companies pioneering nuclear power technology had to be given the discretion to choose plant designs and get them built without a lot of red tape.

The A.E.C. staff was instructed not to formulate rigid safety rules or to undertake laborious independent reviews and double-checking of the designs that applicants proposed to build. It would issue the necessary licenses to industry and then get out of the way. A.E.C. regulations were not intended to restrain the industry, Chairman Strauss emphasized, but to "open the way to all who are interested in engaging in research and development or commercial activities in the atomic-energy field."

The A.E.C.'s hands-off approach toward the regulation of the industry was more than a reflection of Strauss' pro-business philosophy. Even if it had wanted to play a more activist role, the agency's staff lacked the basic knowledge needed to do so. Before the A.E.C. could develop and enforce comprehensive safety standards, research would have to be completed on the long list of "unknowns" that A.E.C. safety advisers had identified. This could take years, and no one wanted to wait, least of all the Joint Committee. It insisted that the A.E.C. forswear the creation of an elaborate regulatory program and told the agency to process license applications as quickly as possible. The committee and its staff believed that cooperation on the part of the A.E.C. was essential if industry was to be encouraged to join the nuclear program. The new Staff Director of the Joint Committee, the architect of the A.E.C.'s friendly partnership with the nuclear industry, was former A.E.C. lawyer James T. Ramey.

On paper, the A.E.C.'s informal regulatory program may have closely resembled the loose contract that Ramey had negotiated with Westinghouse. As implemented by the agency's tiny regulatory staff—which at this time could fit in one small office—it was only a pale imitation of the arrangement that Rickover had used so successfully in managing the development of the submarine reactor.

Rickover was an engineer, who knew what he wanted and personally made sure that the industrial engineers working on his program were doing exactly that. The A.E.C.'s regulatory effort, in contrast, was led by lawyers, who were specifically instructed to delegate management authority to the industry. Harold Price, the chief regulatory officer, was a former Agriculture Department lawyer who had served on the staff of the War Production Board before joining the Commission. He and his staff did not go down into the trenches, like Rickover, and wrestle with the engineering details of reactor design. Instead, following the Commission's directives, they exercised a loose château-generalship over the commercial reactor-development effort. They stayed in A.E.C. headquarters and handed out licenses to those who wanted to build the plants, being careful to stay far away from the front lines where the plants were being designed and constructed. Indeed, to speed the program along, Price and his staff issued construction permits without even seeing detailed designs for the proposed facilities. (The companies preferred not to get locked into fixed designs and typically gave A.E.C. only very sketchy outlines of the kinds of nuclear-reactor system they intended to build.) Price and his staff made it clear to the industry that safety was the industry's responsibility.

THE ONE IMPORTANT INDEPENDENT CHECK on safety in the A.E.C.'s regulatory program was the Advisory Committee on Reactor Safeguards. Its fifteen experts reviewed each proposed nuclear plant and wrote a report to the Commission on the adequacy of its safety precautions. As the number of proposed plants increased, so did the responsibilities of the committee, although not its popularity.

The committee came into sharp conflict with the A.E.C. after the Commission, in August of 1955, approved one of the showpieces of its Power Reactor Demonstration Program: the proposed "breeder reactor" that a consortium of utility companies, led by Detroit Edison, wanted to build on the western end of Lake Erie, midway between Detroit and Toledo.

The most advanced reactor that had ever been proposed, the breeder operated on principles different from those of the water-cooled reactors, like the PWR, that have become the mainstay of the United States nuclear power industry. These ordinary reactors are fueled with uranium, which they use up as they operate. Some new fuel is also produced, as a byproduct of the chain reactions, when some of the uranium is converted into plutonium. The resulting plutonium, however, is insufficient to make up for the U-235 consumed.

Breeder reactors, on the other hand, such as the one proposed in 1955, which was to be named after Enrico Fermi, would use plutonium as a fuel. The plutonium in the "core" of the Fermi reactor, moreover, would be surrounded by a "blanket" of uranium. As the reactor operated, the fissioning of plutonium would provide the heat that, as in any power plant, nuclear or otherwise, is used to create steam to drive a turbine generator. But it would also do something more. As it fissioned, plutonium would give off extra neutrons that would convert some of the uranium in and around the core into more plutonium. The Fermi reactor, it was hoped, would "breed" more plutonium fuel than it used. On its ability to do so, moreover, rested the A.E.C.'s hopes that nuclear power would provide an inexhaustible energy source for the future. "Our main belief—I guess it's still my belief—is that nuclear energy is barely worth the candle, I guess you'd say, unless you develop the breeder," Alvin Weinberg said. For if breeder reactors could be successfully developed, the commercial nuclear program would be able to bootstrap itself along, one generation of breeder reactors creating the fuel for the next in an ever-expanding nuclear power industry.

The problem with the proposed breeder reactor, from the point of view of the Advisory Committee on Reactor Safeguards, was one of safety. Unlike ordinary reactors, fueled by relatively dilute U-235, which cannot explode, the Fermi reactor would be fueled with highly concentrated plutonium, the kind of material used in nuclear bombs.

The plutonium core of the Fermi reactor could indeed explode—and during certain kinds of accidents, safety analysts worried, it might. (They were concerned about a small, "low-order" explosion, not the kind of blast that a nuclear weapon produces.) The Fermi reactor, in addition, would be cooled by a liquid metal, sodium, which explodes when it comes into contact with air or water, a chemistry that made the possibility of sodium leaks a serious problem. The reactor would have a much more compact and powerful core than ordinary reactors, and there was the concern that it might overheat, as had already happened in an experimental breeder reactor at the A.E.C.'s testing station in Idaho. What would then happen was very uncertain, but the Advisory Committee was concerned that some sequence of events might get started and cause a disastrous release of radioactive materials from the plant into the surrounding region.

On top of all the technical issues was the most worrisome problem of all: the siting of the proposed Fermi reactor in a heavily populated region. There were Detroit, twenty-nine miles to the north, and Toledo, thirty miles south, not to mention nearby Dearborn and Ypsilanti, Michigan, and the Canadian city of Windsor, Ontario, across the lake. Millions of people might be affected by any large accidental radiation release from the plant.

Detroit Edison engineers and advisers—including Nobel laureate Hans Bethe, one of the few Manhattan Project physicists who remained close to the reactor-development effort—met with the Advisory Committee on Reactor Safeguards and tried to convince the members that the proposed plant could be operated safely. The committee was perturbed, nevertheless, by the fact that the theoretical calculations used to predict how the new reactor would perform had "not been established experimentally, and must be so before the operation of a reactor could possibly be recommended for a site so close to a populated area." After a number of private meetings with plant designers and with its own consultants, the chairman of the Advisory Committee, C. Rogers McCullough, wrote a report on its behalf to the A.E.C., on June 6, 1956, recommending against the construction of the plant. "[T]here is insufficient information available at this time to give assurance the [Fermi] reactor can be operated at this site without public hazard," he concluded.

The negative letter from the committee forced the A.E.C. to choose between its ambitions and its prudence, a choice that it had no difficulty in making. The Commission ignored the letter from its "Brake Department," did not make it public, withheld it from the Joint Committee, and issued a construction permit for the Fermi plant.

The A.E.C. authorization for the Fermi breeder reactor was subsequently challenged by the United Auto Workers—on behalf of the union's members who lived in the region—and the project became embroiled in a protracted lawsuit that went all the way to the Supreme Court. At issue was the A.E.C. policy, which it acknowledged, of issuing nuclear-plant construction permits before all safety issues were resolved. The A.E.C. did so, it explained, on the basis of the assurances by the builders that all safety problems would be resolved prior to operation. The A.E.C. said that it would verify this before issuing an operating license.

The Supreme Court ruled, in June 1961, that the 1954 Atomic Energy Act had given the A.E.C. broad discretion to regulate the nuclear program as it saw fit, and that the agency had acted within the limits of its authority when it approved the Fermi reactor. The ruling, by a vote of seven to two, cleared yet another obstacle from the way of the nuclear industry.

Justices Hugo Black and William O. Douglas dissented from the Court's majority, arguing that once the A.E.C. gave permission for plant construction the momentum behind the project would be so great that it would very likely be allowed to operate, in spite of unresolved safety questions. No A.E.C. official, they said, would dare leave the companies with a hundred-million-dollar "White Elephant" on their hands. "When millions have been invested, the momentum is on the side of the applicant, not on the side of the public," Douglas wrote. He called the A.E.C. practice, sanctioned by the Court's majority, of approving plant construction despite major, unsolved safety problems "a lighthearted approach to the most awesome, the most deadly, the most dangerous process ever created."

THE JANUARY 2, 1961, issue of *Time* displayed cover photographs of fifteen American scientists to whom the magazine had given its "Men of the Year" award for 1960. It had been another "golden year in the ever advancing Age of Science . . . a year of massive advance on nearly all scientific fronts," the editors wrote. They listed the giant strides that scientists were making in molecular biology and particle physics, in chemistry and radioastronomy, and, especially, in the United States space program. "Almost inevitably, space science was the glamour science," they noted.

Nobel Laureate Glenn Seaborg, who would shortly arrive in Washington to become the Chairman of the A.E.C., and who coveted a place in history, was not among the fifteen celebrated scientists. Nor was there any mention in *Time*'s catalogue of America's recent scientific progress of the nuclear power program into which the federal government had poured hundreds of millions of dollars. There were clear reasons for the omissions.

By January 1961, only two reactors built under the Power Reactor Demonstration Program were operating. Shippingport, completed in 1957 under Rickover's watchful eye, had been a technical success. The Dresden plant in Illinois, built by General Electric, was also working, although somewhat less successfully. (Its boiling-water reactor, or "BWR," the kind G.E. specialized in, and the principal commercial rival of Westinghouse's PWR, had to be shut down immediately after it was started up in 1959 as a result of defective equipment, troubles that were dismissed as mere shakedown problems.) Five other small prototype reactors were under construction. That was the extent of the United States nuclear power program, for the electric utility companies had no plans to build a large number of additional reactors.

The nuclear power program was a small, government-subsidized sideshow, as far as the electric utility industry was concerned, and it was going nowhere. Even federal support for the program was on the wane, with the Bureau of the Budget considering a cutback in the subsidies for nuclear-plant construction. "What has happened is that the glamour has gone out of atomic power," *Science* magazine, once an enthusiastic backer of the program, commented. "Space has taken over most of the position that atomic energy so recently held as a field to be pursued, quite aside from its intrinsic value, as a symbol of national prestige and technological supremacy. Accordingly, the goal of economically competitive nuclear power, once talked about almost in the way the race to the moon is discussed now, has lost much of its urgency."

There were no political, legal or bureaucratic obstacles to the nuclear program—Congress, the Eisenhower Administration, and the A.E.C. had eliminated them all—but there was one fundamental problem. Economically, nuclear power did not look like a winner. Coal, the major fuel used by the electric utilities, was in plentiful supply. Improvements in the efficiency of coal-burning power plants, moreover, had been dramatically reducing the cost of the electricity they generated. Even under the most favorable assumptions, nuclear power appeared to be decidedly more expensive than the electricity generated using this orthodox fuel.

"Such competition is indeed formidable," the head of the A.E.C.'s reactor-development effort, Frank Pittman, admitted in 1961. Others put the doubts about nuclear power in starker terms. The atomic power program "has been quite a flop, and is not to be taken seriously," former A.E.C. Chairman Lilienthal told an interviewer. "Our economic expectations concerning cheap nuclear power have, so far at any rate, failed us rather completely," Manhattan Project physicist Eugene Wigner said. *Newsweek,* which had been highly optimistic about nuclear power, conceded that "the dream of atomic electricity 'too cheap to meter' " was "dead," but it insisted that it would be available at "reasonable prices"—an assertion that utility companies in 1960 did not find convincing.

The nuclear plants that had already been built had been much more costly than expected—Consolidated Edison's Indian Point plant, for example, had cost about $110 million, instead of the $55 million originally projected—and the A.E.C.'s estimates that year still showed that the electricity from nuclear plants would be about 30 to 60 percent more expensive than from conventional power stations. Nuclear power plants, like Shippingport, might work technically, but as investments they didn't appear to pay.

Given the widespread disillusionment with atomic energy, President John F. Kennedy asked Chairman Seaborg, in March 1962, to prepare a report that took "a new and hard look at the role of nuclear power in our economy." The dean of America's scientific optimists and head of the agency promoting nuclear power was thereby offered the opportunity to write the official reassessment that would determine future federal policy on nuclear power. Seaborg accepted the assignment "with enthusiasm," as a power hitter might swing at an easy pitch. The resulting document—*Civilian Nuclear Power: A Report to the President 1962*—argues that "the development and exploitation of nuclear-electric power is clearly in the near- and long-term national interest and should be vigorously pursued."

Economics was the key issue. Seaborg's report said that despite the high costs of the early reactors, major breakthroughs would permit the cost of future nuclear plants to drop substantially. "Happily . . . much progress has been made" and the "difficulties . . . in developing a technology that is economically competitive with conventional power generation methods" have been "progressively overcome." "We conclude that nuclear power is on the threshold of economic competitiveness and can soon be made competitive in areas consuming a significant fraction of the nation's electrical energy." The federal program for subsidizing nuclear-power development should be continued, the A.E.C. argued, because "economic nuclear power is so near at hand that only a modest additional incentive is required to initiate its appreciable early use by the utilities."

With a keen understanding of the role of self-fulfilling prophecies in government policy making, the A.E.C. report offered the confident prediction that nuclear plants by the year 2000 would supply half of the electric power consumed in the United States. How could the Bureau of the Budget even think of cutting off support for the development of a technology on which the nation was to depend so heavily?

The report included few details on how the A.E.C. arrived at its favorable estimates of the economics of nuclear power. Its findings were not, in fact, the product of a purely independent A.E.C. analysis. In preparing the report, the A.E.C. had met with representatives of each of the reactor manufacturers. The "manufacturers' current estimates" of nuclear-plant costs were then used as the principal basis for the agency's conclusions. In an appendix to the report, fourteen tables of numbers were provided to document its economic assumptions. The footnotes to the tables were said to explain "the basis" for the numbers. No footnote, however, discussed the key numbers in the tables, the very low estimates that were given for the cost of building the plants. Those estimates, the A.E.C. asserted in the text, were based on "extensive evaluation" by its staff. The report did not present the details of this work.

The A.E.C. staff was able to offer a favorable assessment of the cost of electricity from large nuclear plants without fear of contradiction, for none had ever been built. As long as you were talking about the future, former A.E.C. General Manager Carroll Wilson observed in a recent interview, "You could be as rosy as you wanted without anybody calling you out."

Chairman Seaborg "was not a forceful, driving manager," according to A.E.C. historian Richard Hewlett. Unlike Rickover, whose attention to detail became legendary, Seaborg was a visionary, dreaming of the future. He left the day-to-day running of the agency to others. "People didn't see in Glenn what they liked in John Wayne," one of his senior aides recalled. "They didn't think he was a crisp decision maker."

In overseeing the preparation of the 1962 report, Seaborg did not demand a searching reappraisal of the suitability of Westinghouse and General Electric reactor designs for use in a large commercial power program. Nor did he insist on a systematic review of the long list of safety "unknowns" that had been identified in the 1950s. He was satisfied when the agency's staff—a bureaucracy that had staked its future on the idea of a large nuclear program—presented an optimistic report on the "marvels" that it expected the industry to accomplish. He passed it on to President Kennedy. It was not so much the requested rethinking of the nuclear program the President asked for as it was a selling document, designed to put the best face on the prospects for an atomic-powered future. One former presidential science adviser characterized Seaborg as "a weak leader, easily influenced by the whim of the bureaucracy." His former associate at Berkeley, John Gofman, feels that Seaborg was "used" by the A.E.C. as "a marvelous front man for the wonderful things the atom could do." He was a Nobel laureate and he gave the A.E.C.'s judgments an air of scientific impartiality.

THE A.E.C.'S PREDICTIONS on the economics of nuclear power helped to support the sales campaigns of General Electric and Westinghouse. The principal selling point they emphasized was the "economies of scale" in nuclear power generation. As nuclear plants got bigger, they proposed, they would be able to produce power more cheaply, at prices competitive with fossil-fuel-burning power stations. The four power reactors operating by the end of 1962 had the capacity, on the average, to produce about 150 megawatts of electric power. Shippingport had a rated capacity of 90 megawatts, and even the largest among them, at Indian Point, had an output of only 270 megawatts, and of that only about half the power came from the plant's reactor. (Indian Point was actually a hybrid nuclear and oil-burning power plant.) The manufacturers said that much larger plants could be built. This looked like idle talk, however, until December 1963, when the General Public Utilities Company of Parsippany, New Jersey, announced that it had purchased, without federal subsidy, a 515-megawatt plant at Oyster Creek from General Electric.

Chairman Seaborg led the applause for the Oyster Creek plant and declared that this sale "proved" that nuclear power had become economically competitive. In fact, all that the sale demonstrated was the successful marketing strategy of General Electric. A very low price—$60 million—had convinced the buyers that it could be competitive with coal. The plant, however, was sold far below its true cost. As in retailing, when stores advertise heavily discounted items to lure customers inside, General Electric was using Oyster Creek as a "loss leader." It was gambling that it might open up a large market for additional nuclear plants, and other utility companies did indeed begin to take nuclear power much more seriously. They did not recognize, until several years later, that Oyster Creek was, as *Business Week* described it, the "greatest loss leader in American industry." General Electric has never disclosed its loss, but it is estimated that it may have been upwards of $30 million.

The Oyster Creek sale marked a turning point in the commercialization of nuclear power. General Electric and Westinghouse approached the major utility companies during the next few years with increasingly daring proposals. Although larger than any power plant that had ever operated, nuclear or conventional, Oyster Creek was soon dwarfed by the new units proposed by the manufacturers. They would be 800-megawatt plants, 1,000-megawatt plants, or even larger. "Back in '58," James Young, a vice-president of General Electric, told reporters, "we wondered how we could ever make a three-hundred-megawatt reactor. Now it's reasonable to make a plant of two thousand megawatts and we could even go to eight thousand." To make it all the easier for the utilities to get into the nuclear power business, the reactor manufacturers proposed "turnkey" contracts under which they would provide not just a reactor but a complete power plant. The owners would just have to pick up the "keys" to turn them on. By 1964, it looked as if nuclear power, which had, a few years earlier, been all but written off as a viable commercial enterprise, was suddenly about to come of age. Glenn Seaborg said that economic nuclear power was "an absolute certainty."

THE ISSUE OF REACTOR SAFETY had been barely discussed in Seaborg's 1962 report to President Kennedy; it had received less than a page. In preparing the report, the A.E.C. consulted with the Federal Power Commission, the Department of the Interior, the Bureau of the Budget, the Joint Committee on Atomic Energy, and the Atomic Industrial Forum, among others. It did not seek the advice of the one official body concerned with safety, its own Advisory Committee on Reactor Safeguards.

In its reports to the A.E.C. over the years, the safety committee had identified a number of unsolved safety problems. The 1962 report did not attempt to assess whether satisfactory progress had been made on any of these matters. Nor did it analyze the kind of safety problems that might affect the new, large reactors that the industry wanted to build. In its final pages, the report observed, in passing, that "vigorous efforts" must be made to "maximize the inherent safety of nuclear power."

Chairman Seaborg preferred to avoid detailed public discussion of nuclear-plant risks. He customarily dismissed the subject with the categorical statement that safety was "an overriding consideration" and that "every possible precaution" was being taken to protect the public. He expected the public to trust the agency to do the right thing. He himself paid no close attention to the subject, leaving this work to the A.E.C. staff. The Commission staff, in turn, following the informal regulatory arrangements it had adopted in the 1950s, delegated the responsibility to the nuclear industry.

Safety was a factor in plant design, but it was more a kind of background noise that the designers could not tune out, rather than their "overriding consideration." "I was involved very much in initiating the pressurized-water reactor," Alvin Weinberg, who shares the original patent for the device, said in a recent interview. "Safety was always a consideration, but I guess one would have to say that in the original conception of the light-water reactor, the primary concern—of course, it was a military device—was 'would it work?' " Having demonstrated, on the *Nautilus* and at Shippingport, that it did, designers then scaled up the small reactors they had developed in order to make a commercial-size nuclear-power system. In the process, they made repeated safety compromises, with A.E.C. approval, in order to keep costs down. "Every possible precaution" was not taken. The nuclear industry couldn't afford them if it wanted to compete with fossil fuels.

"There was a fundamental tug of war," Weinberg said, "between 'as safe as possible' and 'as cheap as possible.' . . . When the nuclear business got started, the price of electricity from coal was 3 or 4 mills per kilowatt hour," he explained. "Nuclear had to get into that ball park or there wouldn't be any commercial nuclear power." The economics of the early reactors, such as Shippingport, was decidedly unfavorable—that plant producing power at a cost of about fifty mills per kilowatt hour. If nuclear power was to compete, the designers knew, he said, that they would have to "sharpen their pencils" and look for ways to cut costs.

"The reactor designer is responsive to the pressures that are applied," Theos J. Thompson, a member of the Advisory Committee on Reactor Safeguards, wrote in a 1965 internal memo to his colleagues. "During the past few years the economic factors have received the most emphasis. Even five years ago it was not clear whether coal or oil or nuclear power would in the long run be more economic. Now, I believe, it is quite clear that nuclear power can hold its own end of the economic race with more conventional fuels. The economic pressures now are those of an extremely competitive market . . . These pressures tend always to reduce the margin of safety conservatism."

In reactor siting, for example, the companies pressed for permission to build nuclear plants close to the urban centers that would be consuming the power—rather than pay the cost of transmitting the power from remote sites. This greatly increased the risk of exposing a large number of people to nuclear-radiation injuries in the event of a serious mishap. Seaborg and the A.E.C. staff were willing nevertheless to accommodate industry's demand for more convenient sites. Abandoning its early siting practices, the A.E.C. allowed reactors to be built close to major metropolitan areas, although not, as some builders proposed, in the middle of cities. (Consolidated Edison, for example, applied for permission to build a nuclear plant in the Ravenswood section of Queens, across the East River from midtown Manhattan; five and a half million people lived and worked within five miles of this proposed site.)

To justify siting in more densely populated areas, "containment" buildings were put up around the reactors; these buildings were supposed to prevent the escape of radioactive material during serious accidents. As reactors increased rapidly in size, accidents affecting them would become more difficult to control and the containment buildings would become less of a barrier against the leakage of radioactive materials. Plants were still licensed for heavily populated areas, a further compromise that was rationalized by pointing to the "engineered safeguards" that were being added on to the plants. The effectiveness of these novel devices was uncertain, however, because proper testing of them had not been completed. The A.E.C. recognized the urgent need for such research, but allowed the companies to do it on a deferred schedule. Plant construction, in the meantime, was allowed to proceed.

The greatest safety compromise of all was allowing very large reactors to be built, to enable the industry to exploit "economies of scale." In a more orderly development program, the industry would have first been required to gain operating experience on small and intermediate-size reactors before proceeding with the building of mammoth ones. "The business grew at a phenomenal rate, and sizes kept getting larger and larger," Weinberg said. "I think there are some in the business—the old-timers—who have argued that it would have been better if it had gone slower, if it hadn't gone to thousand-megawatt plants before you had had fifteen years' experience with, say, 600-megawatt plants, and so on. That's an arguable question, of course."

A carefully managed development effort would also have required the building of prototypes for the large plants, just as Rickover did with his submarine reactor, which was thoroughly tested in a full-scale experimental facility at the A.E.C.'s remote testing station in Idaho. The A.E.C. did not impose such controls on the nuclear industry, which, as officials later acknowledged, rushed "from Kittyhawk to the Boeing 747 in two decades." The "experiment" of operating large reactors, whose advanced designs relied on complex, untried technology, was performed not in a faraway desert but at sites chosen by the utilities on the perimeter of the country's major metropolitan areas.

Larger and more powerful reactors, A.E.C. safety advisers told the Commission, would necessarily be harder to control. Their nuclear fuel would overheat more quickly in the event of cooling system malfunctions. They would also contain much more radioactive material, and this would greatly increase the loss of life in the event of a major accident. By the middle 1960s, A.E.C. safety advisers had identified one particular "sequence of events" that became the focus for much of the subsequent concern about the safety of large reactors. They called this safety problem the "China Syndrome."

The large reactors being proposed by Westinghouse and General Electric would use ordinary water to cool their nuclear fuel. The safety of these machines, A.E.C. experts concluded, would be dependent on the plumbing systems that delivered vital cooling water to the reactor. In the event of a pipe rupture or other major interference with the normal cooling system, the reactor's hot uranium fuel could quickly overheat. In fact, if such reactors were suddenly deprived of needed cooling water, the uranium fuel in them could rapidly begin to melt and form itself into a heavy, white-hot blob of molten metal that could penetrate through the reactor and melt its way down through the basement of the plant, into the ground. (It was said, facetiously, that the molten fuel would be heading in the general direction of China.)

In older reactors, the small uranium cores could not overheat enough to melt, or if they did, they would not be able to penetrate the containment buildings. Unfortunately, with reactors that were being proposed—ten times larger than the early ones such as Shippingport—all this was changed. "Meltdown" accidents, accordingly, became a real threat, not just to public safety but to the ambition of Seaborg and the A.E.C. for a large nuclear power program.

THE SAFETY RISK associated with large reactors was explored in a study that the A.E.C. began, in secret, in the summer of 1964. It was directed by an ad hoc steering committee composed of senior officials. Dr. Clifford Beck of the A.E.C.'s regulatory staff headed the effort. A physicist by training, he had been one of the original members of the regulatory staff that had worked under the direction of Harold Price since 1955. The new study was intended to update WASH-740, the A.E.C.'s 1957 report on potential nuclear accidents and their consequences. Scientists at the Brookhaven National Laboratory, in Long Island, where the original study was done, were called upon to carry out the detailed technical analysis needed for the revised version.

The minutes of the early meetings of the steering committee note that the official motivation for the inquiry—which was requested by the Joint Committee on Atomic Energy—was the same question of accident liability addressed in WASH-740. The Price-Anderson Act was going to expire in 1967; it had been adopted as a temporary device to overcome industry's jitters about entering the nuclear business, and the Joint Committee wanted to know whether its liability limits needed to be amended. An "updated" version of WASH-740 was, therefore, desirable.

The 1957 study, moreover, had caused public-relations problems for the industry, since it contained such fearsome estimates of the injuries that might result from potential reactor accidents. There was the feeling that a more sophisticated look at the subject, reflecting all the insights into reactor safety that had been gained over the years, might lead to a less pessimistic assessment of the consequences. "A major reason for reconsidering WASH-740," according to A.E.C. internal documents written in the summer of 1964, "was that many people feel that new estimates [of accident consequences] will be lower." Publishing such results would secure a public-relations windfall for the A.E.C.

One member of the steering committee, U. M. Staebler, of the A.E.C.'s Division of Reactor Development and Technology, argued that public-relations factors should be ignored. The A.E.C. should simply do a "scholarly job" and "let the chips fall where they may," he told his colleagues. Other officials warned that the study was too sensitive to be done in such a manner. "Great care should be exercised in any revision [of WASH-740] to avoid establishing and/or reinforcing the popular notion that reactors are unsafe. Though this is a public-information or promotional problem that the A.E.C. now faces with less than desirable success, I feel that by calculating the consequences of hypothetical accidents the A.E.C. should not place itself in the position of making the location of reactors near urban areas nearly indefensible," according to a note written to Dr. Beck by S. Allan Lough, another member of the steering committee.

Brookhaven scientists worked through the summer and early autumn of 1964 preparing the technical material needed by the steering committee. On October 21, 1964, the full steering committee, led by Dr. Beck, met with the Brookhaven team. They were performing computer calculations of the potential consequences of meltdown accidents, and the steering committee wanted a status report on how the work was going. "Dr. Beck asked if the computer programs were ready," the minutes of that meeting read. "Mr. Downes replied that they were running, but the results were frightening." They had found that as many as 45,000 people might be killed by a major reactor accident. (WASH-740, in contrast, had estimated only 3,400 fatalities in the most extreme accident it had considered.)

According to the update, moreover, property damage might be as much as forty times greater than the seven-billion-dollar figure in the earlier study. The steering committee learned that its "fond hope that some of the pessimism reflected in the WASH-740 hypothetical models could be reduced by new information" had been shattered.

Kenneth Downes of the Brookhaven staff explained to the steering committee that the results were almost identical with those obtained in WASH-740, "the only difference being the extension to higher power levels." The nuclear accident considered in WASH-740 involved a reactor that produced only about 185 megawatts of electric power, a reactor that was considered "large" in 1956. By 1964, however, 1,000-megawatt nuclear plants were being proposed, and it was a plant of this size that Brookhaven scientists were considering in the update.

Such a plant would routinely hold more long-lived radioactive material than would be produced by the detonation of a thousand Hiroshima-size nuclear bombs. The release of any substantial fraction of that inventory could spread radioactive contaminants over a wide area. "The possible size of the area of such a disaster might be equal to that of the state of Pennsylvania," the Brookhaven scientists told the steering committee.

The committee was appalled by the results. At its urging, the Brookhaven group—which included physicists, chemists, meteorologists, medical experts and other specialists—investigated every possibility they could think of to come up with less gruesome estimates. They tried, for example, to determine whether there were any possible mechanisms, as some A.E.C. officials hoped, that would limit the release of radioactive materials from nuclear fuel that had overheated and melted. The Brookhaven experts said no, and that to the contrary there was "abundant evidence that all the inventory of specific fission products"—such as the radioactive iodine produced as a reactor operates—"would be released" when the core melted.

The steering committee asked whether more refined methods of calculating the consequences of meltdown accidents would produce lower estimates. The Brookhaven scientists, in a report to the committee, again said no.

> In reexamining the details of calculational methods, we have, on the basis of improvements in knowledge and techniques, been able to include formulas, values of parameters and methods of handling the data which permit more accurate and more detailed calculations. This has been particularly true for fission-product releases from melted fuel, atmospheric dispersion of airborne materials, and the mechanics of processing of data by computer machines. In total, however, these refinements contribute to accuracy and clarification in degree and in detail, but the over-all magnitude and character of damaging consequences which would result from major releases of radioactivity are not different from what they were calculated to be in 1957. That is, if large quantities of fission products escape into the environment, the resulting damages will depend on prevailing weather conditions and, if these are unfavorable, large damages will result.

Hoping for favorable results, the A.E.C. learned from the Brookhaven team that

> we have found in our present study nothing inherent in reactors or in safeguard systems as they now have been developed which guarantees either that major reactor accidents will not occur or that protective safeguard systems will not fail. Should such accidents occur and the protective systems fail, very large damages could result.

Brookhaven's pessimistic conclusions alarmed the steering committee. According to the minutes of subsequent meetings, the members were worried that "these results would strengthen opposition to further nuclear power" and might jeopardize all of the A.E.C.'s plans for approving nuclear plants in populated areas. Technically, accidents of such catastrophic magnitude were theoretically possible, all of its experts agreed. Still, the official policy of the A.E.C. was that such accidents were "incredible events," so exceedingly unlikely that they posed no real threat to public safety. The committee wanted accident "probability estimates" prepared that would prove this.

One member of the committee, Dr. David Okrent, who was also a member of the Advisory Committee on Reactor Safeguards, questioned the unscientific attitude of the steering committee in trying to direct the study toward preordained conclusions. He challenged the assumption that catastrophic accidents were necessarily "incredible events." He noted that various events previously declared incredible by nuclear-plant designers on the basis of their presumed low probability were subsequently found to be credible—after they had actually happened. The minutes of one meeting included Okrent's observations that "people are unhappy with the catastrophic results and . . . they secretly hope that some other group will supply optimistic probabilities that can be applied, and this disturbed him."

At another meeting, "there was considerable divergence of opinion within the committee on the matter of probability of highly improbable accidents. Dr. Beck noted that this was the most difficult problem encountered in the writing of WASH-740. . . . There was a general consensus that, while a maximum degree of objectivity in the balancing of hazard and gain was desired, the report must avoid the twin pitfalls of overpessimism, which might produce great difficulties in gaining public acceptance of nuclear energy, and underpessimism, which might appear to be a 'white-wash' of the problem."

To the dismay of the steering committee, the optimistic probability estimates that were desired were not readily forthcoming, because the Brookhaven scientists refused to work on them. Nuclear power was a new technology, and there was so little reactor-operating experience, they believed, that there was no dependable statistical basis for estimating the probability of serious reactor accidents.

"The matter of probability was brought up, and the BNL [Brookhaven National Laboratory] representatives stated that, in their opinion, no significant scientific progress could be made and they proposed not to study it . . . The BNL people . . . insisted that they not consider probabilities of accidents," the minutes of one steering committee meeting noted. Further meetings were held at Brookhaven on this subject, but the staff scientists there remained adamant that "a quantitative determination of reactor accident probabilities cannot be made at this time due to the paucity of input data."

Dr. Beck decided that he would prepare a chapter on accident probability himself so that a treatment of this key topic could be included in the update. He concluded, however, after writing several drafts of this chapter, that he could make no technically defensible estimate for the chances of serious accidents. Nuclear plants, he wrote, in one of his drafts, were subject to "mishaps of many kinds . . . breakdown of machinery, malfunction of instruments, deviations from established [operating] procedures, operators' errors." They did have various safety systems, but "many of the more imaginative and extensive safeguard systems designed for power reactors have not yet been proven out by simulated tests or operating experience," nor was there assurance that "all possible paths leading to catastrophe have been recognized and safeguarded."

Of particular concern was the complexity of nuclear plants,

which meant that small, seemingly inconsequential problems could easily be overlooked even by diligent safety reviewers. Such difficulties could some day set the stage for a serious mishap.

> Totally unexpected abnormal situations do occur, and it is the case that relatively minor events in themselves, in combination with other abnormalities, can turn an insignificant situation into a major accident . . . Reactor technology is still in a relatively early stage of development and it is not yet certain that all possibilities of unsafe behavior have been identified and appropriately safeguarded.

Beck concluded that the "most baffling and insoluble enigma" of nuclear technology was that "it is in principle easy and straightforward to calculate potential damages that might be realized under . . . postulated accident conditions," but "there is not even in principle an objective and quantitative method of calculating probability or improbability of accidents or the likelihood that potential hazards will or will not be realized." Beck's various drafts were distributed to the steering committee members, and his conclusion stated that "It is not at all assured that the conditions [assumed by Brookhaven] cannot happen. [We feel] that we cannot predict if, or when, it might happen." The attempt to find optimistic probability estimates—in order to lift what the steering committee called the "pall of gloom" from the Brookhaven calculations of accident consequences—ended in failure.

By the end of 1964, the steering committee was anxiously discussing the impact of its findings on the future of the nuclear-power program. The members of the steering committee were reluctant to publish any report that could "strengthen opposition to further nuclear power." According to the minutes of one meeting, they believed that the "impact of publishing the revised WASH-740 report on the reactor industry should be weighed before publication." The release of the results was far too sensitive a matter to be arranged by the steering committee itself, and the members decided, accordingly, during their meeting of December 19, 1964, that "the results of the study must be revealed to the Commission and the JCAE [Joint Committee on Atomic Energy] without subterfuge although the method of presentation to the public has not been resolved at this time." Chairman Seaborg and the other leaders of the United States nuclear power program would have to decide what to do.

"AS WE LOOK AT THE STATUS of nuclear energy development, we see something solid," Glenn Seaborg, the head of the United States delegation to the U.N. Conference on the Peaceful Uses of Atomic Energy, said in Geneva, in September 1964. "We find that quietly, without fanfare, the thing we have been waiting for has happened: the age of nuclear power has begun." A few weeks later, in Vienna, at the General Conference of the International Atomic Energy Agency, he noted the "atmosphere of confidence [that] pervades the international nuclear community." The prevailing optimism, he said, was "rooted in experience" and reflected the "great strides" that had been made in nuclear technology and the fact that "the time has arrived when we have the capability of producing nuclear power economically." The economic competitiveness of nuclear power was even better than it was estimated to be in his 1962 report to the President, he said, and he announced that the A.E.C. now believed that "perhaps as much as half" of the power plants purchased by United States utilities "in the decade or so ahead" would be nuclear.

"One of our primary concerns, of course, is safety," Seaborg told his international audiences, noting the goal of developing safety devices for the plants "without adding unnecessarily to capital costs by overdesigning." The safety "challenges have been met successfully" on existing reactors, he added, and "there was no reason to believe that they will not be met as successfully in building the reactors which now are on the drawing boards." He did not mention the major A.E.C. study of reactor safety then in progress at Brookhaven.

No nuclear plants were purchased by United States utility companies in 1964, but companies in several parts of the country were actively reviewing bids from the competing reactor manufacturers. Seaborg's assessment of the high level of interest in nuclear plants was certainly correct. With the utilities on the verge of a major commitment to nuclear power, senior A.E.C. officials were acutely concerned about possible public opposition to the program. To date, there had been little controversy. There had been the lawsuit over the Fermi plant, but many observers felt that it had been inspired more by partisan politics—unions who supported the Democrats using it as a way to embarrass the Eisenhower Administration before the 1960 elections—than by a real concern about safety.

At any rate, that controversy had been settled by the Supreme Court. There had also been local opposition to a few plants. Residents of Malibu, a posh California beach community, had objected to the building of a proposed plant there, and a group calling itself the Northern California Association to Preserve Bodega Head and Bay was protesting the building of a plant near an earthquake fault. The principal factor in the opposition to these plants was local concern about the particular sites, rather than a general concern about nuclear safety.

Under the Atomic Energy Act of 1954, the A.E.C. was required to hold a public hearing every time it wanted to issue a construction permit for a nuclear plant. Any local residents who objected to the proposed plant could participate. The hearing was a formal legal proceeding in which the parties—the utility company applying for the construction permit, the A.E.C. regulatory staff, which reviewed proposed applications, and any "intervenors" who opposed the plant—were represented by counsel. The A.E.C. did not want the public hearings to impede the reactor program, and the rules governing the hearings, which it wrote, were designed with its priorities in mind.

Before the hearing, the A.E.C. staff and the utility company worked out their differences in private so that they would present a united front before the hearing board. The three-member hearing board, whose members were selected by the A.E.C., did not carry out an independent evaluation of the safety of the plant. The board's assigned role was to determine whether the proposed plant was consistent with established A.E.C. policy. Citizens challenging the utility company seldom had the resources or technical expertise to examine the safety of the proposed facility in detail, and the A.E.C., under the hearing rules that it wrote, refused to grant them access to the agency's own data about potential safety problems.

"The only consensus among all of the parties to the proceedings appeared to be a general evaluation that the whole process as it now stands is nothing more than a charade, the outcome of which is, for all intents and purposes, predetermined," according to a 1973 study of the A.E.C.'s hearing process sponsored by the National Science Foundation.

"Seaborg tended to have the elitist attitude," A.E.C. historian Richard Hewlett noted in an interview. "In fact, he might be the epitome of the elitist attitude—that 'Daddy knows best.' He believed that a Nobel Prize winner knew more than a good physicist, that a good physicist knows more than the man in the street." As the rules for the A.E.C. hearings demonstrated, there was never any doubt in Seaborg's mind as to who should make the decisions about the licensing of nuclear plants.

There was one check on the Commission's authority, however—the Federal Court of Appeals, which had the power to review all the Commission's decisions—and officials worried about what might happen if the results of Brookhaven's update of WASH-740 were made public and used in lawsuits by "intervenors" who were opposing nuclear-plant licenses. According to the minutes of a January 1965 meeting of the steering committee, Dr. Richard Doan, of the A.E.C.'s regulatory staff, which was responsible for issuing plant licenses, warned his colleagues that there "was a possibility that someone will take legal action against further reactor construction on the grounds that in light of this report A.E.C. was being irresponsible in granting licenses. He stated that, if greater confidence [in safety] cannot be expressed, it would be difficult to continue granting licenses."

Stanley Szawlewicz, of the A.E.C.'s Division of Reactor Development, wrote a memo to the other members of the steering committee on the particular "dangers of publishing a revised WASH-740." First, rebutting the study's pessimistic conclusions would require "experimental proof" that the safety systems that were going to be installed on reactors would provide reliable protection against catastrophic accidents. Such proof would be "difficult and expensive to achieve," he said, and waiting for it could cause a big delay in plans for reactor construction.

Second, the public might be badly frightened by the finding that a hypothetical reactor accident could have consequences "more severe than those equivalent to a good sized [nuclear] weapon." Szawlewicz added that "this correlation can readily be made by experts if the [Brookhaven] results are published." Finally, the Brookhaven "results could easily be extrapolated to the next round of [proposed] reactors. This might have serious consequences in obtaining site approval for such reactors." The Oyster Creek reactor, in particular—the showpiece of "competitive nuclear power" that was being built on a site in New Jersey that had more than 136,000 people living within twenty miles—might be jeopardized, he said, if the report were published.

On January 28, 1965, the steering committee, led by Dr. Beck, met privately with the Atomic Industrial Forum, the nuclear industry's principal trade organization. Seventeen representatives of the major companies in the nuclear power industry attended the meeting, including those of Westinghouse, General Electric, Babcock & Wilcox and Combustion Engineering, the four principal reactor manufacturers. "Draft copies of [the revised] WASH-740 were forwarded to the A.I.F. . . . prior to the meeting so that the discussions could proceed on a logical basis," an A.E.C. internal memo noted. Dr. Beck described the background of the study, and "then defined the present dilemma"—which was how to publish the results of the study in a way that "does not jeopardize economic reactor development."

Industry representatives replied that they had not had time to study the draft report in detail, and they asked for a review of the technical basis for the conclusions drawn by Brookhaven, which Kenneth Downes and other scientists from the lab then provided. The industry representatives suggested that more emphasis should be put on the low probability of the kinds of accident that Brookhaven was analyzing, but Dr. Beck explained the frustration of the steering committee in trying to make defensible statements about probability. "Considerable discussion on probability theory then ensued with no outstanding new information or conclusions," the minutes of the meeting stated.

Dr. Beck advised Chairman Seaborg and the other commissioners of the results of the WASH-740 update. He also told them of the steering committee's discussions with the Atomic Industrial Forum on the problems of publishing the study. Harold Price, the Director of Regulation, wrote a memo "To the Files" in March 1965; it noted that "the final handling of the 'revised Brookhaven report' has been comprised of a long series of complicated maneuvers and negotiations during efforts to arrive at a final written document which would be acceptable to all parties responsible. . . . By way of oral transmission, essential elements arising out of the efforts devoted to this project were transmitted to the Commission," he noted.

The Commission itself formally took up the subject in May, when the commissioners directed that private talks be held with the staff of the Joint Committee on Atomic Energy to decide what to do with the study. (They directed that a draft copy of the results be given to the Committee.)

On June 4, 1965, Seaborg and the commissioners met personally with Congressman Chet Holifield of California, the chairman of the Joint Committee, to discuss the report. They suggested to Holifield that he might prefer a report on the safety systems that were being developed to prevent major accidents "as an alternative to an updated Brookhaven report."

At the end of all the "maneuvers and negotiations," the Commission itself determined the fate of the WASH-740 update. Dr. Beck had advised the Commission that the Atomic Industrial Forum strongly urged "that the revised Brookhaven study not be published in any form at the present time" and that the Commission "simply report in a very brief letter to the Joint Committee" the need for a renewed Price-Anderson Act to protect the industry from the liability for serious accidents. He gave the Commission the draft of a letter "along the lines discussed between the forum and the steering committee members."

The Commission accepted industry's recommendations and withheld the WASH-740 update from publication. Chairman Seaborg sent a brief letter, as recommended by the industry representatives, to the Joint Committee, which had already received a private copy of the report. He wrote, for the public record, that "a restudy of the theoretical consequences of hypothetical accidents by our staff and that of Brookhaven has led us to fairly predictable conclusions. Reactors today are much larger than those in prospect in 1957 . . . Therefore, assuming the same kind of hypothetical accidents as those in the 1957 study, the theoretically calculated damages would not be less and under some circumstances would be substantially more than the consequences reported in the earlier study." This finding, he concluded, "accentuate[s] the need for Price-Anderson" protection of the industry. Seaborg's three-page letter contains no additional disclosures about the study or its findings.

Dr. David Okrent had told his colleagues on the steering committee that the new estimates of the consequences of major accidents called for a more cautious attitude in the A.E.C.'s safety program, in its licensing process and especially in its policies relating to the siting of nuclear plants near urban populations. Given the profound implications of the findings, he said, "there was no alternative to a public document" that disclosed the study's results, and he recommended that a report of the findings be published "without glossing over" the severity of potential accidents. Chairman Seaborg and the commissioners did not agree.

The A.E.C. answered subsequent inquiries about the study with the response that it was "never completed," a statement that is inconsistent with A.E.C. internal documents in which the Brookhaven scientists reported that their "technical job was essentially finished in December 1964." (This was noted by Dr. Beck in his opening statement at the January 19, 1965, steering committee meeting, in which he thanked the Brookhaven staff for the work they had done and told them that it "closely approximated the report desired.")

In contrast to its public rationale for not publishing the study, an A.E.C. internal summary of the project, written in 1969 by Forrest Western, one of the members of the steering committee, noted that "an important factor in the decision not to produce a complete revision of WASH-740 along the lines proposed by the Brookhaven staff was the public relations considerations." W. B. McCool, the Secretary of the Commission and its official record keeper, wrote a subsequent memo to the commissioners that also referred to the WASH-740 update. McCool mentioned an article in *The Nation,* dated October 18, 1965, written by David Pesonen, a law student in California who was leading the opponents of the proposed Bodega Bay reactor. "The article reiterates his views that the A.E.C. had 'abandoned or suppressed the updated report—a major research project of potentially widespread public importance,' " McCool wrote. "The article contains rather convincing support for this point of view, including [mention of the] recommendations from industry that the A.E.C. drop the planned updating of the report."

FOR TWO FRUSTRATING DECADES the prospects for commercial nuclear power rose and fell in regular cycles of optimism and despair. By 1965 it looked as if the on-again, off-again nuclear power program was finally about to become established as a major commercial enterprise. United States utility companies were sitting down, at long last, to talk terms with the reactor manufacturers. Under discussion were orders for dozens of large nuclear plants.

Chicago-based Commonwealth Edison was negotiating the purchase of an 800-megawatt plant. The Tennessee Valley Authority was studying a proposal from General Electric for two 1,100-megawatt plants. The T.V.A., one of the nation's largest electric utilities, had access to very inexpensive coal, but it ultimately chose nuclear power instead. Like the Oyster Creek sale, the T.V.A.'s decision seemed to provide dramatic evidence of nuclear energy's new-found competitiveness. ("AN ATOMIC BOMB IN THE LAND OF COAL," the headline in *Fortune* read, when the deal was announced.) Actually, General Electric had once again used a "come-on bid" to help create the impression that nuclear power was highly economical—a bid that it would not subsequently repeat, even for additional nuclear plants for the T.V.A. Other utilities were weighing their own ambitious plans to enter the nuclear power business.

The delicate negotiations then in progress with the utilities would have been upset by any sudden official doubts about the safety—and licensability—of nuclear plants. The Commission's decision to quash plans for publishing a WASH-740 update spared the nuclear program from the lawsuits, investigations and public controversy that would have dashed the tenuous plans for nuclear-plant construction.

None of those who knew the results of the WASH-740 update—a group that included Glenn Seaborg, his fellow commissioners, the senior management of the agency, the steering committee, the scientists at Brookhaven, all the reactor manufacturers, and the chairman and the staff of the Joint Committee on Atomic Energy—spoke out about the study as the A.E.C., in the year after it was completed, issued construction permits for thirty large nuclear power stations. The plants would be built near New York City, Chicago, Boston, Miami, and other metropolitan areas. For each plant the A.E.C. regulatory staff issued a "Safety Evaluation Report," which concluded there was "reasonable assurance" that the facility could operate "without undue risk to the health and safety of the public."

The reports did not mention the possibility of catastrophic meltdown accidents of the type analyzed by Brookhaven, or of the fact that A.E.C. scientists could not say "if or when they might occur." "There are no secrets," the narrator says in one of the A.E.C.'s educational films describing the nuclear-plant licensing process. But in fact there were.

Glenn Seaborg, the number-one "salesman" for the program, continued to focus public attention on "the dream of abundance" that would be fulfilled in the "truly remarkable world" that he was working to create. The spectacular gamble that the A.E.C. was taking—that a satisfactory means for preventing the China

Syndrome would be found by the time the plants were ready to operate—was not discussed. With the record number of construction permits issued in 1965 and 1966, commercial nuclear power was well on its way to becoming the dominant technology for electric-power generation in this country. As far as Chairman Seaborg was concerned, nuclear power was firmly established. He concluded that the next and "most interesting challenge to nuclear science and technology" was not in the United States, or even on this planet. The next frontier, he announced, was the colonizing of the moon and beyond—with power provided, of course, by nuclear energy.

PART TWO
HERETICS

THE FIRST TIME I met Philip Rittenhouse, in November 1971, he was wearing a bright orange necktie and a dark purple shirt. In the following months, I met with him several times, saw more of his colorful ensembles—a colleague referred to him as a "candy dude"—and learned a great deal about the research that he carried out for the U.S. Atomic Energy Commission. Rittenhouse headed a team that was trying to find out what would happen, during major accidents, to the hot uranium fuel inside nuclear power reactors. His preoccupation with potential catastrophes did not seem to affect his general disposition, which was that of a rather flippant, happy-go-lucky guy. Rittenhouse was an amateur auto racer, I learned, and the technology that really excited him was in the modified MG Midget or Porsche 912 in his driveway at home.

Rittenhouse was born in Piqua, Ohio, in 1934. His father was in the shoe business, and the family moved from one town to another in the South and Midwest as he grew up. He attended the University of Tennessee, where he studied chemical and metallurgical engineering, and graduated in 1956. Unlike Glenn Seaborg, he had no strong interest in basic scientific research, nor was he gripped by a driving ambition to make a name for himself in history. Rittenhouse went into engineering because "I heard at the time that engineers might be able to make ten thousand dollars a year." Having worked during two of his college summer vacations at the A.E.C.'s Oak Ridge National Laboratory, in Oak Ridge, Tennessee, he took a full-time job there after graduation. He joined the more than two thousand technical specialists who worked at the laboratory, the anonymous journeymen assigned to do the detail work for the nuclear-powered world envisioned by the A.E.C.

For his first twelve years at Oak Ridge, Rittenhouse studied the properties of some of the special metals used in nuclear reactors. His research—on the best kinds of metals to use, on the factors that might cause them to corrode, and on how common alloys used by reactor builders might be improved—had obvious practical implications. Over the years Rittenhouse and other metallurgists at Oak Ridge developed considerable expertise on a particular metal alloy know as Zircaloy. This is the material used to make the slim tubes—called fuel rods—that hold the uranium fuel that is placed inside conventional power reactors. He got a number of offers to work for the nuclear industry, but he liked Oak Ridge and decided to remain there.

By 1968 Rittenhouse had become a group leader for a small staff of metallurgists. He got a call one day to go to a meeting about a new safety research program that was being started at the request of the A.E.C. Until that point, his work had not focused on safety problems, but his superiors handed him a new general assignment: to look at what would happen to the hot Zircaloy fuel rods in the reactor if they accidentally overheated.

"No strong worry had set in about nuclear safety. The lab was like a university at the time, and safety was almost an academic subject," Rittenhouse said. "I always looked at it like they wanted me to be a devil's advocate—that's the impression I had." When the research staff was instructed to look at the behavior of reactor fuel rods under accident conditions, fellow Oak Ridge metallurgist David Hobson said in an interview that the members took it as "just another job." "I don't guess anybody appointed us down here as a conscience for the nuclear industry," Rittenhouse said. "We just did what we were assigned to do. It could have been studying the corrosion of garbage cans. They could have assigned us that." He cannot recall that any deadline was set for his research, but he does remember "a little bit of a tone of urgency" when senior laboratory officials asked him to undertake the project. Data from Rittenhouse's research would help to determine how susceptible nuclear reactors might be to what A.E.C. officials were privately calling the "China Syndrome."

IN APRIL 1965 the Commonwealth Edison Company of Chicago asked the A.E.C. for permission to build another nuclear power plant in Morris, Illinois, next to the Dresden Nuclear Power Station, which the company had been operating there since 1960. The new plant, to be known as Dresden 2, would be more than four times as large as Dresden 1. In December of that year, the Consolidated Edison Company of New York filed an application for an additional nuclear plant to be built on the same site as its Indian Point Nuclear Power Station, which had been operating in Buchanan, New York, since 1961. Indian Point's second reactor would be almost six times as large as its first, and larger than any ever considered for licensing.

A few months later, topping all previous proposals, the Tennessee Valley Authority requested construction permits for the Browns Ferry Nuclear Power Station, to be built near Decatur, Alabama, which would incorporate two mammoth reactors, each of which would be larger than the giant new one to be installed at Indian Point 2. Glenn Seaborg, the chairman of the A.E.C., saw the rapid increase in plant size as evidence of the nuclear program's coming of age. The members of the A.E.C.'s Advisory Committee on Reactor Safeguards, on the other hand, debated whether they ought to send a "warning letter" to the Commission about the safety problems of these large new plants.

The A.C.R.S. was required by law to review the safety of each proposed plant. Its meetings were closed to the public, but after the A.E.C.'s failure, in the late 1950s, to disclose its negative findings on the Fermi breeder reactor, Congress amended the Atomic Energy Act to require that reports from the committee be made public. The spirit of the law could easily be circumvented, however. The A.E.C.'s Director of Regulation, Harold Price, told the committee that the candid expression of its views could create "difficult public-relations problems" for the A.E.C. Industry representatives also warned the A.C.R.S. that its questions about plant safety might be "aired by the press," to the industry's embarrassment.

The industry and the A.E.C. wanted the committee to raise its safety concerns in private, off-the-record discussions, without the public's being informed, and the A.C.R.S. was willing, by and large, to oblige them. When it did issue the mandatory written reports on the safety of proposed plants, it kept them short and obscure.

When the Dresden, Indian Point and Browns Ferry applications came before the A.C.R.S., its fifteen members debated, behind closed doors, whether they finally ought to write a stiff public letter to the A.E.C., and possibly to "call a halt" to the increase in plant size. The A.E.C., they noted, had been dispensing one construction permit after another. All unresolved safety questions, the Commission confidently assumed, would be settled by the time the plants were ready for operation. As the larger and more complex plants came up for operating licenses, A.C.R.S. member Stephen Hanauer, a nuclear-engineering professor from the University of Tennessee, noted that "in none of these are the problems which were of concern during construction even close to being solved."

Indian Point 2, in particular, which would be operating only thirty-five miles north of New York City, aroused special safety concerns. Dr. David Okrent, a physicist on the committee, believed that "economics tend to color technical judgment." Indian Point, he believed, "looked like a site much worse than others they had been considering." Approximately 10 percent of the population of the United States lived within a fifty-mile radius of the site, which one federal nuclear-safety official many years later called an "insane" place to put a large nuclear power plant. A.E.C. regulatory staff engineers who reviewed the safety devices at Indian Point used to joke half-seriously among themselves that Buchanan, New York—which was north of Croton-on-Hudson and Hastings-on-Hudson—should be renamed "Hiroshima-on-Hudson."

There was no risk of a nuclear detonation at Indian Point 2—its uranium fuel was too dilute to explode—but there was the terrifying danger of an accident in which the reactor's uranium fuel overheated and melted. Such an accident could cause a large leak of radioactive materials from the plant. The consequences of this had been studied during the A.E.C.'s 1964–65 update of WASH-740, of course, but the Commission was extremely reluctant to provide the detailed results of that study to the A.C.R.S. The A.C.R.S. knew about the study—member David Okrent had been on the steering committee that directed it—and the committee exerted "considerable pressure" on the A.E.C., according to Okrent, in order to obtain the data it produced.

A.E.C. officials considered the possibility that the results of the study might be written down, for internal use, in some way that disguised its government auspices—for example, not identifying its authors and using plain paper rather than A.E.C. or Brookhaven letterhead—but even this was judged too risky. Dr. Clifford Beck, the director of the WASH-740 update, finally agreed to a meeting, in May 1966, at which the A.C.R.S. could talk to two of the scientists from the Brookhaven National Laboratory who worked on the study. The minutes of that meeting state that Dr. Beck did not allow the Brookhaven conclusions to be written down.

Okrent, however, in an executive session for A.C.R.S. members only, told his colleagues, that the Brookhaven results showed, among other things, that an accident involving a reactor located "thirty miles from a city," under some circumstances, could be more severe than if the reactor were right in the city. This was so, he said, because the winds could spread out the radioactive debris from the reactor in "a wide enough plume to give the whole city a lethal dose." He added that the Brookhaven scientists had "not been allowed to write this up in a manner that is really intelligible."

"An item of special interest" in the minutes of another A.C.R.S. meeting with Dr. Beck noted his acknowledgment that the overheating and melting of the uranium-fueled core of a large reactor "would not only lead to melt-through of the reactor vessel but that calculations indicated the core would melt through the concrete of the containment floor into the earth. . . ."

The A.C.R.S. concluded that there were a number of possible equipment breakdowns that might bring about the China Syndrome. Okrent worried about the possibility that the reactor itself—the steel tank that holds the uranium fuel—might have a "catastrophic rupture" as a result of some undetected flaw in its thick steel walls.

Theos J. Thompson, a Professor of Nuclear Engineering at the Massachusetts Institute of Technology, and a member of the committee, thought that "the most vulnerable area" was the bolts that held the top of the reactor in place. Reactors operate at high pressure, and if some of the bolts break, the top head of the reactor might fly off and crash through the containment building. The reactor would lose its cooling water when it was abruptly decapitated, and a meltdown would ensue, one that would be all the worse since the escaping radioactive materials would be vented directly into the outside through the punctured roof of the containment building.

Another potential problem involved the control rods that were relied upon to shut off the chain reaction in an emergency. The A.C.R.S. concluded that the "reliability" of these systems "cannot be accurately established" and that, if they failed when needed, an uncontrollable accident might develop.

Of all the safety issues raised by A.C.R.S. members, the most sharply focused questions dealt with a key piece of safety apparatus known as the emergency core-cooling system, or "E.C.C.S." This was the principal device counted on to prevent accidents from developing into the China Syndrome. The hot uranium fuel in a nuclear power reactor must be constantly bathed in water so that its temperature remains safely under control. In normal operation, the required cooling water is pumped into and out of the reactor by means of an elaborate plumbing system. However, if one of the pipes in this system ruptures, the normal cooling-water supply could be suddenly lost. (Since reactors operate at high pressure, the normal cooling water would be rapidly blown out the hole caused by a broken pipe.)

Emergency cooling equipment therefore had to be provided to cool the uranium fuel during such emergencies—which were known as "loss-of-coolant" accidents. The E.C.C.S. was supposed to resupply the reactor, very quickly, with additional cooling water to make up for what had been lost as the result of an uncontrollable leak.

The A.E.C. had not required that emergency core-cooling systems be installed on the smaller, early reactors, but such equipment was mandatory for the large new ones. E.C.C.S. designs, however, had been something of an afterthought—additional pumps and piping that was tacked onto the plants at the last minute. The A.C.R.S. was unsure that the untested E.C.C.S. systems would work satisfactorily and felt that much more research on the subject was needed. Moreover, because of the potentially catastrophic consequence of E.C.C.S. failure, several members also felt that additional safeguards should be provided to deal with the meltdown accidents that might result from poor E.C.C.S. performance. They wanted the A.E.C. to force the industry to develop new safety systems—such as some kind of supercontainment or "core-catcher"—that would stop a molten core from melting through the reactor building and into the ground, if the E.C.C.S. didn't work. The industry did not see the necessity for any additional safety apparatus.

THE MEMBERS OF THE A.C.R.S. discussed their concern about the China Syndrome and other problems directly with Glenn Seaborg and his fellow commissioners. Cooperating with the official desire to "avoid public attention" to reactor safety problems, the committee made it a practice to send the Commission draft copies of sensitive reports and to confer privately with the commissioners, or other appropriate officers of the agency, before releasing them publicly.

In May 1965, the A.C.R.S. drafted a letter warning of the dangers of siting reactors in metropolitan areas, and met with Chairman Seaborg and his colleagues to discuss it. The heads of the agency, according to the internal A.C.R.S. minutes of that meeting, "indicated a desire to avoid any interpretation which might preclude large reactors near large cities."

The "public relations" and "political" problems raised by the reactor-siting issue were subsequently reviewed at another Commission meeting by Harold Price, the Director of Regulation. If reactors were not safe enough to site in metropolitan areas, he explained, the A.E.C. would then have the problem "of convincing people near the presently approved sites that the nuclear units are adequately safe." The A.E.C., that is, would have to tell people why a given plant, which wasn't considered safe enough to put in a more populated area, was safe enough to operate in their neighborhood.

Price told the A.C.R.S. that the commissioners "were not inclined at this time to take any stand against metropolitan reactors." The draft A.C.R.S. letter, accordingly, was never made public. On this and numerous other occasions, the A.C.R.S. was told that the Commission "would prefer not to receive" its unfavorable report on reactor safety. Glenn Seaborg, in a recent interview, was asked to explain the Commission's treatment of these reports but said, "I have only the vaguest recollection of the A.C.R.S. meetings."

On August 16, 1966, the A.C.R.S. concluded its review of Indian Point 2. Its public report to the Commission—a four-page letter—was vague and conditional. It described the emergency cooling system to be installed, for example, and noted that "improvements" in the design "may be appropriate." It mentioned "various items" that might affect the safety of the plant, and said that they "can be resolved during construction." (The letter did not mention Dr. Hanauer's observation that it was unlikely that they *would be* resolved, since the industry's past record in doing so was not very encouraging.) It concluded that the proposed reactor could be constructed at the Indian Point site "with reasonable assurance" that it could be operated "without undue risk" to the health and safety of the public. What the risk would be, the committee didn't say, or even hint at.

The same day it sent its official letter on Indian Point 2 to the A.E.C., the A.C.R.S. sent a second, private memo to the agency. This was a more general and more critical draft letter on the problem of pipe ruptures in reactor cooling systems that might lead to the China Syndrome. This second letter expressed the A.C.R.S.'s concern about the possibility of "a functional failure of the emergency core cooling system" of the type to be installed on Indian Point 2 and other large reactors. "Additional precautions" needed to be taken, the committee said, and "future reactors" similar in design to the one at Indian Point, without improved safety devices, would not be suitable for populated areas.

This was a major safety-policy recommendation of the A.C.R.S., and it had taken the members seven drafts to prepare it in final form. (Several of the members had agreed to the other public letter on Indian Point on the condition that this second letter also be released.) Before making this second letter public, they reviewed it with Seaborg and the other commissioners.

Seaborg strongly objected to the letter on meltdown accidents since its "impacts on the industry might be serious." He told the committee any such letter "should await more study." The draft letter was therefore tabled. The A.C.R.S. itself could still have sent the letter and made its concerns public, but it wanted, as one member noted, to avoid "any action which would result in a moratorium" on reactor construction. For the next several years, the A.C.R.S. continued, in a gentlemanly way, to press its recommendation that steps be taken to develop a means for coping with the China Syndrome. The Commission received this advice politely and continued to ignore it.

The A.C.R.S. also urged a broad range of other corrective measures to deal with reactor safety problems. Few of its suggestions were acted upon by the A.E.C. because of the expense they might cause the industry. Chairman Seaborg repeatedly told the A.C.R.S.

about his "concern over the costs and economics of safety" and cautioned against "going to extremes without consideration of costs." James Ramey, the former staff director of the Joint Committee on Atomic Energy who became a commissioner in 1962, and who had very close ties to the industry, told the A.C.R.S. that the "utilities and equipment manufacturers have held discussions with the Commission and have expressed their concern over snowballing safeguards requirements leading to increased costs."

Similar views were expressed by the members of the Joint Committee on Atomic Energy, which assented to the A.E.C.'s rejection of the safety recommendations being made by the A.C.R.S. and even threatened to abolish the committee. Complaining that the A.C.R.S. had become "an Advisory Committee on Reactor Redundancy," Congressman Craig Hosmer of California, a senior Republican member, said that the A.E.C.'s chief safety advisers were standing in the way of the government's program for getting "kilowatts to the people." At one industry meeting he spoke out against the "lopsided" emphasis on safety that was hurting the economics of nuclear power, and he called for "burning the Advisory Committee on Reactor Safeguards at the stake." He received a standing ovation.

One concession to the A.C.R.S. concerns over meltdown accidents was the Commission's appointment, in October 1966, of a task force to study the problem. The group was chaired by the late W. K. Ergen of the Oak Ridge National Laboratory, an engineer who had formerly served on the A.C.R.S. and was a consultant to the committee during its review of Indian Point 2. In that capacity, Ergen had told the A.C.R.S., in a memorandum submitted in September 1966, just before his special task force was formed, of some of the factors that contributed to the risk of the China Syndrome—a term which he invented.

"Extreme care" would have to be taken in constructing nuclear plants so that pipes and other components of the reactor's cooling system would not rupture, Ergen said. Yet "there are limits on how far one can go in this direction in a price-competitive industry." "The same care with respect to the emergency cooling system" was also required, he said, adding that "the same difficulties apply here." Moreover, "violent accidents" that cause normal cooling water to be lost might also "impair the emergency cooling system." Finally, Ergen's memorandum noted that "the test of emergency cooling systems under operating conditions and inspection of such systems in operating power reactors have not been reassuring."

The public report of Ergen's task force, which was issued a year later, did not contain such frank reservations. It did acknowledge areas where more research was needed, but it said that "sufficient test data are available" to indicate that the industry's current "approaches to emergency core cooling" were "satisfactory." Ergen's skepticism about the adequacy of the existing E.C.C.S. designs was not shared by the industry representatives on the A.E.C.'s task force, a group in which they happened to hold the majority. Never excessively scrupulous about conflicts of interest, the A.E.C. had given the industry a large role in reviewing the adequacy of their own E.C.C.S. designs. The industry representatives gave themselves high grades.

THE JOB THAT HAD BEEN ASSIGNED to Philip Rittenhouse was reasonably straightforward. The Ergen report had recommended that research be undertaken to learn more about what would happen to reactor fuel rods when they accidentally overheated. Accordingly, he began to take sample fuel rods, to heat them in a special furnace, and to study what took place. He was trying to simulate, in his laboratory, what might occur inside a reactor if its cooling water were suddenly lost and the temperature of its fuel began to increase uncontrollably.

The pencil-thin fuel rods used in United States nuclear plants are twelve feet long and are stacked upright inside the reactor. The fuel rods consist of hollow tubes made of Zircaloy—an alloy of zirconium—which are filled with pellets of uranium dioxide fuel. (The Zircaloy tube is sometimes referred to as the "cladding" for the uranium fuel.) There are thirty to forty thousand Zircaloy fuel rods in a large nuclear reactor, and they are packed together tightly to form the reactor's "core"—which is typically only twelve to fifteen feet in diameter.

During normal operation, a continuous river of cooling water flows upward through the narrow channels between the fuel rods. The flowing water keeps the fuel rods at a normal temperature of about 600 degrees Fahrenheit. During an accident in which the normal cooling water is lost as a result of a major pipe rupture, emergency cooling water is supposed to be injected into the reactor. It would also have to flow through the tiny channels in between the fuel rods.

Since it would take several minutes, even under the most favorable circumstances, before the normal cooling water could be replaced, the temperature of the fuel rods inside the reactor would increase temporarily before they were doused with emergency cooling water. The fuel-rod temperatures might increase from 600 degrees to more than 2,000 degrees within the first few minutes of a serious loss-of-coolant accident.

This was worrisome to safety analysts for several reasons, and one particular concern was that the fuel rods, as they heated up, might begin to swell. The rods were spaced together so closely that if they expanded substantially, they might block the channels through which emergency cooling water was supposed to flow. "Flow blockage" caused by swollen fuel rods could delay the arrival of emergency cooling water in parts of the core, allowing the fuel-rod temperatures to increase. If the blockage was bad enough, it might possibly allow some of the fuel to begin to melt. Rittenhouse's task was to find out how much fuel-rod swelling might take place. The A.E.C. made him the "coordinator" for A.E.C. and industry research on this subject.

The reactor manufacturers, on the basis of their own tests, assured the A.E.C. that flow blockage was not a problem. They told Rittenhouse that the fuel rods would only swell up slightly, their diameters increasing no more than 10 to 30 percent, and that the flow blockage resulting from this would have an inconsequential effect on the performance of the E.C.C.S.

Rittenhouse wasn't so sure. He was critical of the in-house tests that the companies had run—he did not think that the kind of electrical heating device they used provided a fair simulation of conditions inside a reactor, for example—and he therefore started from scratch to design his own experiments. His team at Oak Ridge soon found that Zircaloy was much more ductile than reported by the industry. Its strength, that is, declined rapidly as it heated up, making it likely that the Zircaloy fuel rods would increase a great deal in size during a serious loss-of-coolant accident.

"O.R.N.L. experiments . . . demonstrated that swelling greater than one hundred percent was possible, under realistic conditions, over significant portions of the core," a 1970 report from his laboratory to the A.E.C. stated. The fuel rods, when subjected to higher than normal temperatures, "ballooned out," Rittenhouse discovered, and in photographs the bulges on them made the normally slender rods look like a snake that had swallowed a mouse. The resulting flow blockage, he told the A.E.C., might "undermine" the effectiveness of the emergency cooling equipment that was being counted on to prevent meltdown.

Rittenhouse had more bad news for the A.E.C. Not only would the hot fuel rods swell, but they would also undergo a fundamental change as they heated up. The chemistry of Zircaloy was such that at temperatures above about 1,400 degrees, it would start to react chemically with the hot steam that would be present in the reactor. Above about 2,000 degrees, the reaction rate increased dramatically. The Zircaloy metal, in effect, would begin to burn, and the fuel rod would become transformed from solid metal into brittle, crumbly zirconium oxide. The effects of this reaction had been overlooked in the Ergen report, and had been dismissed by the industry.

Rittenhouse and his co-worker David Hobson found that the reaction would take place so quickly that much of the core could be destroyed by it. It was not enough to keep temperature in the core below the melting point of Zircaloy—3,300 degrees—as the A.E.C. and the industry had thought. The emergency cooling devices would also have to prevent the Zircaloy-steam reaction, which took place at far lower temperatures, from destroying the core.

In February 1971, in a general meeting with A.E.C. and industry experts who were studying reactor cooling problems, Rittenhouse and Hobson brought with them a sample of Zircaloy that Hobson had heated up in the presence of steam. Hobson tossed it onto a conference table, where it shattered on impact, leaving a pile of loose gravel on the table. "It was a demonstration for effect," Rittenhouse said.

The results of the ongoing Oak Ridge research on fuel-rod problems were presented to the A.E.C. in a series of research reports, which were also publicly disseminated by the laboratory. The unfavorable results annoyed the Commission officials sponsoring the research. For years, Oak Ridge had published the journal *Nuclear Safety,* and its editor, physicist William Cottrell, said in an interview recently that he "used to have running battles" with the A.E.C. over what he put into it. Milton Shaw, the director of the A.E.C.'s Division of Reactor Development and Technology, which controlled the money for safety research, "didn't want anything that diverged from the safety philosophy he was promoting" to be published by Oak Ridge, Cottrell stated. "Shaw certainly was not for a general discussion of those things the public didn't know."

The industry similarly objected to the published reports of Rittenhouse and his colleagues, which some critics of nuclear power were beginning to cite as evidence of serious reactor-safety problems. In early 1971, with much of Rittenhouse's scheduled work on fuel rod failure still to be done, the A.E.C. decided to cut off the funding for all research on the subject at Oak Ridge. Milton Shaw bluntly told laboratory officials that the safety researchers there were "causing more problems than they were solving."

THE RECOMMENDATIONS of the Ergen task force for more research on emergency cooling gave as many headaches to George Brockett as to Philip Rittenhouse. One of the leading experts on E.C.C.S. problems, Brockett managed a large engineering staff at the A.E.C.'s National Reactor Testing Station in Idaho, a major center for the country's nuclear-safety research effort. Run for the

A.E.C. by a succession of different contractors—including the Phillips Petroleum Company, the Idaho Nuclear Company, and Aerojet Nuclear Company—the testing station was spread out over almost nine hundred square miles of empty desert on the Snake River plain. According to the "Water Reactor Safety Program Plan," which the A.E.C. published in 1970 and which Brockett and his staff helped to write, emergency-cooling-system effectiveness was the Commission's "most urgent" research priority.

In 1963, Brockett and his associates had begun the construction of a small test reactor that would be deliberately sacrificed—subjected to an uncontrolled loss-of-coolant accident—so that they could study what happened during a meltdown. In 1967, the research objective was modified. The A.E.C. decided to include an emergency cooling system on the reactor so that its effectiveness could be observed under realistic accident conditions. The A.E.C. also asked that other devices be built—such as small-scale reactor mock-ups—so that additional experimental studies could be done to help find out what might occur during loss-of-coolant accidents. All the data from this research could then be used to check the adequacy of the emergency cooling apparatus on commercial nuclear plants. Nuclear-plant designers, with A.E.C. approval, had relied heavily on computers to predict how well these safety systems would perform during accidents. Experimental data were needed to determine whether the computer predictions were correct.

The nuclear industry was moving ahead rapidly and had not wanted to postpone plant construction while extensive safety research programs were completed. Consequently, the designs for emergency cooling devices had been selected on the basis of very limited knowledge of what would happen inside nuclear reactors during a serious cooling crisis. To account for the large uncertainties, industry designers had attempted to make what they termed "conservative assumptions"—that is, to "err on the safe side." But without tests to verify these assumptions, their predictions that the apparatus would work satisfactorily remained highly speculative.

The A.E.C. took the position, nevertheless, that when appropriate safety research was completed, the results would "confirm" the adequacy of the designs chosen by the reactor manufacturers. Nature, of course, owed the A.E.C. no favors, and research on complicated problems sometimes produces surprising results. The research at Idaho and Oak Ridge, after all, was being done because so much was unknown about the subject. The confidence that future research would demonstrate the adequacy of the industry's safety systems reflected what one A.E.C. engineer later referred to as "the triumph of hope over reason."

Like the researchers at Oak Ridge, Brockett and his co-workers found themselves the bearers of frequent bad news. To check the industry's computer predictions, they had developed independently their own computer methods for assessing loss-of-coolant accidents. Their results were strikingly more pessimistic than those presented to the A.E.C. by the reactor manufacturers. According to the industry, a major pipe rupture in the reactor's primary cooling system would cause a relatively gradual increase in the temperature of the Zircaloy fuel rods. From a normal temperature of 600 degrees the fuel would heat up within a few minutes to a peak temperature of about 1,600 degrees. At that point, the industry predicted, the E.C.C.S. would curtail further heat-up and quickly lower the temperature to safe limits.

According to the more detailed analyses done at the Idaho laboratory, the fuel in the reactor could get much hotter, much faster. Within a few *seconds,* the temperature of the fuel might soar above 2,000 degrees, and the temperature increase might already be out of control long before emergency cooling water reached the fuel rods. The industry had used a simplified model of the reactor's cooling system and had assumed that the normal cooling water, on its way out of the reactor through a broken pipe, would first flow *through* the core, providing ample cooling of the fuel. The more elaborate analyses done at Idaho showed that this probably wouldn't happen. The Idaho researchers reported to the A.E.C. that instead of the abundant flow predicted by the industry, the flow rate would be nearly zero.

But this was not the worst of the news from Idaho. The industry had predicted that the E.C.C.S. in pressurized-water reactors would be able to deluge the core with water, quickly refilling the reactor and terminating the difficulties caused by the loss of normal cooling water. The industry's calculations showed that the "reflooding rate"—the speed at which the water level inside the reactor increased following the injection of E.C.C.S. water—would be about one foot per second. Since the fuel rods in the core are twelve feet high, it would therefore require only about twelve seconds to flood the core with cooling water once E.C.C.S. water arrived on the scene.

Brockett and his associates, however, reported that the reflooding rate might be one *inch* per second, or less. The industry's analyses, they showed the A.E.C., had overlooked the fact that the steam pressure inside the reactor would drastically limit the rate at which emergency cooling water could rise up into the core. Because of "steam binding," they said, the current E.C.C.S. might have only a "marginal" capability for preventing the China Syndrome.

The most shocking results from the research effort in Idaho came from tests performed on a tea-kettle-size model of a pressurized-water reactor. Part of a program of "semiscale" experiments, the model consisted of a tiny "reactor," which contained electrically heated rods designed to simulate the heat produced by uranium fuel rods. Like a real PWR, the experimental apparatus had inlet and outlet piping, a main pump for circulating its primary cooling water, an E.C.C.S., and other auxiliary equipment. It operated at the same pressure (2,200 pounds per square inch) as a commercial PWR. Its tiny "core," however, was only nine inches in diameter, and many of its other features necessarily had to be scaled down in ways that did not accurately represent the characteristics of a real reactor. Still, it provided the most realistic emergency cooling tests that had ever been carried out. The tests scheduled to be performed in Idaho on an actual reactor were many years away.

During the winter of 1970–71, six tests were run. In each test, one of the pipes in the model reactor's cooling system was deliberately ruptured in order to create a loss-of-coolant accident. The high-pressure cooling water inside was rapidly blown out the hole, as one would expect. The E.C.C.S. equipment was promptly and automatically activated in each test, also as expected, but to the dismay of the A.E.C., the vital backup cooling apparatus did not work as predicted. Instead of cooling down the model reactor, and refilling its core, the emergency cooling water escaped out the same break in the pipe as the normal cooling water. It "bypassed" the core, the experimenters reported.

When I visited the Idaho laboratory a few months after the experiments, I saw a photograph of the semiscale test apparatus on the wall. Coming out of one of the pipes was a dark purple spray. I asked George Brockett why the water was purple. He explained that some of the people in the industry couldn't believe that the emergency cooling water was going out the same hole as the normal cooling water. The experimenters, accordingly, added colored dye to the emergency cooling water.

THE NEWS OF THE EMERGENCY-COOLING-TEST failures caused consternation at A.E.C. headquarters in Washington. As of January 1971, fifty-three large nuclear power plants were under construction, and many of them were nearing completion. Doubts about E.C.C.S. performance raised embarrassing questions about the licensability of these plants and jeopardized plans for further reactor construction. The A.E.C. made no public announcement of the unexpected test results, but officials recognized that it was only a matter of time before they became known and were cited as evidence of safety inadequacies.

The A.E.C. formed an ad hoc task force to review the emergency-cooling problem. The group was headed by Dr. Stephen Hanauer, who had served on the A.C.R.S. and had recently become a full-time member of the A.E.C. regulatory staff. The other members of the task force, all of whom worked in the A.E.C.'s Division of Regulation, were Frank Schroeder, Edson Case, Marvin Mann, Victor Stello, Thomas Novak, Norman Lauben, Richard Tedesco, Warren Minners, Denwood Ross, Howard Richings, Paul Norian, Morris Rosen and Robert Colmar. All of the members of the task force were engineers. Some of them had limited acquaintance with E.C.C.S. problems, but none was recognized as an expert in the field.

Their assignment was not to do a detailed technical study, but to review the data and policy recommendations to be provided by the industry and by the Commission's experts. The plan was for the task force to prepare a general policy statement on emergency cooling requirements, and for George Brockett and his staff in Idaho to prepare the backup report that established the technical basis for the A.E.C.'s conclusions.

The Hanauer task force held extensive meetings with representatives of the reactor manufacturers. Industry experts provided the A.E.C. with reports that summarized their computer predictions of how well the E.C.C.S. would perform if it ever were needed. The industry cited its own experimental data as proof that the assumptions behind their computer models were correct, and it rejected the Idaho semiscale tests as any kind of proof of their designs. The tiny apparatus, industry experts insisted, was too unlike a commercial reactor for the tests to be taken as a demonstration of adequacy or inadequacy of an emergency cooling system.

Although relying heavily on computer predictions to establish the effectiveness of their E.C.C.S., the manufacturers did not provide the A.E.C. with a complete description of their computer analysis methods. They provided what were usually just summary descriptions. (They considered the actual techniques they used to predict E.C.C.S. performance as "proprietary information"—that is, as commercial or trade secrets that they did not wish to make known to their competitors.) According to its philosophy of industry self-regulation, the A.E.C. customarily licensed plants on the basis of summary descriptions of plant designs—rather than on detailed engineering information—and officials were willing, similarly, to accept the industry's general accounts of how its computer methods worked.

The A.E.C. had commissioned the researchers at Idaho to develop the A.E.C.'s own computer methods for assessing E.C.C.S. performance. Officials believed that this would provide a satisfactory independent check on the industry's conclusions.

George Brockett organized a crash program at the Idaho lab to prepare the technical backup record needed by the A.E.C. Dozens of engineers there, the A.E.C.'s leading experts in the field, worked on the document, which was intended to summarize the "state of the art" in emergency-cooling technology. The planned report was to be in two volumes: one focusing on pressurized-water reactors (the kind manufactured by Westinghouse, Combustion Engineering, and Babcock & Wilcox) and the other on boiling-water reactors (the type made by General Electric).

The two-volume "Brockett Report," as it was later called, was completed within weeks and was submitted to the A.E.C. in April 1971. It was a compendium of basic data and frank technical judgments, and like Rittenhouse's reports on flow blockage, it caused more problems than it solved for the A.E.C.

The Idaho experts concluded that reactor-cooling problems were so complex, and the available data so limited, that "the complete and correct analysis" of such accidents "is beyond the scope of currently used techniques and in some areas beyond present scientific knowledge." The principal difficulty was simply that no one really knew what would happen inside a nuclear reactor that was in the throes of a major cooling crisis. The existing computer models took a stab at predicting what might take place, but they made a number of arbitrary assumptions. Firm data to confirm these assumptions, and the overall validity of the predictions, Brockett and his associates reported, were just not available.

The industry admitted that there were gaps in the available knowledge on what happened during loss-of-coolant accidents but said that its "conservative assumptions" satisfactorily covered the uncertainties. That is, in calculating how fast the water would leak out of the reactor through a broken pipe, how quickly the core would heat up, and so forth, the industry said that it took a deliberately pessimistic point of view in order not to underestimate the problem that would have to be controlled by the E.C.C.S. It also claimed to make a set of conservative assumptions when it analyzed E.C.C.S. performance, in order not to overestimate its capabilities.

Even taking such an exaggerated view of the difficulties of controlling serious loss-of-coolant accidents, the industry told the A.E.C., the computer analyses predicted that existing E.C.C.S. systems were fully capable of keeping core temperatures within safe limits. It was possible, the industry acknowledged, that future research, like the tests, might show unexpected results. They insisted, however, that large "safety margins" had been built into their E.C.C.S. designs. The industry claimed to have an adequate hedge—like cash reserves put into a contingency fund—against any E.C.C.S. problems that might arise in the future.

Brockett and the staff at Idaho, who had spent years developing their own computer-analysis methods, cautioned the A.E.C. about relying on illusory margins of safety. It was all well and good to *attempt* to make conservative assumptions, they said. But unless one really knew what would happen during loss-of-coolant accidents, it was difficult to know whether such assumptions really were conservative. There had already been repeated instances in which supposedly conservative analyses had been proved to be optimistic rather than pessimistic. Moreover, since no reliable quantitative measure was available of *how* conservative the industry's assumptions really were, the nominal safety margins would remain ill-defined.

As to the tests that the manufacturers had performed, the A.E.C. experts in Idaho disputed many of the interpretations that the industry drew from them. One particular testing program was especially controversial. A key factor in emergency cooling is the rate at which "heat transfer" takes place—that is, how efficiently the emergency cooling water would remove heat from the hot uranium fuel rods. To study this, the A.E.C. wanted full-scale studies carried out in which bundles of simulated fuel rods, twelve feet in length, would be heated up and then cooled down under realistic accident conditions.

The tests were known as the Full-Length Emergency Cooling Heat Transfer Tests (FLECHT). Rather than have this work done at one of its own research laboratories, the A.E.C. initiated a "cooperative" research program under which the work was delegated to the reactor manufacturers. Westinghouse performed the FLECHT test of the pressurized-water-reactor E.C.C.S., and General Electric performed the FLECHT test of the boiling-water-reactor E.C.C.S. The A.E.C., that is, paid the manufacturers to perform the critical tests needed to determine adequacy of the equipment the manufacturers had already installed on current reactors.

In reviewing the FLECHT tests, the A.E.C.'s experts in Idaho found so many inadequacies that some of them suspected that the manufacturers might have rigged the experiments to prevent weaknesses in their E.C.C.S. from being exposed. "There are, as you know, a number of problems in the . . . FLECHT program," one internal memo on the program by the Idaho research staff noted. "A great deal of this is caused by the G.E. [General Electric] determination to prove out their ECC systems. Their role in this program can only be described as a conflict of interest as is the Westinghouse portion of PWR-FLECHT. Because the GE systems are marginally effective . . . there is little constructive effort on their part."

During the tests, the reviewers at Idaho noted, the temperature-measuring devices failed repeatedly, the electric heaters did not work properly, and they had considerable difficulty getting data about the tests from G.E. "The combination of poor data acquisition and transmission, faulty test operations (probably caused by crude test facilities) and the marginal nature of these tests has produced a large amount of questionable data," they concluded.

In one key test by General Electric, designated test ZR-2, the E.C.C.S. had great difficulty in keeping the temperature of the fuel-rod bundle under control. In fact, the temperature was satisfactorily brought under control only after several of the electric heaters, which were used to simulate the heat that would be produced by the radioactive materials inside real uranium fuel rods, short-circuited and failed.

"The 'why' of the situation has come down to the simple fact that we believed GE was doing the job for which they were paid

. . . The GE effort in heater development has been demonstrated to be seriously inadequate," Idaho researchers wrote. Test ZR-2, they concluded, "was not [a] satisfactory demonstration test—same need still exists today—in fact need is greater because [safety] margin appears to be less than originally expected."

THE BROCKETT REPORT fueled a major debate in the Hanauer task force. Its members had been struggling to find some way to keep the nuclear program moving ahead despite the test results and other evidence of E.C.C.S. problems. The alternative, of course, was for the A.E.C. staff to admit, publicly, that it had blundered and had permitted dozens of plants to be constructed but was now unsure that they could be operated safely. Every bureaucratic tendency operated against making such an admission of incompetence. "The Regulatory Branch is guided by a desire to avoid establishing obstacles to the licensing of plants," the minutes of one A.C.R.S. meeting that spring noted.

The industry wanted the A.E.C. to approve its present E.C.C.S. designs on the basis of the available computer predictions. Several members of the task force wanted to do just that, while perhaps adding the requirement that further conservative assumptions be included in the computer analyses. Other task force members had profound doubts about taking what they regarded as a business-as-usual approach. Dr. Morris Rosen, the head of the Division of Reactor Standards, and his deputy, Robert Colmar, wrote an internal memorandum to other members of the task force on June 1, 1971, setting out their specific concerns.

Rosen, who had a Ph.D. in mechanical engineering from the Rensselaer Polytechnic Institute, had been one of the principal A.E.C. officials assigned to monitor progress in emergency-cooling technology. He also served as a regulatory staff liaison with the A.C.R.S., whose members had strong reservations about the existing E.C.C.S. designs. Colmar also had experience in the area, having been a program manager for some of the studies that the A.E.C. had commissioned on E.C.C.S.

The joint Rosen-Colmar memo to the Hanauer task force noted that "the multiplicity of computer coding techniques, of various reactor-system designs, of assumptions regarding fundamental physical events, the general interpretation of the limited available experimental information . . . have all served to raise serious questions regarding the basis for reasonable assurance concerning the operation of these complicated systems." The memo outlined some of the technical difficulties with the computer methods, and concluded—in capital letters—that "THE CONSUMMATE MESSAGE" from the studies to date was that the "THE SYSTEM PERFORMANCE CANNOT BE DEFINED WITH SUFFICIENT ASSURANCE TO PROVIDE A CLEAR BASIS FOR LICENSING."

Licensing reactors, of course, was just what the A.E.C. wanted to do. Setting aside the qualms of Rosen and Colmar, and of all the A.E.C.'s principal experts, Hanauer presented the conclusions of his task force to Chariman Seaborg and the other commissioners. He recommended that the Commission do exactly as the industry had suggested and approve current emergency-cooling-system designs on the basis of the industry's favorable computer predictions of how well they would work under accident conditions. The task force prepared no technical report to justify its confidence in these controversial computer predictions. Nor did it explain to the Commission how it was able to take such a position in the face of all the reservations that had been expressed by the Commission's leading experts.

Seaborg and his colleagues, without pausing for detailed deliberation, accepted the task force recommendations, having first met privately with industry representatives to discuss them. On June 19, 1971, the Commission issued its formal policy statement on emergency cooling—a brief document that simply set forth the conclusions of the Hanauer task force. The A.E.C. said that its approval of current E.C.C.S. designs would go into effect immediately. The A.E.C. licensing staff would thus be able to move ahead quickly with the issuance of operating licenses for the dozens of plants waiting to receive them.

Hanauer appeared at a press conference on June 19 to explain the new policy statement. Harold Price, the Director of Regulation, and Peter Morris, the Director of Licensing, accompanied him. Hanauer briefed the press and explained how the E.C.C.S. was supposed to deliver water "to that nice warm core" and "do a good cooling job before the core gets too hot." The A.E.C. was "confident," Price stated, "that the emergency cooling systems will perform adequately to protect the temperature of the core from getting out of hand."

The three A.E.C. officials did not refer to the doubts about E.C.C.S. design and performance that some of the committee's own experts had expressed. There was no reference to flow blockage, to steam binding, to the China Syndrome, or to the numerous criticisms that its experts had raised about the industry's computer methods. Nor did they make any mention of the two-volume Brockett report, which the A.E.C. decided not to publish although it had specially commissioned it to provide a technical basis for its policy statement on E.C.C.S. The authors of the report were told that "The existence of this document should not be discussed with outsiders." (Several months later, Hanauer acknowledged that the Brockett report existed, but he said that he had not read it. He had "leafed through it" and found that it "did not help me any.")

The A.E.C. had no technical backup report to accompany its policy statement on emergency cooling but decided to publish it anyway. Glenn Seaborg retired later that month, after ten years as A.E.C. Chairman, having made this one last major decision.

NO ONE ON THE HANAUER TASK FORCE had bothered to consult Philip Rittenhouse, or anyone else at Oak Ridge. The subject of flow blockage had been mentioned briefly in a meeting of the task force a few days before it concluded its work, but in its haste to finish no detailed review was undertaken. Nor did the task force take the time to confer with Oak Ridge experts about their work on other aspects of Zircaloy behavior during loss-of-coolant accidents.

Technically, the research at Oak Ridge and all of the other safety research done for the A.E.C. were sponsored and supervised by the Division of Reactor Development and Technology, not the Division of Regulation, for which Hanauer and his colleagues worked. The A.E.C. branch responsible for safety and licensing, accordingly, had never had a close working relationship with the A.E.C.'s principal safety-research scientists.

When the staff at Oak Ridge received a copy of the June 1971 policy statement, they were struck by its technical naïveté. According to the statement, the A.E.C. wanted to make sure that the Zircaloy-water reaction, which occurred at high temperatures, did not proceed unchecked during loss-of-coolant accidents and destroy the core. It therefore required that the E.C.C.S. be designed to limit the fuel-rod temperature to 2,300 degrees.

The Oak Ridge researchers knew, however, that the damage done by these chemical reactions depended not just on high temperatures but on *how long* the fuel rods remained at high temperatures—that is, on the "integrated time at temperature." (The simple principle of chemistry behind their observation is taught to high-school chemistry students.) They knew from their experiments that even at temperatures below 2,300 degrees, the Zircaloy-water reaction was strong enough to destroy the core if it was given enough time.

The A.E.C.'s handling of flow blockage raised similar objections from the Oak Ridge staff. The policy statement contained language to the effect that the E.C.C.S. should keep the "core geometry" in a configuration "amenable to cooling," but it did not define what this meant. The computer methods that the A.E.C. had approved as the means for determining E.C.C.S. performance, moreover, were incapable of assessing the distortions to core geometry that swollen fuel rods would produce. They begged the question by making the simplifying assumption that there would be *no* changes in core geometry during loss-of-coolant accidents. (The complex, three-dimensional geometry of the core was too much for the existing computer programs to handle; they were capable only of performing one-dimensional analyses.)

Some of the defects in the policy statement on E.C.C.S. were obvious even to outside observers who had little of the expertise of the A.E.C.'s own researchers. In the spring of 1971, together with other members of the Union of Concerned Scientists, I had begun to study the E.C.C.S. issue as part of a review of the safety of the Pilgrim Nuclear Power Station, in Plymouth, Massachusetts. Rumors about the semiscale test results had prompted a special interest in the subject of E.C.C.S.

One member of the U.C.S., Henry Kendall, a professor of physics at the Massachusetts Institute of Technology, prepared his own update of WASH-740 in order to estimate the potential consequences of meltdown accidents. (We had no knowledge of the fact that the A.E.C. had already prepared, but not published, a similarly revised version of the study.) Kendall and other members of the U.C.S. also reviewed the semiscale results, as well as the reports from Oak Ridge, Idaho, and other research centers where studies on E.C.C.S. had been performed. (We also had no knowledge of the unpublished data and analyses from these laboratories that were being reviewed by the Hanauer task force, nor did we know of the existence of the task force.)

The U.C.S. analyses of the E.C.C.S. problem and of the possible deficiencies in the Commission's policy statement were published in July and October 1971. In November 1971, together with Kendall and another physicist, James MacKenzie, the chairman of the U.C.S., I visited Oak Ridge to try to get more information about the work that Rittenhouse and his colleagues had done.

Rittenhouse, who was wearing the colorful outfit I still remember, briefed us on his work. We explained to him and his co-workers some of the conclusions that we had drawn from their published reports. The Associate Director of the Oak Ridge laboratory, Donald Trauger, subsequently sent a report on our visit to Milton Shaw at A.E.C. headquarters.* "We felt that the technical publication of this group, as well as their professional integrity, justified our meeting with them," Trauger wrote. "However, in-

* An unofficial copy of this letter was given to me privately some months later.

asmuch as the Union of Concerned Scientists has intervened in the hearing on the ... Pilgrim reactor, we also felt that you should be aware of the nature of our discussions."

Trauger's summary of those discussions stated that

> H. W. Kendall (MIT-UCS) showed us how he has used our data ... to demonstrate that approximately 85 per cent of the fuel rods are "candidates" for producing ... coolant channel blockage in the range 90 to 100 per cent. Kendall had reached this conclusion independently, and wanted to know if he was using our data properly—which he was, within the limits of its accuracy.

Following the discussion of flow blockage, Trauger reported to the A.E.C., there was

> a general discussion of water reactor safety, including the October U.C.S. paper. The three members of the Union of Concerned Scientists who visited here appeared to be well educated and dedicated people. According to them, they had not received satisfactory answers from either the utility or the [reactor manufacturer] in the case of the Pilgrim reactor as to some of the issues raised in their papers, so they felt compelled to undertake the intervenor's role. In pursuit of this role they have become intimately familiar with the relevant published literature and have even received some "proprietary" information from at least one vendor. Their experience led them to examine this situation very closely, and they have become aware of various deficiencies in the case for E.C.C.S. performance.

Rittenhouse's formal briefing did not tell us anything that we had not already learned from his published reports. A representative of A.E.C. headquarters had sat in on the meeting, and his presence may have inhibited the discussion. At lunch, however, he happened to sit at one end of a long cafeteria table, and Rittenhouse at the other. I sat next to Rittenhouse and asked him what people at Oak Ridge thought of the principal conclusion of the October 1971 U.C.S. paper—namely, that there was inadequate proof that the E.C.C.S. would be able to do what it was supposed to do.

He said that he and his colleagues agreed with that finding. There had been no public indication whatever of an internal A.E.C. controversy over E.C.C.S. His answer, which surprised me greatly, was the first hint.

During subsequent visits to Oak Ridge, I learned that a number of scientists in the A.E.C. laboratories and in the agency's senior staff had privately expressed doubts about E.C.C.S. performance. During the next few months, I met with some two dozen of them, at various A.E.C. installations around the country. Many asked to meet privately rather than at their offices, and some insisted on elaborate meeting arrangements. Senior researchers at one A.E.C. laboratory asked that I fly in to a town fifty miles away and stay at a hotel where they could come during the evening for extensive discussions. They said they would stay all night, if necessary, rather than risk my being seen entering their homes. (Several of their neighbors also worked at the lab.)

In addition to describing their own concerns about the China Syndrome, A.E.C. scientists disclosed that many major studies on the problem had not been made public by the Commission. Many of these reports, during the next few months, were sent to me anonymously. None contained information that was "classified" as "secret" or "confidential"; they simply contained material that the A.E.C., for policy reasons, had decided not to make public.

Much of the material in them consisted of detailed technical analyses of the problems with current emergency cooling-system designs. There were also more general, summary accounts of E.C.C.S. problems written by some of the agency's senior management. Milton Shaw, for example, as Director of the A.E.C.'s Division of Reactor Development and Technology, headed the civilian nuclear power program in the United States. He was also a leading spokesman for the agency's official safety policies and had frequently ridiculed the contention that the precautions at United States nuclear plants were inadequate to protect the public from catastrophic accidents.

In one A.E.C. internal memo written in February 1971, however, Shaw stated categorically that "although test information is available on the response of simulated fuel [rod] bundles to a range of emergency coolant-flow conditions, no assurance is yet available that emergency coolant can be delivered at the rates intended and in the time period prior to [Zircaloy] clad and subsequent fuel melting . . ." The work of the Hanauer task force in the next few months did not alter the conclusions reached by Shaw and his staff. A major internal report on safety-research needs prepared by his division in November 1971 concluded, once again, that "present experimental data and analysis techniques are not now sufficient to provide the degree of ECC assurance deemed necessary by the A.E.C." The computer methods relied upon by the A.E.C. to predict E.C.C.S. performance, the report continued, "are unable to describe important physical phenomena [that occur during loss-of-coolant accidents] and therefore unable to confidently define safety margins."

Another document that provided an overview of E.C.C.S. problems, and that the A.E.C. chose not to make public, was written by William Cottrell, the director of the Nuclear Safety Program at Oak Ridge. Cottrell and some of the researchers at Oak Ridge decided, on their own initiative, to file their views on the June 19 policy statement with the Commission. Cottrell set out their conclusions in a detailed letter dated December 6, 1971, which was addressed to L. Manning Muntzing, the A.E.C. Director of Regulation. (He specialized in administrative law and was a lawyer for the Chesapeake and Potomac Telephone Companies when he was appointed to the A.E.C. by President Nixon in late 1971.)

"To summarize what follows herein," Cottrell wrote, "we are not certain" that the E.C.C.S. policy "adopted by the A.E.C. will, as stated . . . 'provide reasonable assurance that such systems will be effective in the unlikely event of a loss-of-coolant accident.' " Their work at Oak Ridge, they noted, had shown that "there seems little chance of preventing at least some degree of fuel rod swelling and rupture" during loss-of-coolant accidents. The resulting flow blockage would depend "on a large number of factors" and could range from minimal closure of the channels through which emergency coolant would have to flow up to "total blockage." Yet the policy statement gave "no consideration" to the problem of flow blockage, nor did it address "other phenomena which could adversely affect E.C.C.S. performance."

The six-page letter from Cottrell, and its twenty-page technical attachment, if treated in the customary fashion, would have been "docketed" by the Secretary's office at the A.E.C. That is, since it related to a formal legal matter pending before the Commission—public hearings on the June 19 E.C.C.S. policy that were scheduled to begin the following month—it should have been placed in the official file for that case in the A.E.C.'s Public Document Room in Washington. Doing so, of course, would have disclosed the fact that some of the A.E.C.'s own experts questioned the official optimism about E.C.C.S. performance. Muntzing did not send the letter to the Secretary's office for docketing. He sent it back to Oak Ridge.

IN JANUARY 1972, the A.E.C. began formal hearings on the adequacy of the June 1971 policy statement on E.C.C.S. The Commission had no sudden desire to open up its decision making on reactor safety to the public. The hearings were an administrative maneuver aimed at limiting public questioning of E.C.C.S. adequacy. The parties contesting the licensing of Indian Point 2, Midland, Pilgrim and other plants had pressed the E.C.C.S. issue after learning the results of the tests. Lawyers for the utility companies complained that the controversy about E.C.C.S. was creating "chaos" in the reactor-licensing process. The June 1971 policy statement had been written to put an end to this bothersome controversy. It provided a blanket A.E.C. approval of the current E.C.C.S. designs and the computer methods used by the industry to assess E.C.C.S. performance. Under the A.E.C.'s licensing procedures, these subjects could, therefore, no longer be raised in the individual licensing hearings since adequacy of the plants' emergency cooling devices had already been certified by the Commission's new ruling. (According to the A.E.C.'s rules, the parties to its licensing hearings were not allowed to challenge A.E.C. rules.) Having no technical report to justify its position, the A.E.C. attempted to settle the E.C.C.S. debate by administrative fiat.

The opponents of individual nuclear-plant licenses persisted, nevertheless, in raising the issue. The legal challenges to the nuclear power program were being raised by individual citizen activists, local and national environmental organizations, "public interest" law firms, and ad hoc groups opposed to the siting of nuclear power stations in their localities. The Vietnam war protests had prompted widespread attacks on "Establishment" endeavors, and the environmental movement—which had been battling to curb air pollution, strip mining, pesticide use, and federal projects such as the supersonic transport—finally turned its attention to the nuclear power program. Nuclear power still enjoyed strong support in Congress and in the general public, but the A.E.C. was worried by the increasingly successful tactics of the vocal minority who were opposing nuclear-plant construction. They threatened to take the A.E.C. to court for foreclosing examination of the E.C.C.S. question in the licensing hearings.

To extricate itself from the growing legal challenges, the A.E.C. decided that instead of fighting the issue over and over again in individual cases, it would hold a single, consolidated "rulemaking" hearing to try to settle the E.C.C.S. controversy once and for all. The parties to the separate licensing hearings agreed to participate in this unprecedented hearing—the first major public hearing the Commission had ever held on reactor-safety policy—if the A.E.C. would allow them to cross-examine the government's experts on E.C.C.S. Some sixty environmental and public-interest groups joined together to participate in the hearing. The Union of Concerned Scientists was part of the coalition, and since the A.E.C. rules allowed nonlawyers to do the questioning on technical subjects, I participated in this capacity.

The prospect that criticism of E.C.C.S. adequacy might undermine public support for nuclear power was definitely on the minds of A.E.C. officials as they made the arrangements for a hearing on this subject. Containment buildings are intended to limit the accidental escape of radioactive materials from nuclear plants. Similarly, the ground rules for the hearing were designed to limit the adverse public-relations fallout from a public discussion of E.C.C.S. problems.

According to the A.E.C.'s plan, the hearings that would begin in January 1972 would be a brief exercise, lasting perhaps six weeks. The Hanauer task force would appear in public, and its testimony would provide the technical justification for the June 1971 policy statement—and thus end the embarrassment caused by the lack of a technical backup report. (The written testimony of the task force would replace the aborted Brockett report.) The environmental groups who criticized the policy statement would then be allowed to make their case, and the nuclear industry could also add whatever information it wanted to the record. After the hearings, the A.E.C. could deliberate, behind closed doors, and then issue a "final" policy statement on E.C.C.S. to supersede the "interim" one released the previous June. The controversy on this subject, then, would be settled.

The testimony that the Hanauer task force prepared for the hearing did not discuss the Brockett report, or any of the other internal studies that conflicted with the official optimism about E.C.C.S. performance. It did not mention the fact that two of its members, Morris Rosen and Robert Colmar, had strongly disagreed with its findings. When the task force appeared at the hearing to present its testimony, members Rosen and Colmar were not among them. The A.E.C. did not explain or note their absence.

The week before the hearing was to begin, Rosen had been told that the A.E.C. staff was being "reorganized," and he had found himself reorganized out of his job. When he explained to his superiors that this might look suspicious—that they might be accused of stifling dissent—he was given a job in another part of the staff, one where he no longer had any responsibility for E.C.C.S.

The testimony presented by the Hanauer task force also made no reference to the dissenting opinion on the June 1971 policy statement that had been expressed by the A.C.R.S. The committee's experts on E.C.C.S. privately informed the Commission that the policy statement was "inadequate to protect the public health and safety" and that new E.C.C.S. designs were needed. They also cautioned against adopting any "quick fix" to the problem, noting that "neither the A.E.C. nor the [reactor manufacturers] understand the problems of E.C.C.S. well enough to know what is an improvement in system design."

In December 1971, in preparation for the upcoming hearings, the A.C.R.S. drafted a formal report on the policy statement and some of the members met with Chairman James Schlesinger*—Seaborg's successor—and the other commissioners to discuss it. The minutes of that meeting state that "the A.C.R.S. representatives agreed to withhold the report." They did so in order that the committee might consider the "Commissioners' suggestions" regarding "the desirability" of "a more positive statement" on E.C.C.S. adequacy. They were also warned by the commissioners about the possibility that the members might be subpoenaed to testify at the hearings and asked to answer questions on their views if they dissented from the policy statement.

The A.C.R.S. did not want to be forced to answer public questions about its deliberations or to come into open conflict with the A.E.C. The members therefore revised their report on E.C.C.S. The solution they ultimately worked out with the A.E.C. was quite simple. The A.C.R.S. wrote an ambiguous public report, which appeared to support the policy statement. The Commission then adopted hearing rules which specified that the A.C.R.S. members could not be called for questioning on what they had actually meant.

This left the A.E.C. with one remaining "containment" problem: how to limit what the A.E.C. witnesses who *would* appear at the hearing might reveal. The A.E.C. had reluctantly agreed to allow its witnesses to be cross-examined and to present as witnesses some of its experts from Idaho and Oak Ridge. The Commission staff worked with the Idaho and Oak Ridge experts on the preparation of their written testimony, which simply presented background data about E.C.C.S. and avoided any appraisal of the adequacy of the policy statement. This still left the problem, though, of what these witnesses would say during cross-examination.

* Schlesinger, a former RAND Corporation economist, had been a member of the White House Office of Management and Budget before his appointment to the A.E.C.

Shortly before the hearing the management at the Idaho lab met with staff researchers there and told them that they were free to say whatever they wanted at the hearing. But the management could not assure them that they would still have a job after the hearing if their testimony displeased the A.E.C.

Charles Leeper, the president of Aerojet Nuclear, the company that ran the Idaho facility for the A.E.C., subsequently explained that it was essential for his company to maintain good relations with its "customer." (Aerojet Nuclear was a "captive contractor," one that worked exclusively for the A.E.C.) Each member of the staff at Idaho had to recognize, Leeper said, that if his expressed opinions "sour his relationship with the customer, we cannot guarantee that after some time has elapsed that he will still be in the same position." Leeper added that Aerojet Nuclear would "make every effort to find him a suitable opening in this organization, or elsewhere in Aerojet, or allow him to look beyond the company."

A.E.C. lawyers, at a meeting for A.E.C. staff witnesses a few days before the start of the hearing, also addressed the question of what the staff would say during cross-examination. The A.E.C. witnesses were given a one-page instruction sheet entitled "Hints at Being a Witness." It contained fifteen numbered instructions. Some of them were noncontroversial, lawyerly instructions that told the A.E.C. staff witnesses to be on time for the hearings, to wear a suit if they had one, not to fidget while on the witness stand or to make faces or laugh while their colleagues were testifying. The A.E.C. witnesses were also told not to volunteer any information not directly requested. And, although they were appearing as expert witnesses and were testifying under oath, item number ten on the list admonished them: "Never disagree with established policy."

THE MEMBERS OF THE HANAUER TASK FORCE, minus Morris Rosen and Robert Colmar, took the witness stand on January 27, 1972. They had submitted one hundred and twenty pages of written testimony, and during the next five weeks they struggled to defend its conclusions.

Shortly before the hearing, I met one evening with a group of A.E.C. scientists who told me that some of their colleagues had put together a line-by-line critique of the task force's testimony. (They had done an analysis of it on their own initiative and had not submitted the results to A.E.C. management; they were afraid that they might be fired for having prepared such a document.) One of them had a copy of the critique, but he did not want to make it public, insisting that it was too sensitive a document. He was willing to discuss its contents, however, but at the rate at which he was going it would take several days to go through its account of the technical flaws in the testimony.

Finally, he stepped out of his living room and returned with a kitchen wastepaper basket. He placed it in the middle of the room and then dropped the document into it, repeating that he was not at liberty to release it. "Now, on the other hand, if you just happened to find it in the trash . . ."

Cross-examination on the technical weaknesses in the official testimony—formulated on the basis of the A.E.C. scientists' private critique—created several problems for the A.E.C. The agency's embarrassment was compounded by the internal working papers of the Hanauer task force, which the A.E.C. finally made public in response to a threatened Freedom of Information Act lawsuit. The documents, released while the Hanauer task force was still on the witness stand, included the dissenting memo by Rosen and Colmar, as well as several additional memos that Colmar had prepared in the late fall of 1971 on the problem of flow blockage. (Colmar was working on the subject because he was the most knowledgeable member of the Hanauer task force on this issue; after he prepared the memos, which described the inadequate treatment of the subject in the June policy statement, he was removed from the task force.)

The working papers of the task force also revealed the existence of the Brockett report. The A.E.C. did not make that document public along with the other Hanauer task force papers, but its release soon became a moot point. An anonymous A.E.C. scientist decided to "leak" a draft copy of it.

Far more sensational than the original Brockett Report, however, was an additional study that Brockett and his staff had prepared for Milton Shaw in August 1971. The centerpiece of this supplementary Brockett report was a simple table that summarized the current state of knowledge on E.C.C.S. In the left-hand column, it listed the twenty-nine major technical areas where information was needed in order to make a satisfactory computer prediction of whether the E.C.C.S. would work. Another column summarized the "current status" of the A.E.C.'s information in each of those categories.

Going down that column, one reads that the available information is "Incomplete," "Preliminary," "Unverified," "Inadequate," "Incomplete," "Unverified," "Inadequate," "Unverified," "Inaccurate," "Uncertain," "Imprecise," "Inadequate," "Inadequate," "Uncertain," "Inaccurate," "Incomplete," "Inadequate," "Inadequate," "Inadequate," "Inadequate," "Incomplete," "Uncertain" and "Uncertain."

In the remaining seven of the twenty-nine categories, there is no rating of the adequacy of available information, because the A.E.C. did not have any information at all on those subjects. In those areas, the information was reported simply as "Missing." Another column in the table defines the "Urgency" that the A.E.C. experts attached to various research programs on E.C.C.S. Two of the research programs are listed as "Low" priority, five as "Medium" priority, fifteen as "High" priority, and eight as "Very High" priority. The table prepared by Brocket and his co-workers was a convenient report card on what the A.E.C. knew and didn't know about loss-of-coolant accidents and E.C.C.S. performance.

"A.E.C. documents have come forth as a hesitant series of tidal waves," George Freeman, the attorney who represented the nuclear-plant owners at the hearings, noted in an article recounting them. The "continuing stream of documents . . . strained the capacity of participants in the rulemaking to almost the breaking point," he added. There was a rule that stated that parties who wanted to refer to a document during cross-examination had to notify the other parties five days in advance. When the supplementary Brockett report was suddenly introduced into the hearing, a contribution from an anonymous A.E.C. official, Freeman suggested that perhaps the "leakers" also be asked to observe the five-day rule.

As more internal A.E.C. documents became available, additional issues kept arising and thus caused the hearing to expand into one of the longest and most complex rule-making proceedings that the government has ever held. As it departed from the short, pro-forma exercise that the A.E.C. had planned, the hearings also became a protracted public-relations debacle for the agency. The industry newsletter *Nucleonics Week* observed that the hearings had "opened up a Pandora's Box of scientific doubts and bureaucratic heavyhandedness."

AFTER THE HANAUER TASK FORCE testified, the E.C.C.S. experts from Oak Ridge and Idaho were scheduled to take the witness stand. It was obvious from their internal reports that these scientists had serious reservations about E.C.C.S. The key question was whether they would actually express their views candidly on the witness stand. They could easily try to mute their objections, or even retract them, to make their position more in line with "established policy." Or, at great risk to their careers, they could speak out about the problems.

Already, during the questioning of the Hanauer task force, one witness, G. Norman Lauben, an A.E.C. regulatory staff engineer, had dissented from one item in the task force's prepared testimony. He had raised his hand in response to a general question put to the task force: did any of them think that there were parts of the policy statement that were not conservative enough? Practically in tears, he acknowledged in a quaking voice that he did not think certain heat-transfer coefficients used in the industry computer methods were conservative enough. He did not make any broad challenge to the overall adequacy of the computer methods, merely this single objection. Still, it was obvious that it required considerable courage to take even this one minor exception to the official policy.

Philip Rittenhouse was to be the lead witness from the A.E.C. laboratories. He took the stand on March 7, 1972, looking as dapper as usual but uncharacteristically grim. He was on the spot, and he knew it. He had told A.E.C. lawyers privately, in a prehearing meeting, that he regarded the June 1971 policy statement on E.C.C.S. as "technically indefensible." If he testified in public to that effect, it would be the most sensational testimony at the hearing to date—and probably the end of his career as well.

Before the hearing, Milton Shaw, the head of the A.E.C. division that funded the research at Oak Ridge, had invited Rittenhouse to lunch. "I'd never had lunch with him before—or since, for that matter," Rittenhouse said. Shaw had not discussed Rittenhouse's upcoming testimony, Rittenhouse said. Shaw had merely told him what his own views were on E.C.C.S. Before the hearing Rittenhouse and other Oak Ridge staff members who would testify also spoke with Alvin Weinberg, the director of the Oak Ridge lab. Unlike the managers at Idaho, Weinberg told his researchers to "act responsibly and tell the truth."

At the outset of his testimony, Rittenhouse acknowledged, in response to the questioning, that flow blockage had long been of concern to him because of its potential detrimental effect on E.C.C.S. performance. His answer brought him into immediate conflict with the Hanauer task force, which had declared that flow blockage would not have a detrimental effect and could even be a positive benefit.

Rittenhouse did not shy away from the conflict. In response to further questions, he stated that the A.E.C.'s analysis was simply incorrect, technically. Asked to comment more specifically on the task force's testimony concerning several key experiments, Rittenhouse called the official interpretation of those tests "unreasonable and arbitrary." He was shown a copy of William Cottrell's December 6, 1971, letter.* The A.E.C.'s explanation for its return to

* A "leaked" copy of this document had been introduced at the hearing shortly before Rittenhouse testified.

Oak Ridge was that it was "withdrawn" because it was a draft document that did not properly express the views of the researchers at Oak Ridge.

Rittenhouse testified that he, in fact, had helped to draft Cottrell's letter and that at the time it represented his views. Moreover, with a few minor amendments to update it, he said that he would still stand by its conclusion that the June 1971 policy statement was seriously deficient. As he gave one answer after another at odds with established policy, he appeared to be so drained emotionally from the strain of giving this testimony that the pattern of questions had to be altered. He needed time to recover from answering difficult questions. Henceforth these would have to be interspersed with ones on noncontroversial topics. The questioning would have to be spread out over a period of days.

At the beginning of his second day on the witness stand, Rittenhouse was asked about his role as a consultant to the Hanauer task force. He had not been consulted when the June policy statement was being prepared. Just before the hearing, however, he had been asked to review the testimony that the task force had prepared on the subject of flow blockage. That testimony included optimistic estimates about the maximum degree of flow blockage that might occur in a reactor core during a major loss-of-coolant accident. When questioned about these estimates, the task force members replied that they had done supporting calculations—but had lost them.

Rittenhouse testified, however, that in reviewing the draft of the task force's testimony, he had learned that the estimate had not been made on the basis of calculations. Pressed to explain the basis of the estimates, Victor Stello, a member of the task force, had told Rittenhouse that he had "guessed" how much flow blockage might occur, Rittenhouse testified. The A.E.C. staff had also made other "extrapolations" from the limited available data to estimate the extent of the possible flow blockage. Rittenhouse testified that the staff did not have any metallurgists who really understood the issue and that its estimates did not reflect "good engineering practice." "I have decided that the kindest thing I can say is that they weren't very smart," Rittenhouse said in a recent interview.

Finally, by the end of his third day on the stand, Rittenhouse seemed to be ready to answer the ultimate question. Was there enough solid technical evidence to show that the emergency cooling equipment on current plants was capable of preventing the China Syndrome? Posing the question to him brought immediate objections from the lawyers representing the nuclear industry. Answering Rittenhouse's question, they said, went far beyond his expertise since he was a metallurgist, not an expert on heat transfer, computer analysis, or the other special fields involved in the study of E.C.C.S. performance. After protracted legal argument about the scope of his expertise, and the exact formulation of the question, the hearing board overruled the objections and allowed him to answer.

"Are you having trouble remembering the question, Mr. Rittenhouse?" the hearing transcript reads, when his turn to answer finally came.

"Not at all," Rittenhouse replied. "It'll be in my mind forever, I'm afraid."

There was laughter in the hearing room, followed by a hush as Rittenhouse began his answer. He noted that he had "really been asked to pass a judgment, an opinion, as a personal opinion," on what the whole hearing was about, to answer the question that the "entire task force of the regulatory staff" had sought to answer in its testimony.

> I have worked in the fuel rod failure program [studying] the questions of fuel cladding and swelling, subsequent blockage, and the possible effects of this blockage on cooling effectiveness . . . As far as these points, in which I am an expert, there is not the information available to objectively confirm, by scientific or technical procedures, what exactly these materials-related phenomena . . . what effect they may have on the E.C.C.S. in the course of a loss-of-coolant accident.
>
> Beyond that, I can only say that I have talked to a number of [A.E.C. experts], people who work in the area of E.C.C.S., both

> the materials people, people who work primarily with [computer] codes, people who are experts, if you will, in heat transfer, fluid flow. And I get the genuine feeling from all of these people that they believe there are things we just do not know well enough yet. . . . They have too many reservations—I believe shared too generally—for me to pass off. These reservations are primarily that certain phenomena, portions of the loss-of-coolant accident—maybe they're not quite sure what's going on.

He concluded by noting that, "Certainly many of the things that we toss around in computer codes and use to predict maximum temperatures or to predict the course of the loss-of-coolant accident . . . have not been verified experimentally." Pausing after his answer, Rittenhouse looked out into the hearing room and then said into the microphone, his own voice barely audible, "It's awfully quiet in here."

The A.E.C. hearing examiner asked him "Are you through, Mr. Rittenhouse?" He replied, "I think I am," the look on his face suggesting that he was thinking at that moment that both his testimony and his career in the nuclear program had been concluded. "I just knew I'd blown a lot of jobs with the reactor manufacturers," he said in a recent interview.

Patricia Rittenhouse had come to Washington to be with her husband as he testified. I met them in the lobby of a restaurant, near the hearing room, at the end of his first day on the witness stand. "I told him if he didn't tell the truth, not to come home," she said. "I didn't want to have to live with him, moping around for the rest of his life, because he had an opportunity to do the right thing and didn't do it."

"A.E.C. EXPERTS SHARE DOUBTS OVER REACTOR SAFETY," the headline in *The New York Times* read. The testimony of A.E.C. scientist Philip Rittenhouse, the accompanying story said, had "severely shaken" the A.E.C. After his revelation, at the end of his third day on the witness stand, that doubts about the E.C.C.S. were widely shared among his colleagues in the safety-research program, Rittenhouse was asked for the names of those who had expressed reservations. He requested that he be given an evening to put together the list. The following morning he slowly read into the record the names of thirty scientists and engineers at Oak Ridge, in Idaho, and on the Commission's headquarters staff. His list was practically a "Who's Who" of the A.E.C.'s leading safety experts. George Brockett, Morris Rosen, Robert Colmar, George Lawson, Lawrence Ybarrando, Roger Griebe, Rex Shumway, and others named by him were called to the witness stand in the following weeks. They described their own conclusions about the defects in the A.E.C.'s approval of current emergency-cooling-system designs. Rittenhouse's testimony opened the floodgates, and the internal controversy about E.C.C.S. that the A.E.C. had tried for so long to keep secret was finally made public.

The E.C.C.S. hearings continued for almost two years, until December 1973. During these twenty-three months the hearing record grew to include more than fifty thousand pages of evidence. The industry and A.E.C. staff filed testimony to rebut what Rittenhouse, Brockett, Rosen, Colmar, and the other scientists from the A.E.C. laboratories had said on the witness stand. All of the concerns expressed by these scientists, the Hanauer task force asserted, had been resolved. (The A.E.C. hearing board refused to allow further questioning of these A.E.C. experts, however, to determine whether they agreed with the resolution of their concerns.) At the conclusion of the hearing, the A.E.C. staff, led by Stephen Hanauer, recommended that the A.E.C. reaffirm its June 1971 approval of the existing E.C.C.S. designs—and the Commission did so. Its "final" policy statement on E.C.C.S. left its June 1971 "interim" policy statement essentially intact.

The outcome of the E.C.C.S. hearing was not particularly surprising, since the Commission's predispositions on the controversy had already been indicated as early as July 16, 1972. While the hearing was still in progress and testimony critical of its policy was still being entered into the record, Edson Case, the Deputy Director of Licensing, told the *The New York Times*, in response to an inquiry, that "no costly changes" would be imposed on the industry as a result of the hearings. There might be some "technical changes" in a few of the rules governing E.C.C.S., Case remarked, but "the overall result will be substantially the same."

This was not the first occasion on which agency officials had indicated their prejudgment of a pending case—which, given the judicial role of the Commission, is highly improper. At a congressional hearing some fifteen years earlier, A.E.C. Chairman Lewis Strauss inadvertently disclosed his plans to attend the groundbreaking ceremonies for the Fermi breeder reactor. (He was being badgered by Congressman Clarence Cannon about the lack of progress in getting the Fermi project started, and told of his plans to go to the Fermi plant as evidence that things were moving ahead.) Strauss' announcement that he would go to the groundbreaking caused some controversy—since the A.E.C. had not yet completed its safety review of the proposed plant or issued a construction permit for it. His disclosure was just one more indication of what Thomas E. Murray, a fellow commissioner who opposed the Fermi plant, described to Senator Clinton Anderson as the A.E.C.'s intention "to ignore the signs of danger and grant the construction permit anyway."

Case's *faux pas* in disclosing the A.E.C.'s intransigence on E.C.C.S. was the subject of a sardonic private note that Edward J. Bauser, the staff director of the Joint Committee on Atomic Energy, sent to A.E.C. Director of Regulation Muntzing. "The recent article in *The New York Times* which is enclosed would, in my view, be very disturbing to those who still have faith in the integrity of the administrative process," he wrote. "It could also be useful to anyone who wishes to discredit the integrity of the A.E.C. licensing process."

THE E.C.C.S. ISSUE settled to its satisfaction, the A.E.C. went about its normal course of business: promoting nuclear power expansion. No major change was made in E.C.C.S. designs in the dozens of plants it licensed in the next few years, but there were some noticeable changes in A.E.C. personnel rosters.

Philip Rittenhouse was removed as head of the fuel-rod-failure program at Oak Ridge under orders from Herbert Kouts, who was the senior A.E.C. official in charge of safety research. Alvin Weinberg, who had sent his own letter to the Commission backing up the concerns of his researchers, was replaced as director of the laboratory. Rosen and Colmar had already been reassigned prior to the hearing, but Rosen decided subsequently that his chances for advancement were better outside the agency, and he left it. At the Idaho lab, senior personnel who had criticized the "established policy" found themselves, as one of them noted, switched from responsible positions to "nothing jobs." Some of them, like George Brockett, took advantage of the company policy that encouraged those who criticized A.E.C. policies to "look outside the company" for a new job.

Stephen Hanauer, Victor Stello, and other task force members who defended the June 1971 policy statement were given "Distinguished Service Awards" by the agency. Most of them have been steadily promoted and currently hold senior positions as regulators of the United States nuclear industry.

A decade after the E.C.C.S. hearings, Rittenhouse is a different man. He has become a kind of Flying Dutchman, cut off from the nuclear-safety program by the A.E.C. and by his own unwillingness to get involved in any further controversy. He returned to Oak Ridge after the hearings and was given a job in a different part of the laboratory. He then found work for a few years in England and, after that, in Germany. He had returned to Oak Ridge and I interviewed him there recently, but he said that he had his eye out for the next opportunity to work abroad. The flashy clothes that seemed to be his trademark had been replaced by a muted plaid shirt and dark brown trousers. He seemed sad and bitter.

His removal from the safety-research program at Oak Ridge had not surprised him. "There was no way in the world," he said, "that the program could be continued if I were deeply involved. What I've done with the last few years is just try to forget the whole goddamn thing. I had a bunch of papers, mementos, a couple of volumes of the hearing transcripts, and so forth. I took these and I threw them in the trash. I do not want to see them again." He would give no opinion on whether the flow-blockage problem had been resolved over the past decade. "All I know is that they've done a hell of a lot of work on it. I don't know anything else about it—and I don't want to know anything else about it. Purposely not. I do not want to be involved in that area anymore, ever, thank you. I've been a lot happier since I've been divorced from that. I don't read anything on reactor safety anymore."

"Phil got blackballed," his wife said, "but I'm still glad he did it. It was for the good of us all that he spoke out. What if there were a bad accident and a lot of people got killed? I didn't care if he lost his job. It was one of those causes in life. I seriously didn't care. I thought it was his job to tell what he'd learned. He'd been asked by the A.E.C. to find these things out. He had to speak out truthfully."

Both Rittenhouse and his wife believed in nuclear power, and, they said, they still do. "I think nuclear power is going to be terribly important, regardless of what people say," Pat Rittenhouse explained. Her attitude a decade ago, she continued, was that "If there is a problem, it should be corrected now, while we're on the ground floor. I think we should get into it in the right way. So what if G.E. and Westinghouse had to back up and do things a little different? Wouldn't it be better to make a few adjustments now?"

"We really believed that we'd done what they'd asked us to do, which was to identify some problems," Rittenhouse said of his work for the A.E.C. "We just identified the things that we believed were problems and that people were trying to sweep under the rug in the hope they'd go away. I can't understand why I didn't get a gold medal like Stello did."

PART THREE

THE BIBLE

THE UNITED STATES ATOMIC ENERGY COMMISSION had a problem with its public image, James Schlesinger observed. With unabashed enthusiasm, the agency had championed nuclear power development for more than two decades. "Atomic power for peace" was widely popular; but now in the early 1970s, the A.E.C. was at the center of a bitter controversy. Appointed by President Nixon in July 1971 to be the new chairman of the agency, Schlesinger could see that the environmental movement—which was leading the attack on the A.E.C.—was growing, that public sympathy with its general objectives was increasing, and that the agency had failed to calm the growing controversy that was threatening plans for a large nuclear power program.

A few weeks after his appointment, Schlesinger got a clear indication of the diminished esteem in which the A.E.C. was held. In a landmark environmental decision, the United States Court of Appeals for the District of Columbia ruled that the agency had violated the National Environmental Policy Act of 1969. It had failed in its licensing procedures, the court said, to give due regard to the environmental impact of proposed nuclear plants. The

Commission's "crabbed interpretation" of its responsibilities in this area made a "mockery" of the 1969 law, the court concluded.

The A.E.C. was ordered to prepare detailed "environmental impact statements" and to consider the adverse environmental effects of proposed plants before making further licensing decisions. In 1961, in better times, the Supreme Court had afforded the A.E.C. broad powers to license nuclear plants as it saw fit. A decade later, the judiciary was no longer convinced that the A.E.C. used its discretion wisely.

Having regarded the nuclear program uncritically for two decades, the news media detected the scent of a potential scandal, which in the normal course of events it would be likely to dramatize and to build into an even bigger controversy. Schlesinger realized that if the nuclear program was to expand, as planned, public trust in the A.E.C. would have to be restored. Creating a new image for the A.E.C. was one of his highest priorities.

Schlesinger promptly announced that the agency would accept the decision of the Court of Appeals and would prepare environmental-impact statements, as the court said the law required, before deciding whether to license proposed plants. A few weeks later, in a widely publicized speech at an industry meeting in Bal Harbour, Florida, he took further steps to rectify the image of the agency as a conscientious regulator of the industry. He admitted that an overfriendly relationship between the A.E.C. and the industry had developed during the early days when the A.E.C. "fostered and protected" the "infant" nuclear industry. The industry had grown rapidly—"Perhaps in some respects the pace has been too swift," he added, without elaboration—and had finally reached "relative maturity." A new A.E.C. policy was, therefore, appropriate, and the industry would have to realize that the Commission "exists to serve the public interest," not just to promote nuclear power.

"Environmentalists have raised many legitimate questions," he said, and in the future the A.E.C. would respond to these questions "as a referee serving the public interest," not as an exclusive agent of the industry. The industry had not done all that it should to ensure safety, he added—noting, in particular, that the quality of workmanship at some nuclear plants gave the industry "reason to blush." The A.E.C. would set "tough" new regulations for the industry to follow, and "although we sympathize with the difficulties that you are facing . . . we have no intention of evading our responsibilities under the law."

Having introduced the A.E.C.'s new image to the press, who received it favorably, Schlesinger turned his attention to other matters, taking no major steps to change the actual regulatory program of the A.E.C. Environmental-impact statements would have to be written, of course. These reports would mean more paperwork, for which the agency would need more staff, but the new documents would not dramatically affect the reactor-licensing process. After all, the law required that the A.E.C. "consider" environmental impacts, and it would now do so in multivolume reports. This exercise completed, the A.E.C. would then be able to proceed along its traditional course and issue nuclear-plant construction permits to each utility company that asked for one. No real change of attitude on the part of the A.E.C. staff was called for by the new chairman, who left in place the program of industry self-regulation that the A.E.C. had adopted in the 1950s.

Schlesinger's intent, it soon became clear, was to change the public's perceptions of the agency's regulatory program, not its substance. A suitable new image formulated and announced, he began work on his other priorities. The A.E.C. also had responsibilities for nuclear-weapons development, and Schlesinger was personally far more interested in the "military side" of the A.E.C. than in its civilian power programs.

The attempted image switch was not immediately successful, for the critics of the agency did not readily accept the chairman's declaration that the A.E.C. staff would emerge, overnight, as "born again" regulators. Nor did the press show an inclination to abandon its skepticism on nuclear power. The controversy continued. In response to the persistent questioning of plant safety, Schlesinger argued that the chance of a catastrophic accident was "virtually zero." Yes, such accidents were theoretically possible, but so many precautions were taken at nuclear plants, agency officials explained with increasing exasperation, that there was no appreciable risk of any kind to the people living nearby. The chance of a catastrophic reactor accident, Seaborg wrote, in a book published shortly after his retirement, was comparable to "the probability that all of the airplanes circling in the vicinity of New York's airports might collide over Shea Stadium during a Sunday afternoon baseball double-header—with the wreckage falling into the stadium."

But, as the agency ridiculed the critics for ignoring the "vanishingly small probability" of serious accidents, it found itself in the embarrassing position of not being able—with proper technical evidence—to say what the odds really were. In the hearings on emergency cooling systems, for example, the A.E.C. staff had been challenged to provide a technical assessment of the likelihood of serious loss-of-coolant accidents, but it had none to offer. When the staff was then pressed to justify its assertions that such accidents were "highly unlikely," it avoided the issue by contending that such questions were "beyond the scope of the hearing."

Similarly insistent questions about the A.E.C.'s probability claims were raised by the U.S. Environmental Protection Agency. (One of the E.P.A.'s jobs was to comment on the technical merits of the environmental-impact statements that other federal agencies prepared.) The A.E.C.'s impact statements had to analyze, among other topics, the effects of reactor accidents on the environment. To do so, the A.E.C. divided potential accidents into eight categories, ranging from trivial equipment breakdowns (Class 1 accidents) all the way up to major disruptions of the plant (Class 8 accidents) that would require the emergency operation of plant-safety systems. A.E.C. analysts concluded that there would be no major environmental impact, even during the worst Class 8 accidents, because existing safety systems could be counted on to work satisfactorily.

It was possible, of course, that the safety devices might fail, but the A.E.C. staff concluded that such failures were so "highly unlikely" that they created no "credible" safety problem. All such "incredible" accidents were lumped together into one catch-all category—"Class 9 Accidents," they were called—and their consequences were not discussed in the environmental-impact statements. The E.P.A. questioned the peremptory exclusion of Class 9 accidents, and A.E.C. officials acknowledged, privately, that they had no satisfactory justification. "Associating technically defensible probabilities with Class 9 accidents is not possible at this time," the Director of Licensing, Dr. Peter Morris, wrote in an April 1972 A.E.C. internal memorandum. "To develop a basis for this is, and has been, the subject of much discussion among the top Regulatory Staff and the Commission," he added.

A study had already been under way, in the A.E.C.'s Division of Reactor Development and Technology, to establish the comparative risks of nuclear power and other energy sources. The study had been lagging because of other demands on the division and because of the difficulty and complexity of the project. Earlier attempts by the A.E.C. to establish the probability of reactor accidents had fared no better, leaving the A.E.C. in the uncomfortable position of being unable to support, by reasonable technical evidence, the central premise on which it based its conclusions about nuclear-plant safety.

In light of the growing debate over nuclear power, Chairman Schlesinger decided that it was time for the A.E.C. to launch a major, high-priority study to prove, once and for all, how exceedingly safe nuclear plants really were. The official dogma about the "low probability" of serious accidents needed to be backed up by an authoritative bible on the subject. The project to prepare such a probability assessment became known as the Reactor Safety Study.

THE PROBABILITY OF AN EVENT indicates how likely it is to happen under particular circumstances. There is a fifty–fifty chance, for example, on the toss of a symmetrical coin, of getting heads. There is one chance in fifty-two of getting the ace of spades in a draw from a well-shuffled deck of cards. There is one chance in sixty-five thousand of getting a straight flush. In each of these cases, the probability of various outcomes can be determined in advance by straightforward methods, since the boundaries of the problem are so well known. There are only two sides of the coin, only fifty-two cards in a deck, only a specific number of possible hands that can be dealt. The "laws of probability," as the mathematicians call them, can be applied easily and with confidence.

In the case of nuclear-plant accidents, on the other hand, the boundaries of the problem are not clear-cut. A nuclear plant is very complex—having thousands of pumps, pipes, motors, valves, electrical circuits, instruments, and the like—and the possible malfunctions range from simple failures (a valve stuck open) all the way up to massive breakdowns of key pieces of equipment. Exceedingly bizarre accidents can get started, moreover, as one failure leads to or combines with other failures in a sequence of events that plant safety devices may or may not be able to control. Possible failures in the safety devices themselves, of course, greatly complicate the outcome of a given accident.

Unlike a card game, in which all of the possible outcomes are known in advance, the full range of potential accidents that can occur in a nuclear plant is impossible to define. Many "unexpected" accidents are therefore possible—and in fact, have occurred. Classical probability theory tells one how to estimate the likelihood of known possibilities, but it does not explain how one is to calculate the odds of an unpleasant surprise that plant designers failed to anticipate.

In March 1972, the A.E.C. began to make concrete plans for its study of accident probabilities. It was L. Manning Muntzing, the Director of Regulation, and Dr. Stephen Hanauer, his technical adviser, who took responsibility for setting up the study, along with other senior A.E.C. aides. They recognized, as Hanauer noted in a memo that month, that it was not at all obvious that probability analysis could be successfully applied to predict the likelihood of reactor accidents. "Do we dare undertake such a study until we really know how?" Hanauer wrote to his colleagues. "Are we willing to be told that the task is impossible of achievement with presently available resources (information, theoretical bases, man-years)?"

There were, of course, recognized experts in statistics and probability theory who could have advised the A.E.C. on how such a study might be undertaken, but the A.E.C. did not turn to them. Nor did the agency ask any of the experts from the Apollo program to head the study. (The Apollo program had done a great deal of pioneering work in the field of "reliability analysis" in order to assess the likelihood of possible malfunctions in the lunar spacecraft.) The A.E.C. decided that it would do the study "in-house," with its own staff, so that the Commission would have tight control over the undertaking.

The Commission wanted, however, to have the study appear to be an independent work and—to give it the color of independence—was eager to recruit an outsider as its titular director. Accordingly, Schlesinger asked Dr. Manson Benedict, the head of the Nuclear Engineering Department at the Massachusetts Institute of Technology, to take charge of the study. Benedict was not a specialist in reactor safety, but he was a longtime supporter of the nuclear program. He also had very close ties to the industry; he served, for example, as a member of the board of directors of the Atomic Industrial Forum, the nuclear industry's principal trade organization. (The group had successfully lobbied the A.E.C. in 1965 when it asked that the agency not make public the unfavorable results of its 1964–65 study of the risk of catastrophic accidents.)

Benedict, citing "personal reasons," declined the invitation, but he offered an alternative. In a letter to Schlesinger dated March 17, 1972, he nominated Dr. Norman C. Rasmussen of M.I.T. as the study director. Benedict referred to Rasmussen as "my colleague in the M.I.T. Nuclear Engineering Department whose professional specialization has been in the reactor safety field."

Like Benedict, Rasmussen has had a number of ties to the nuclear industry. He has worked as a consultant for the Nuclear Energy Liability Property Association, the New York State Atomic and Space Development Authority, Burns and Roe (nuclear-plant architect-engineers), and Reddy Communications (a public-relations firm that specializes in teaching firms in the nuclear industry how to debate the critics of nuclear power). He was also an original member of the board of directors of Americans for Energy Independence, a group organized and funded by the Westinghouse Electric Corporation to lobby in suport of nuclear power, and he presently serves on the board of Northeast Utilities.

Rasmussen is a physicist by training, his interest in the subject cultivated by a high-school physics teacher. "If I'd had a good chemistry teacher, maybe I would have done that," he said in an interview. He grew up on a dairy farm in Middletown, Pennsylvania, he explained, and "anybody who grows up on a dairy farm will want to do something else." (His family's farm, near the Susquehanna River, was a few miles from Three Mile Island, which would later become the site for two large nuclear power stations.) He studied physics and played football and basketball at Gettysburg College before attending graduate school in physics at M.I.T. After receiving his Ph.D. in 1956, he dropped out of physics and went into engineering, joining the nuclear-engineering department at the Institute.

Rasmussen's professional specialization was not, as Benedict wrote in his letter to Schlesinger, "in the reactor safety field." His career, which had not yet been rewarded with great prominence, had actually been spent in the unrelated field of gamma-ray spectroscopy. Rasmussen, in fact, had never published any technical papers on any aspect of nuclear-power-reactor safety. Nor, according to Rasmussen's own description of his background, was he a specialist in statistical methods, probability analysis, reliability-assessment techniques, or any other technical specialty applicable to the probability study that the A.E.C. wanted to undertake.

"At the time, I had only a vague idea of how to carry out such a study," Rasmussen said. His limited involvement in nuclear safety was as head of an annual summer lecture program on that subject at M.I.T. In that capacity, he had come to know the senior A.E.C. staff people, Stephen Hanauer and Saul Levine, who were organizing the Reactor Safety Study.

Rasmussen's only prior publication relating to nuclear safety was a four-page, nontechnical article entitled "Nuclear Reactor Safety—An Opinion," which appeared in the industry magazine *Nuclear News* in January 1972. In the article he stated his belief, supported by reference to industry reports, that the emergency cooling systems installed on American nuclear plants were adequate to prevent meltdown accidents. The risk of major accidents was "very small" and "insignificant," he said. Two months later, the A.E.C. appointed him director of the Reactor Safety Study.

BENEDICT AND RASMUSSEN prepared a basic outline for the Reactor Safety Study, as they envisioned it, and submitted it for A.E.C. approval. Their seven-page letter, dated March 17, 1972, discussed the goals of the study, the general technical issues that it would address, how the information that it developed would be controlled, and the means of organizing the effort. (Their letter, and other internal working papers of the Reactor Safety Study, were released by the A.E.C. in response to a formal request that I made for these documents under the Freedom of Information Act.)

They told the A.E.C. that there would be "very difficult problems" in trying to develop valid accident-probability estimates. Nuclear plants had a large number of components, they said, and in many cases "we do not have meaningful statistical information" from which component-failure probabilities could be derived. (Good statistics on equipment-failure rates were unavailable, since few reactors had built up substantial operating experience.) "It is not clear," they added, "whether it would be possible to achieve any kind of consensus" on what the correct probabilities were. The numbers that were ultimately chosen "for these poorly known probabilities will have a large effect on the results of the study and will be the aspect of it most open to criticism."

Despite the difficulties, the two industry consultants concluded that carrying out the study "in the light of present-day information is a manageable task that might have significant benefit for the nuclear industry." They suggested that the project be guided by a steering committee that would include M.I.T. faculty members and "possibly representatives from the principal reactor manufacturers and the E.P.A." They added that "the report to be useful must have reasonable acceptance by people in the industry."

This was a noteworthy and peculiar condition, applying as it did to what would later be presented to the public as an "objective, scientific study" of nuclear-plant safety.

According to the memorandum from Benedict and Rasmussen, the A.E.C. would have control over the important decisions that had to be made during the study and on how the results of the study would be made public. The A.E.C. would approve, in advance, the basic methods used to estimate failure probabilities and the appointment of all project staff and consultants.

Benedict and Rasmussen also stated that we "must recognize that once we start our results may become public" and that "the sensitive nature of these studies will require careful control of all official information releases." They said that the A.E.C. would have control over the final report so that its conclusions "on this controversial subject" would be put "into a form which the A.E.C. would be willing to issue." The A.E.C. stated publicly, at the completion of the study, that it "took care to assure the independent nature of the study group," although it is hard to reconcile this statement with the veto power over all aspects of the study that Benedict and Rasmussen assured the Commission that it would have.

Some dismay was voiced by a few A.E.C. officials over the orientation of the Reactor Safety Study toward a report that would serve the purposes of the nuclear industry. Jerome Saltzman of the A.E.C. staff wrote a memorandum in which he expressed concern about the "tone, credibility and appearances" of the proposed effort. He noted that the study should be done "for the A.E.C. and not the nuclear industry. Any benefit or detriment for the nuclear industry that might result from the study should be considered incidental." He added, "In light of this, I am bothered by statements such as . . . 'it seems to us that the problem . . . is a manageable task that might have significant benefit for the nuclear industry' and . . . 'the report to be useful must have reasonable acceptance by people in the industry.' " The senior officials in charge of organizing the study—Hanauer, Muntzing and Schlesinger—had no such reservations. On the basis of the March 17,

1972, memo Rasmussen set to work, with A.E.C. approval, to direct the urgently needed Reactor Safety Study.

Only one significant alteration was made in the plan that Rasmussen and Benedict had proposed. They had suggested that the study be done at M.I.T., but the A.E.C. decided to have the work carried out at A.E.C. offices in Germantown, Maryland. Saul Levine, of the A.E.C. staff, was appointed full-time Project Staff Director; the Director, Rasmussen, on leave from M.I.T., worked part time on the study. The final report of the study, when it was ultimately completed, became commonly known as the "Rasmussen Report," but people close to the study have suggested that, given the respective roles of Rasmussen and Levine, it might, more properly, be called the "Levine Report." "It became clear that Rasmussen didn't really know the specifics of the report," one of the members of a government review committee on the study said in a recent interview. "Whenever there was any kind of technical question on it, he had to turn to Levine to find out what was in the report."

BECAUSE OF THE POLITICAL CONTROVERSY over nuclear power, there was strong pressure on Rasmussen and Levine to get results quickly. As an unfortunate consequence of this, some of the study's key technical work, which, to be done properly, required a great deal of time and effort, had to be done as a rush job—or omitted altogether. The subtle work of developing suitable methods for calculating accident probabilities, for example, was characterized in April 1972 by the A.E.C.'s Dr. Peter Morris as a task that would require "a very substantial technical effort over a considerable length of time."

Rasmussen and Benedict concluded, however, that in "a short project like this"—they estimated that the entire Reactor Safety Study would be completed in eleven months—there would not be time to "produce new concepts" for handling difficult problems in probability analysis. They proposed instead, and the A.E.C.

agreed, that the Reactor Safety Study would use a technique for making probability assessments that had been developed in the United States aerospace and ballistic missile programs. The technique which they borrowed—called fault-tree analysis—had well-known and very serious shortcomings. Rasmussen and Benedict decided to use it anyway.

Fault-tree analysis, in its most general sense, is a straightforward application of logic. The engineers analyze a given system, look at the individual "faults"—such as mechanical breakdowns and human errors—that are possible, and then draw diagrams showing how those independent faults might combine to produce various accident "sequences." (The diagrams, which indicate how accidents can branch out in various directions, resemble complex family trees.) One then takes whatever data are available about the probability of the various individual faults and computes the overall probability that a given *set* of them could occur, one after another, to disrupt the system.

For example, one might want to determine the kinds of accidents that could develop if a major pipe in the reactor's primary cooling system suddenly ruptured. To do this the fault-tree analyst would trace the possible follow-on events that could take place. The emergency cooling system might work to control the resulting leak and halt the accident sequence right there—this outcome would be represented by one branch on the fault tree—or the E.C.C.S. might fail, and the accident would worsen. This possibility would be represented by another, separate, extended branch on the fault tree that showed the possible further stages into which such an accident could evolve.

If the E.C.C.S. failed, the core would melt, and so the next major branching point on the fault tree would indicate whether or not the molten fuel penetrated the containment building. If the containment restrains the molten fuel, then the accident would end at this point, with no release of radioactive materials into the nearby region. On the other hand, if the containment failed, like the E.C.C.S., a large release of radioactive materials from the plant might ensue. But this would not be the end of the fault-tree analysis.

To determine the probability of injury to the public, many more factors would have to be analyzed. (People may or may not be evacuated in time to avoid injury, for example.) All the alternative outcomes would be described as further branches on what would be, by this point, a set of very long and complex fault trees.

When the fault trees are completed, one can use them to estimate accident probability if one has information on the likelihood of the individual faults. Thus, if one knows the probability of pipe ruptures, of an E.C.C.S. failure, of a containment failure, and so on, one could compute the overall probability that a given pipe rupture could lead to a catastrophic accident. Having looked not just at pipe ruptures, but at all possible malfunctions that could lead to large radiation releases, one would then be able to make a summary estimate of the risk to the public from nuclear-plant accidents. This, at any rate, was the theory behind the approach that Rasmussen adopted.

The problem with this kind of probability analysis, the engineers in the space program had learned, was that its results were not very reliable. Fault trees offer streamlined versions of complex events, and the kind of chaos that can prevail in a messy accident is not accounted for by them. Fault-tree analysis can easily handle simple hardware failures (a motor that fails to start) but not design deficiencies (a motor that starts but, because of the designer's error, is not powerful enough to perform the job assigned to it). The fault trees that one prepares, moreover, are a product of engineering judgment, and if there are important kinds of accidents that the engineers have overlooked, the resulting predictions will be too optimistic. This is especially a problem when one is dealing with new, complex systems. How does one know that all possible accidents have been included in the fault trees?

Despite their extensive fault-tree study, the engineers working on the space program found that there were just too many "surprises." Approximately 20 percent of the ground-test failures in the Apollo program, and more than 35 percent of the in-flight malfunctions, were failures that had not previously been identified as "credible" possibilities.

The performance of the Apollo Service Propulsion System engine illustrates some of the problems with fault-tree analysis. This was the main engine of the Apollo Service Module and it powered most mid-course corrections, slowed the service module as it entered lunar orbit, and propelled the spacecraft out of its lunar orbit for return to earth. In the early 1960s, using methods quite similar to those of the Reactor Safety Study, estimates were made of the reliability of this engine. The estimates proved far too optimistic, and the rate of engine failure, after thousands of tests, proved to be forty times higher than predicted.

Although fault-tree analysis can be of some benefit to designers—it is a logical way of searching for potential weak spots in a complex system, for example—it was patently unable to produce reliable probability estimates. Long before the Reactor Safety Study adopted the fault-tree methods for probability analysis, the Apollo program engineers had discarded them. Hanauer himself, in a note written in 1971, had stated, "I do not consider the numerical results [from fault-tree analysis] to be reliable . . ."

THE REACTOR SAFETY STUDY did not do a general study of all the nuclear plants in the United States. To simplify its work, it focused on a pair of "representative" plants that incorporated the two most common types of nuclear reactors. These were the Surry Nuclear Power Station Unit 1 in Surry County, Virginia, which used a pressurized-water reactor manufactured by Westinghouse, and the Peach Bottom Nuclear Power Station Unit 2 in Louisa County, Pennsylvania, which had a boiling-water reactor made by General Electric. The A.E.C. had to go to Westinghouse and General Electric, the two ultilities that operated these facilities, and to the architect-engineers and construction companies who designed and built them, to obtain the detailed information needed for a full-scale fault-tree analysis.

Safety Analysis Reports on each of these plants had already been submitted to the A.E.C. by plant owners, before the plants were licensed, but the information they contained was of a very general nature. They frequently included only simplified schematic drawings for the basic plant systems. (The A.E.C. had so little specific knowledge about the kind of equipment in the plants that its staff safety experts used to refer to engineering drawings that they reviewed as "cartoons.") A substantial body of additional data had to be collected on such particulars as the exact location and dimensions of plant components, the detailed layout of key systems, the response time and other performance characteristics of pumps and valves. Also needed was information about the design assumptions for various components such as the amount of stress or vibration or heating the component was able to take before it failed.

Extensive questionnaires relating to these particulars were forwarded to the various companies involved with Surry and Peach Bottom. Selected checking of some of the responses was possible, through site visits and independent reviews by the Reactor Safety Study staff, but much of the data had to be taken on faith.

The industry did more than supply raw data for the Reactor Safety Study. The role of industry expanded to the point where it assumed a major responsibility for some of the actual analysis that the Rasmussen group published in its final report. At the outset of the study, Chairman Schlesinger held a private meeting with industry representatives, to discuss their "interaction" with the study. Members of Levine's staff were subsequently appointed as "liaison" officers with the industry to coordinate industry's participation. The internal memos written by Levine's staff document the specific parts of the Reactor Safety Study that were handed over as "assignments" to industry analysts.

The industry assumed such a prominent role in the work of the Reactor Safety Study because its experts had much more detailed knowledge than anyone else about the two plants under study, and because the industry had other resources that the Rasmussen group needed. Computer methods, like the controversial ones used to predict emergency-cooling-system performance, are widely used by nuclear-safety analysts. Instead of developing their own methods, Rasmussen asked the designers of the Surry and Peach Bottom plants to do the work using their existing computer techniques. The Rasmussen group did not review the validity of the industry's computer methods—having neither the expertise nor the time to do so. Like the other data provided by the industry, the computer predictions were accepted largely on faith.

The details of the industry's computer methods are generally not made public. The industry regards them as "proprietary." When the study staff did try to look at such information, they encountered difficulties. Stone & Webster, the designers of the Surry plant, insisted on certain "ground rules" before they would permit personnel from the study to visit the company's offices. They stated that the personnel "may inspect S&W [Stone & Webster] calculations in Boston" but would not be permitted to obtain copies of analytical information.

WHILE THE REACTOR SAFETY STUDY was in progress, the Nixon Administration issued a directive to the A.E.C. Safety-review procedures should be streamlined, the agency was told, so that nuclear plants could be licensed faster. An in-house A.E.C. task force was formed, under the direction of Malcolm Ernst of the regulatory staff, to see how this could be done. This special task force covered some of the same ground as the Reactor Safety Study since, before assessing how licensing could be speeded up, Ernst and his colleagues decided to review how well the licensing process was fulfilling its nominal goal: ensuring the safety of nuclear plants.

They concluded, in an October 1973 internal report, that the regulation of nuclear power appeared to have been successful "at least on the surface." Nevertheless, they found that serious safety problems were "besieging reactors under construction and in operation." One indication of these problems, they said, was the approximately eight hundred fifty safety-related problems that occurred at the thirty operating reactors in the eighteen-month period between January 1972 and June 1973. "The large number of reactor incidents, coupled with the fact that many of them had real safety significance, were generic in nature and were not identified during the normal design, fabrication, erection and preoperational testing phases, raises a serious question regarding the current review and inspection practices both on the part of the nuclear industry and the A.E.C.," they reported to the Commission.

The Ernst task force drew a number of conclusions from the data on the frequency and seriousness of plant safety problems. Senior A.E.C. spokesmen had been saying that the chance of a major reactor accident was less than "one in a million" per reactor year, a claim that they hoped would be validated by the upcoming Rasmussen report. The Ernst report, however, said that the Rasmussen study was "no panacea," and it expressed doubt about the validity of the probability estimates that it was trying to make.

So many new and unexpected safety problems were occurring at the operating plants, the Ernst report said, that numerical estimation of accident probability was doubtful "since identification of all possible accident combinations has not been accomplished." Moreover, with so many malfunctions plaguing nuclear-plant safety equipment, the Ernst task force said, it "does not believe" that there is "the required confidence level that the probability for [a major] accident is one in a million or less per reactor year."

In January 1974, the A.E.C. issued an edited, public version of the October 1973 report that was filed by the Ernst task force. The published report described the steps that the group had recommended for streamlining and improving the licensing process. The findings of the Ernst task force that were critical of the state of safety at existing nuclear plants and of the probability estimates in the forthcoming Rasmussen report were deleted.

RASMUSSEN AND BENEDICT'S ORIGINAL PLAN for an eleven-month project was soon abandoned, as the scope and complexity of the Reactor Safety Study became more fully appreciated. After more than a year of work, the end was still not in sight. Lack of required data, unanticipated technical problems and additional complications kept delaying the completion of the study. One such complication, brought to the attention of Staff Director Saul Levine in October 1973, was that some of the study's results might call into question the A.E.C.'s official policy toward nuclear-plant safety.

Quality assurance has been called the "watchword" of the nuclear industry, and it was an essential element in the A.E.C.'s program for ensuring the low probability of serious nuclear-plant accidents. Unlike conventional industries, where product quality can be highly uncertain, the nuclear industry was expected to practice extreme diligence in building and operating nuclear plants according to very strict standards. The A.E.C. did not send out government inspectors to look over each worker's shoulder as the plants were built. Instead, as a key part of the A.E.C.'s program for industry self-regulation, each company was supposed to appoint certain members of its own staff to serve as the "first-line" quality-control inspectors. Other senior company personnel were then responsible for reviewing all reported deficiencies and getting them corrected.

The term "quality assurance" implies management's commitment to procedures that monitor and ensure plant operation in conformance with quality standards. Periodically, the Commission would review a specific management's program of such procedures. A.E.C. inspectors would not physically inspect the actual equipment in the plants, to determine their conformity with appropriate standards, but would look at the documentation each company kept on its in-house quality-control efforts. Company inspectors, that is, checked the equipment, and the A.E.C. "audited" the front-office records of their work.

In addition to the general importance of quality assurance in the A.E.C.'s regulatory scheme, the subject had to be addressed by the staff of the Reactor Safety Study for an additional reason. The study's probability analyses were based on fault trees derived from the "as-built" drawings for the Surry and Peach Bottom plants. In the event of substantial deviations between the drawings and the actual equipment in the plant—as a result of quality-control lapses—the study's results could be invalidated.

The required review of quality assurance presented to the Reactor Safety Study difficulties that were not of a technical nature. As described in the study's internal working papers, the principal problem was the possibility, apparently considered likely, that a comprehensive review of quality control at the two plants might be very embarrassing to the A.E.C. Chairman Schlesinger had already gently chided the industry, in his Bal Harbour speech, about its poor performance in this area. Study officials feared that a detailed report on the subject would expose such widespread quality-control deficiencies that the safety of existing nuclear plants would be put in doubt.

The quality-assurance issue was the subject of detailed discussions among Staff Director Saul Levine and his deputies. On October 12, 1973, they held a meeting at A.E.C. headquarters to discuss the "options" for handling this sensitive topic. Present at the meeting were Levine and three other project officials—T. Cole, John Bewick and Edward Gilbert. Gilbert, who had been working on the quality-assurance problem, prepared a memorandum, dated October 23, 1973, that summarized the meeting.

Gilbert noted the two "approaches" to the quality-assurance problem that had been discussed. One, "Approach A," would be to gather information to support a "pre-determined finding" that the designers and builders of the two plants, and the A.E.C., "did an adequate job of Q-A/Q-C"—quality assurance/quality control—"to assure the safety and reliability of the two plants studied." The other, less ambitious approach, "Approach B," would try to avoid this sweeping, predetermined conclusion, in favor of a narrower one. This alternative approach would not involve a review of the industry's role in quality assurance but would simply describe how well the A.E.C. part of the process—the audit of the industry's quality-assurance records—worked. "Our preference is to reach a finding (supportable by facts gleaned from the A.E.C. records) that all major Q-A/Q-C deficiencies were uncovered by the A.E.C. audit and that they were repaired and/or resolved in a manner which assures plant safety system reliability," Gilbert wrote.

The Gilbert memo discussed the advantages and disadvantages of each approach. The advantages of adopting a predetermined general conclusion, Approach A, would be to "engender confidence" in reactor safety. On the other hand, the "disadvantages" of undertaking a comprehensive review of quality assurance at the two plants, in order to support this preferred finding, was that "the facts may not support our pre-determined conclusions." Another concern was that "the more stages of Q-A/Q-C covered, the more deficiencies . . . will be shown to have been found. This may undermine public confidence in the reliability of plant-safety systems, particularly as the nature of repairs and corrections become better known."

Approach B, on the other hand, had the advantage that such a limited review of quality-assurance practices—focusing solely on the A.E.C.'s part in the process—would reduce the time and manpower that would have to be expended. This was a major concern of the study staff, since they were far behind schedule. Furthermore, by not assuming that the industry had done an adequate job on quality assurance, "our input to the overall . . . study will be more realistic (but not necessarily in the direction of engendering higher confidence . . . in safety system equipment)." On the other hand, Gilbert noted, Approach B had "disadvantages" similar to those of Approach A in that it might still prompt "the objective reader" to question "whether the whole story is not actually *much worse* than the negative picture given by a summary of just the Field audits—i.e., how many defects were found and *improperly corrected* at the earlier stages of vendor and licensee inspections." [Original emphasis.]

After weighing all these factors, Gilbert recommended that no comprehensive review of quality assurance at the two plants be undertaken, thereby ruling out Approach A. There wasn't enough time to do such a review, and he felt that it would be enough if a modified version of Approach B were followed. He recommended that the study should include a report "on just a few pre-selected cases" where the A.E.C. succeeded in identifying and overseeing the correction of quality-assurance problems.

Gilbert's proposal was to "summarize" the quality-assurance review performed by A.E.C. inspectors "as a simple chronology (provide no details)" and then to "pick out three or four" success stories in which the A.E.C. was able to get quality-control deficiencies repaired. "This will show that where serious deficiencies and non-conformancies were found, they were vigorously pursued by the A.E.C."

Gilbert had reservations about doing even this, however. Since the A.E.C. only audited the plant quality-control records selectively and did not perform a thorough review, he feared that the "objective reader" might conclude that "if a number of defects were found in a single system and then corrected, but other systems were not examined for this same defect, how confident could we be that the other systems are free of the same defect?"

Gilbert reported to Levine that he had spent a number of weeks "groping" to find "a positive way" to write a report on quality assurance at the two plants. He continued to work on the problem and prepared a draft report along the lines he had recommended to Levine. As late as April 1974, an outline of the multivolume Reactor Safety Study report that was then being written included Gilbert's section on Q-A/Q-C. The chapter that Gilbert wrote on this subject was never published, however. Levine has stated that the omission reflected the fact that the material was judged "not germane" to the Reactor Safety Study.

Gilbert himself has subsequently explained that the "findings" of his draft report "should" engender public confidence in the effectiveness of the A.E.C.'s quality-assurance effort. On the other hand, he said, the findings could also be "misused" by "professional" critics of nuclear power "in damaging ways." "I think Rasmussen and Levine made the right decision (a tough one) in not including this material in the [published] report," he added.

"PEER REVIEW" is the customary quality-control procedure used in the technical community, before a work is published, to verify its accuracy. A reputable scientific journal will have a group of experts—referees, they are sometimes called—who screen all material submitted for publication. The reviewers can approve the paper, reject it, or ask that it be revised and resubmitted. Their purpose is to try to maintain objective standards and to avoid perpetuating errors.

By the beginning of the summer of 1974, a working draft of the Reactor Safety Study had been completed. It was a multivolume report almost a foot thick. A twelve-member review group consisting of senior A.E.C. officials and consultants was asked to call attention to "omissions," "errors" and "loopholes in the study approach." The 3,000-page report of the study's findings had taken two years to complete; the panel of reviewers was given from June 10 to June 21 to examine it.

The A.E.C. had big plans for the release of the report in August and was unwilling to delay publication to permit a more thorough critique. The twelve reviewers acted as individuals because there was no time to organize subgroups that might concentrate on particular sections of the report. According to the letter from A.E.C. consultant Harold Etherington transmitting the reviewers' comments to Rasmussen, "Time has not permitted any attempt to correlate comments by reviewers or to reconcile any differences of opinion. Indeed, there is a big question whether this would have been desirable."

Some two hundred pages of comments were filed by the members of the review group, who focused on the subjects they found of greatest professional interest. Dr. Daniel Kleitman, a professor of mathematics at the Massachusetts Institute of Technology, reviewed the use of probability concepts and statistical methods in the study. "There are many ways to present statistical data," he wrote. "Some by their nature are put in terms that are confidence expanding—some are frightening by nature—the choice of terms and of comparisons can easily be made so as to bias the appearance of the results in any desired way." He found that the Reactor Safety Study was heavily biased toward optimistic estimates of accident probability.

Instead of following conventional practices, the probability estimates in the study were based on what Kleitman called "fatuous" calculational procedures of the study's own invention. "I think all of your quoted final results are wrong," he said, estimating that they would have been higher by a factor of approximately two and a half if standard computational techniques had been used. He observed that the results of the study would be "not so wonderful" if the failure rates were multiplied by two and a half, and "much worse" if stated in terms of the expected number of core melts in the next twenty years.

Kleitman said that he calculated that with 150 reactors in operation for a twenty-year period "we get four melts, or one every five years. . . . This is by no means reassuring and is certainly worse than present A.E.C. hopes. When it is considered that attempts have been made to be accurate rather than conservative in risk assessment and that unknown factors can only make things worse, this could well be frightening, at least for the future of the nuclear power program if not for public health," he said.

Another error, Kleitman said, that "may invalidate" the study's findings was its handling of what are known as common-mode failures. These are accidents in which a single event or condition causes the simultaneous failure of duplicate safety systems. To make sure that the plant remains under control, designers rely heavily on the installation of extra safety systems that will be available if some of the apparatus fails. "Common-mode failures can have a disastrous effect on system reliability, especially for systems intended to have high reliability," Stephen Hanauer noted in a memo on the subject that he sent to the Reactor Safety Study staff in December 1973. "Such systems usually have multiple redundant components, or subsystems, with the intention that single failures, or even multiple failures, need not induce failure of function. . . . But a common-mode failure involving the redundant components destroys the real redundancy and negates the concomitant benefit in functional reliability of the system."

Hanauer, a leading expert on common-mode failures, had written this memo to emphasize the need for close attention to this problem by the study group. He was also a member of the June review group, and he concluded that the study's "consideration of common-mode failures has been inadequate." The study had overlooked "classical" types of common-mode failures, he said, and some of its estimates of potential safety-system failures were "suspiciously low" as a result of these omissions.

Richard DeYoung of the A.E.C. regulatory staff, another member of the internal review team, concurred. "The discussion of common-mode failures presented in the first 50 pages of Appendix IV is excellent," DeYoung wrote. "The description of the approach used in the study to account for common-mode events indicates that the subject was covered in a thorough and systematic manner. However, in reviewing some of the detailed analyses . . . I was left with the impression that the approach described in Appendix IV was in actual practice often the exception rather than the rule."

Earthquakes are a clear example of the kind of event that can cause damage to multiple plant components and safety systems. DeYoung observed that the study "eliminates earthquakes as a serious concern on the basis of a perfunctory discussion." He rejected the study's finding that common-mode failures were not a significant element in nuclear-plant safety risks. "It seems inconsistent with experience not to include common-mode failures as significant contributors to system failures."

One of the most startling and original conclusions in the study's draft report was that core meltdowns would be much less severe than previously believed. The study's authors concluded that the molten metals trapped under the plant would be unlikely to release large amounts of radioactive materials, because a large number of factors, such as the filtering of these materials by the ground, would keep the materials safely confined. The analysis they used to support this novel conclusion did not impress the members of the review group. They called the appendix dealing with these phenomena "very weak." J. Griffith of the A.E.C. staff, one of the reviewers, called this analysis "subjective and unconvincing," and others raised detailed technical questions about it.

At the time the review was done, important parts of the draft were not even completed. The appendix on design adequacy, for example, was the least complete section. Of the thirty-one design questions relating to the Surry plant, work had been completed on only ten of them, according to DeYoung's count. With so much more work that still needed to be done, "the issuance of the Reactor Safety Study report, in essentially its present or even an editorially revised state, as anything other than an interim status report would be inadvisable and a disservice to the study group.

The report contains deficiencies and inconsistencies to such an extent that to correct them would likely be a major task requiring many more months of effort," DeYoung wrote.

THE ATOMIC ENERGY COMMISSION had no intention of postponing the publication of the already much-delayed Reactor Safety Study. In spite of its technical flaws, it was scheduled to be released on August 20, 1974, a date that the A.E.C. looked upon as D-Day in its battle against the critics of nuclear power. The reassuring results of the study, according to the agency's plan, would be publicized in the biggest media effort the A.E.C. had ever organized, just as senior officials had intended when Chairman Schlesinger commissioned the work in 1972. Schlesinger himself had left the A.E.C., in 1973, to become the director of the Central Intelligence Agency.

Long before the formal release date, and before the study was even reviewed internally, senior A.E.C. officials began giving reporters what they represented as the findings of the study. On January 14, 1974, Dr. Herbert Kouts, the head of the Division of Reactor Safety Research, told the Associated Press that the "preliminary results . . . suggest there will never be a major accident in a nuclear power plant. The odds on a major catastrophe were . . . 'one in one billion to one in ten billion years' for a given reactor. . . ." The AP interview with Dr. Kouts also reported, incorrectly, that "the study was conducted for the A.E.C. at the Massachusetts Institute of Technology." (The study had been carried out at A.E.C. offices in Germantown, Maryland.)

On January 21, 1974, the new A.E.C. chairman, Dr. Dixy Lee Ray, gave a luncheon address at the National Press Club in Washington. (A marine biologist specializing in sea worms, and former head of a science museum in Seattle, Dr. Ray had become a local television personality there; her credentials as a public-relations expert were reportedly a factor in her appointment by President Nixon.)

Chairman Ray, as she preferred to be called, said that she would like to "share" with the media "some significant points we have learned thus far" from the Reactor Safety Study. "Our study is now predicting that the chance of core melting is about one in a million per year for each reactor," she said. Dr. Ray did not present the technical rationale for such an estimate but promised that it would be forthcoming that spring. The A.E.C., in the meantime, would be able to use this result, attributed to the study, for public-relations purposes without having to expose the study's methods and assumptions to technical review. (In fact, when the study was released in August, it estimated that the chances of a meltdown were about one in seventeen thousand per reactor-year, *not* one in a million. The A.E.C. offered no reason that the chances were so much higher—sixty times higher—than Chairman Ray had reported earlier.)

In February 1974, an article on nuclear safety in *The New York Times Magazine,* written by Ralph E. Lapp, offered the public another hint of the study's findings. Lapp identified himself as "an energy consultant and member of the Sierra Club's energy policy committee." He also worked as a consultant to the nuclear industry and, in particular, for Reddy Communications, a public-relations firm that services the industry; Norman Rasmussen has also been associated with the firm, beginning his work for it while the Reactor Safety Study was still in progress.

Lapp wrote that there was a "one in one million" chance of a meltdown and stated that "presumably this is the kind of conclusion that the Rasmussen analysis will reach when the final report is published this summer. The report is going to be backed up by many technical appendices documenting the task force findings . . ." A.E.C. internal records indicate that Lapp had submitted a rough draft of his article to the A.E.C. for review before publication "with an understanding that it would be kept confidential." The A.E.C. subsequently refused to release records relating to its "involvement or non-involvement" with the article.

Finally, on August 20, 1974, after several inaccurate versions of the "results" had been made public by Drs. Kouts, Ray and Lapp, the Reactor Safety Study was released. Rasmussen, one industry newsletter noted the following week, had been set up by the A.E.C. as the "arbitrator" of the nuclear-safety controversy. "In the interim the Commission and the industry have awaited the Rasmussen report like the faithful waiting for word from on high," *Weekly Energy Report* said. "Last week they got the word. And it was good."

A.E.C. officials announced, with unqualified enthusiasm, that the study proved that nuclear power was far safer than just about everything else in modern life. Their most widely quoted condensation of the study's findings—it was the lead sentence in most major news reports on the study—was that "a person has about as much chance of dying from an atomic reactor accident as of being struck by a meteor." The report itself was labeled a "draft," but the Commission lent the full weight of its authority to its conclusions. There was no hint of any tentativeness about the basic data or methods used in the study.

The A.E.C. launched a massive publicity campaign to broadcast the study's results around the country, and it strongly emphasized the "independence" of the study; many news reports referred to it as "the M.I.T. study." The A.E.C. public-relations staff prerecorded a two-and-one-half-minute television message summarizing the study, for distribution to local stations around the country. The A.E.C.'s film clip featured Norman Rasmussen, sitting outside the Student Union at M.I.T., as he was interviewed by an A.E.C. official; it left the strong impression that the A.E.C. was just learning the results of a study that had been done at M.I.T.

In releasing the results of the study, the A.E.C. made no mention of the internal review group—whose two hundred pages of comments on the study were not made public. Levine's staff had not had time to respond to the numerous objections that had been raised by this group of experts, or to make all the necessary corrections, but the Commission decided to release the study uncorrected. Under pressure to produce a response to the critics of reactor safety, the agency could see no alternative. As it had hoped, the A.E.C. immediately received a windfall of favorable publicity as news stories used the Rasmussen findings to declare the reactor-safety controversy finally settled. "Campaigners Against Nuclear Power Stations Put to Rout," the headline in *The Guardian* read. It was a fair summary of the A.E.C.'s public-relations coup.

THE LAUDATORY RESPONSE of the national press to the Rasmussen report contrasted markedly with the study's reception by the scientific community. An editorial in the *Bulletin of the Atomic Scientists* commented in October 1974:

> The report is essentially an in-house study by an agency under heavy pressure to get critics off its back. It is in no sense an independent evaluation of the A.E.C.'s performance or policies in nuclear reactor safety; it is, instead, a defense of them. . . . Whether the conclusions can withstand the close scrutiny they are bound to receive within the next few months remains to be seen.

The A.E.C.'s stated purpose in releasing the draft report was to permit public comments before it was put into final form, which the A.E.C. planned to do as quickly as possible. Reviewing the draft was not an easy task, even for technical specialists. "The report is lengthy and is difficult to review as an entity," the A.E.C. regulatory staff's Systems Analysis Group noted in its comments on the study.

> It is often exceedingly difficult to determine the manner whereby specific system or containment failure probability values were obtained . . . Many of these questions can be answered by extremely careful reading and interpretation of the report. However, in many cases the detailed technical data and drawings needed to permit an independent assessment of accuracy to be made have not been provided.

There was a suspicion among some reviewers that the study's lack of clarity about how it arrived at its conclusions was not unintentional.

Following the release of the draft, the A.E.C. regulatory staff organized a second in-house review group, like the one the previous June, to provide further comments on the study. Directed by Hanauer, the second review group carried out a general reading of the draft and a selective examination of key issues. It had to work hurriedly, since the A.E.C. allowed only sixty days for comments on the study. This second A.E.C. review group identified some of the same flaws in the study as the first—the "shallow" analysis of accidents caused by earthquakes, it repeated, might be "a basic error" in the study—but it also emphasized several additional concerns.

Fires in nuclear plants, for example, might have "severe and widespread" effects; yet the Rasmussen group had neglected such an obvious risk, the panel noted. A few months later, on March 22, 1975, the safety threat posed by fire was demonstrated at the Browns Ferry Nuclear Plant near Decatur, Alabama, where a workman accidently set fire to the insulation on some of its electrical control cables. The fire burned for seven and a half hours, destroyed sixteen hundred cables, and caused one of the most severe accidents in the history of the nuclear program. The possibility of such fires had been overlooked in the draft.

Another specific problem that the study neglected, the review panel observed, was the problem of plant abandonment.

> The Study has given detailed consideration to the possibility of operator errors in performing the manual actions required in so many plant emergency procedures. However, since virtually all of these procedures are based on the presence of trained operators, the Study should also consider the possibility of accident conditions in the plant leading to panic in the crew with subsequent abandonment.

In addition to numerous comments about specific technical issues such as these, the second internal-review panel raised several far-reaching questions about the basic methods used in the study. The Rasmussen staff had carried out a fault-tree analysis, they noted, of *two* plants and then extrapolated the results and drawn general conclusions about the risks associated with the operation of one hundred plants—the number projected by the A.E.C. to be in operation in the early 1980s. This might not be valid, they said, because these two plants—Surry Unit I and Peach Bottom Unit 2—were "atypical in a significant number of instances." Moreover, even if they were representative of the average plant, there was still the possibility that there might be a real "lemon" among the ninety-eight other plants, at which the risk of major accidents was very much higher.

In a telephone conversation on December 5, 1974, Rasmussen and Hanauer discussed the review group's comments. Hanauer's handwritten record of this "telecon" noted that there were "things" that Rasmussen had to "try and improve" in the final report, but that "many Reg [A.E.C. regulatory staff] suggestions" were "beyond capability for final report" consideration. The A.E.C. plan was to proceed as quickly as possible with the preparation of a final report, fixing up minor errors in the draft, and to ignore the more general criticisms of the study's controversial probability analysis. The final report's accident-probability estimates were virtually identical with those of the August 1974 draft.

THE DRAFT RASMUSSEN REPORT, reversing all previous A.E.C. analyses, concluded that meltdown accidents were unlikely to have catastrophic effects. The "discovery" that only a few people might be killed—not the thousands or tens of thousands estimated in the 1965 update of WASH-740—brought great comfort to the A.E.C. and the nuclear industry. The part of the report most heavily criticized by independent experts, however, was the short technical appendix that supposedly demonstrated this welcome result.

Even before the objections were filed and before the draft was released, Rasmussen knew that this appendix "needed more work"—although he did not mention this at the A.E.C. press conference at which the report was made public. Repairing its deficiencies was not possible prior to publication, he said later, because of the schedule set by the A.E.C. Rasmussen and the A.E.C. staff who worked on the study were not the authors of this section of the report, moreover. It was written by Winston Little, an engineer employed by Westinghouse, the leading American reactor manufacturer, who was on loan to the Reactor Safety Study.

The American Physical Society, the professional society of the nation's physicists, gave the A.E.C. the most detailed criticism of the draft report's assessment of meltdown accidents. (This portion of the report was also the subject of extensive comments by the A.E.C. regulatory staff, the E.P.A., and the Union of Concerned Scientists.) Earlier in the year, the A.P.S. had set up a special panel to review the general topic of nuclear-reactor safety. Frank Von Hippel, a theoretical physicist who worked at a number of universities and national laboratories, had organized this study group. An advocate of "public interest science," he wanted to bring together independent experts who had no predisposition for or against nuclear power—"virgins," he called them in a recent interview—to carry out an objective study of this controversial topic. Getting such a committee together wasn't easy.

There are many technical review panels that advise the federal government, and a number of academic scientists make side careers consulting with particular government agencies, which can be both interesting and lucrative. Professional consultants run the risk of jeopardizing their careers if their advice is too openly critical of an agency's policy. Aware of such a potential conflict of interest, Von Hippel wanted to set up an exemplary study group made up of people who would be free to express their own best technical judgment on the subject of reactor safety. His first thought was to ask the National Academy of Sciences to sponsor such a study. "I presented this proposal to them and they were quite disarming about it," he recalled. "They said, 'This is too hot for us to handle.' "

The A.P.S., where some members had already expressed interest in a "summer study" on reactor safety, was next on his list. Von Hippel wanted to get a "well-respected, senior physicist" to chair the project. "I must have asked twenty different people to be chairman, but no one wanted to assume the burden." Finally, A.P.S. officials asked Harold Lewis, a physicist at the University of California at Santa Barbara, and a regular consultant to the Department of Defense, to chair the panel, and he agreed. The A.P.S. agreed to pay the members of the panel and turned to the National Science Foundation, and the A.E.C., to get funding for the study group. Von Hippel himself and eleven other physicists served on the study group chaired by Lewis.

The A.P.S. study group spent August 1974 together, at the A.E.C.'s Los Alamos laboratory in New Mexico. The draft version of the Reactor Safety Study was published that month, and they made an attempt to review key parts of it. Von Hippel was immediately struck by the significance of the study's finding that meltdown accidents would not have particularly dire consequences. "The Reactor Safety Study really did make the reactor safety issue look trivial—if in fact the consequences weren't that serious."

Members of the study group reviewed the basis on which the health effects of a meltdown were calculated in the draft. To do so, they did their own "back-of-the-envelope" calculations. They took the Rasmussen report's estimates, that is, of how much radioactive material would be released during hypothetical meltdowns and then calculated by hand—rather than by computer, as the Rasmussen group had done—what the effects would be on the population "downwind" of the plant. They came up with fatality estimates far greater than the Rasmussen report, and they soon learned the reason why.

The Rasmussen report's calculations, the A.P.S. group discovered, were full of basic errors. The A.E.C.'s fatality estimates, for example, considered the radiation dose to the downwind population only in the first twenty-four hours after the accident. In fact, the radioactive cesium (Ce-137) contained in the fallout from the accident—the substance that would be the principal source of injury to the public—has a half-life of thirty years, and for decades to come would expose the population over an area too wide to be evacuated to its harmful effects. The most serious injuries from the cesium exposure would be latent forms of cancer that would not show up until years after the accident.

The A.P.S. reviewers also learned that the draft Rasmussen report entirely neglected inhaled radioactivity when it calculated the expected incidence of lung cancer among the exposed population and that it made other assumptions which greatly underestimated the incidence of thyroid tumors that would result from the inhalation of radioactive iodine, which would also be contained in the fallout produced by a meltdown.

The criticisms of the A.P.S. study group were communicated, privately, to the A.E.C. at the group's August session in Los Alamos. Saul Levine, Staff Director of the Reactor Safety Study, promised to arrange a meeting so that his experts on accident consequences could discuss the apparent errors in their work with the A.P.S. reviewers. Over a period of six months, however, Levine repeatedly postponed the meeting.

The writing of the A.P.S. report became a touchy political process, because, in addition to the negative findings about validity of certain calculations in the Rasmussen report, other subgroups of the panel were also drafting reports critical of key aspects of the Commission's nuclear-safety program. They found, for example, that the computer methods used to predict the performance of emergency cooling systems had not been satisfactorily verified. "The reactor-safety debate was very hot. Some of the people on the committee became concerned about the possible impact of our report on the reactor-safety controversy. They even worried that it could be the end of nuclear power," Von Hippel said recently. The members discussed how they could "cushion the blow" and say "some positive things" to tone down the negative message in the report they were drafting. There were a lot of "negotiated sentences" and "weasel words" used in the report, members of the panel have stated privately.

One standard method used for handling bad news in official reports is to bury it deep inside, where most readers—and most news reporters, especially—will not delve. A few soothing sentences at the beginning of the report, intended to characterize its findings for popular consumption, helps to effect this strategy. The "Lewis report," as the April 1975 report of the A.P.S. panel became known, began, accordingly, with a summary paragraph that had a positive tone but which the members could agree upon, despite their acknowledgment of weaknesses in the official "proof" of nuclear-plant safety. They could do so because, technically, the summary said practically nothing. "In the course of this study, we have not uncovered reasons for substantial short-range concern regarding risk of accidents in light-water reactors," the introductory paragraph states.

This sentence—which was included in the official press release for the Lewis report—seems reassuring. All it really says is that the panel did not discover a reactor that was going to have a meltdown the following week. This sentence figured prominently in most news reports about the study, which overlooked the qualifying and ambigious phrase "short-range" and described the A.P.S. study as a resounding confirmation of A.E.C. claims about reactor safety.

The news accounts generally failed, however, to note another heavily "negotiated" sentence, on the same page in the Lewis report, which says, politely, that the review panel didn't believe Rasmussen's probability estimates. "Based on our experience with problems of this nature involving very low probabilities, we do not now have confidence in the presently calculated absolute values of the probabilities," the panel wrote. The Rasmussen group knew, of course, about the significant errors that the A.P.S. had found in their work, and they were struggling to find a means to handle this criticism. The months passed and no "final" version of the study appeared.

IN NOVEMBER 1974, in response to the growing controversy over nuclear power, Congress passed an Energy Reorganization Act. To put an end to the persistent criticism that the A.E.C. had an inherent conflict of interest—being both promoter and regulator of the nuclear industry—Congress decided to place those functions in separate agencies. The A.E.C. was abolished, and in its place two new agencies were formed. One, which was subsequently renamed the Department of Energy, assumed the promotional role of the A.E.C., broadened to cover nonnuclear energy sources as well. The other new agency, known as the Nuclear Regulatory Commission, would be the "independent" agency in charge of safety. The "new" N.R.C., according to the provisions of the law, would be the regulatory staff of the old A.E.C. under a new name. As its first official act of business, N.R.C. adopted all the safety and licensing regulations of its predecessor.

N.R.C., which formally came into existence on January 19, 1975, assumed responsibility for completing the Reactor Safety Study, which was then being revised. N.R.C. Chairman William Anders, a former Apollo 13 astronaut, told a congressional hearing a few weeks later that N.R.C. would not endorse the study until it had reviewed it properly. "The Rasmussen study was done by the A.E.C. The N.R.C. has only been in business for a little over two weeks. The R.S.S. is out for public review and public comment at this time," he said. "This Commission has not had a chance to look at it as a Commission. We would appreciate the opportunity to review these public comments. . . . At the time when the public comments are in and we are able to review the Report in its final form, then we will be in a better position to discuss this with you and your colleagues. . . ."

N.R.C., in fact, carried out no independent review of the final report prior to releasing it, in October 1975. N.R.C. left the control of the project in the hands of Saul Levine, the former A.E.C. official who remained the study's staff director. Moreover, instead of insisting on time to review the work, the N.R.C. actually speeded up the preparation of the final report, in response to pressure from the Joint Committee on Atomic Energy. The Price-Anderson Act, which protected the industry from liability in the event of reactor accidents, was up for renewal. It didn't expire until 1977, but the Committee felt that doubts about its renewal might make it difficult for utilities to make plans for additional reactors.

Fearing a "standstill" in the nuclear program, Committee Chairman Melvin Price wanted to get the matter out of the way as soon as possible. Since the study dealt with the key questions underlying the legislation, "the Joint Committee hearings cannot be completed until the Reactor Safety Study was issued (this requirement was established by Congress)," an N.R.C. internal memorandum noted. "The original completion date for the Study was

December 1975, however, that date has now been changed by the Commission, to October, 1975, thereby necessitating rapid completion of all work."

Some N.R.C. officials questioned how the defects in the draft could be corrected during the crash program to prepare a final report. "The regulatory staff had voluminous general and detailed comments, amounting to several inches of paper, on the draft R.S.S.," Brian Grimes, the Chief of the Accident Analysis Branch, wrote in an internal memo.

> These substantive comments formulated by knowledgeable staff members probably constituted the best critical review the study received. We do not know, at this point [September 1975], how these comments have been taken into consideration, except that we understand that the consequences model is being completely redone. The final R.S.S. cannot therefore be accepted uncritically and without further review. A substantial review effort will have to be mounted before we know how well the final study will stand . . .

The recommended review was not undertaken. On October 30, 1975, the N.R.C. accepted the final report and made it public. N.R.C. Chairman William Anders issued a press release calling the final report "an objective and meaningful estimate of the public risks associated with the operation of present-day light-water power reactors in the United States. The final report is a soundly based and impressive work."

Joint Committee Chairman Price, urging renewal of the Price-Anderson Act, proudly announced the results of the Reactor Safety Study to his colleagues; he noted that "the final report was almost identical to the original version. The only difference being one or two minor areas where they got together with the people who raised exceptions to figures and there was a final meeting of the minds." Rasmussen himself, briefing Congress on the final report, was asked if there were "substantive scientific group[s] anywhere with whom you find lingering differences?" "None that I am aware of," Rasmussen replied. He did not mention the fact that the study was still at the Government Printing Office, and had not been distributed to the scientific community for review. Indeed, on October 30, the day the final report was nominally "published," I called Rasmussen to see if I could drop by his office to look at a copy. He didn't yet have one, he told me.

THE FINAL REPORT of the Reactor Safety Study totaled 2,300 pages, divided into nine volumes. This hefty work consisted of a short "Executive Summary" intended for the press and nontechnical audiences, a "main report," and a set of eleven appendices. As one moves from the very technical material, which is mostly in the appendices, to the main report, to the Executive Summary—a pamphlet prepared for wide public distribution—a change of tone as well as of technical content is evident.

In the "back" of the study, there are cautionary notes, discussion of uncertainties in the data, and some sense that there may be important limitations to the results. The qualifications successively drop away as one moves toward the parts of the study that the public was intended to see. In the months following the study's completion, the honesty of the official summary of the results—rather than the technical validity of the probability assessment itself—became the most controversial issue.

Frank Von Hippel naturally took an interest in how the final report responded to the comments of the A.P.S. He noted that the specific errors that had been made in the draft report's analysis of the consequences of meltdown accidents had been acknowledged and corrected in the final version. The technical appendix on this subject showed, for example, that the estimated radiation dose to the population downwind was ten times as high as stated in the draft. Other errors too, such as underestimates of water contamination, were corrected. The final report's figure for this was a thousand times as high as the draft version. Surprisingly, however, the Executive Summary showed that the risk to the public was somewhat *smaller* than it was estimated to be in the draft. Something looked fishy.

It turned out that the Executive Summary simply omitted the

most damaging findings in its condensation of the study's results. Exposure to radiation can produce many kinds of injuries. At high doses, the victims die within a matter of days. At lower, but still harmful doses, the radiation exposure can cause cancers and other side effects that might not show up for many years. The radiation injury in such cases has a delayed fuse, as it were, before the results become manifest.

The Reactor Safety Study found, one of its appendices reports, that the dominant effect of serious reactor accidents would be cancer deaths in the long run, not prompt fatalities in the weeks following the accident. The Executive Summary does not make this finding clear. It presents a graph which shows the small number of estimated "fatalities" from major accidents but does *not* explain that these are simply the "early" ones. The *total* number of fatalities that would result, according to the study's detailed analyses, would be vastly higher. Von Hippel noted that on average an accident that the Executive Summary said would cause ten "fatalities" would also cause seven thousand cancer deaths—if one looked up the data in the appropriate technical appendix and had the training that would enable one to interpret it properly.

Other scientists reviewing the final report concurred with Von Hippel that the Rasmussen Report's Executive Summary was misleading—indeed, outrageously so. The subject was brought to congressional attention, during a June 1976 hearing on the study, before Congressman Morris Udall's Subcommittee on Energy and the Environment. Udall subsequently asked the N.R.C. to prepare a new Executive Summary, but it declined to do so. The agency finally agreed, however, in response to continuing attacks on the study, to set up a "review group" to examine the validity of its conclusions.

N.R.C. internal files disclose that the commissioners left the organization of the review group in the hands of Saul Levine, whose work the group was to judge. Levine chose Harold Lewis to head the review group, which also included William Rowe of E.P.A., Herbert Kouts, former A.E.C. director of safety research, Walter Lowenstein of the Electric Power Research Institute, Robert Budnitz of the Lawrence Berkeley laboratory, and Frank Von Hippel of Princeton. The group included both critics and admirers of the study, and they were left to themselves to thrash out their differences and to produce an overall assessment of the validity of the study's controversial findings.

In September 1978, after thirteen months of heated debate, they managed to reach a consensus on all the technical issues before them. "I personally believe that this convergence was only possible because of the basic respect for truth that scientists absorb along with their discipline," Frank Von Hippel commented recently.

The review group concluded that the Rasmussen report's probability calculations were so uncertain as to be virtually meaningless. "Many of the calculations are deficient when subjected to careful and probing analysis," they wrote. The "spectrum of problems" with the report's statistical analysis ranged from "lack of data" to "the invention and use of wrong statistical methods." On key issues—such as the Rasmussen report's dismissal of common-mode failures as a cause of major reactor accidents—it said that the study's "degree of arbitrariness . . . boggles the mind."

The review group repeated, and endorsed, many of the previous technical criticisms of the Rasmussen report, noting that "cogent comments from critics were either not acknowledged or evaded" in several instances by Rasmussen and Levine. "An egregious case in point is the lack of response to the frequent suggestion that summary figures in the Executive Summary be labeled 'early fatalities' as opposed to 'fatalities.' " The Reactor Safety Study was a "substantial advance" over previous attempts to estimate nuclear-plant risks, the group concluded, but it did not succeed.

ADVANCED TECHNOLOGY is so much a part of modern life that major political decisions are increasingly complicated by heated technical controversies. Federal agencies and the Congress routinely face difficult technical questions when they try to assess military requirements, health issues, environmental problems, and many other policy questions. To get the necessary advice on these topics, the government sponsors a large number of scientific studies, a few of which, like the 1961 Surgeon General's report on the health effects of cigarette smoking, play a decisive role in resolving vital issues.

The Reactor Safety Study was one of the most publicized scientific studies the government has ever carried out, and it appeared, when it was initially released, to be the last word on the nagging controversy over nuclear safety. This impression was short-lived. Three years after the Rasmussen report was published in final form and unreservedly endorsed by the N.R.C., the agency began to search for the most polite way to disassociate itself from it. Instead of settling the controversy over reactor safety, the report had expanded it, embarrassed the agency, and given the critics a prominent, vulnerable target to attack.

In January 1979, after four months' pondering the review group's findings, the Commission accepted them and made a terse statement repudiating the Rasmussen report. "The Commission does not regard as reliable the Reactor Safety Study's numerical estimate of overall risk of reactor accident," it announced. The N.R.C. also stated that it "withdraws any explicit or implicit past endorsement of the Executive Summary."

Unlike the publicity that N.R.C. sought when it released the final Rasmussen report in October 1975, it tried to handle the rejection of the report as quietly as possible. No press conference was called, and officials hoped the obituary notice they had written for the study would be relegated to the back pages of the newspapers. Dr. Joseph Hendrie, the former A.E.C. official who was chairman of the N.R.C., was reportedly very annoyed when it received much greater notoriety.

Congressman Udall promptly called Hendrie and the other commissioners before his subcommittee—whose members had been led to regard the study as the gospel on the safety issue—to explain what the rejection of the study meant. Without these reassuring probability estimates, how did N.R.C. know that reactors were safe enough to operate?

Hendrie testified that N.R.C. had not actually depended on the study, which he portrayed as merely a "supplement" to the "traditional engineering analysis" of nuclear plant safety. The Commission relied on its own "regulatory system" to protect the public—its safety reviews of each plant—not on "the ability to make precise quantitative estimates of accident risks," he said. The agency accordingly still believed that the risk of major accidents was negligible.

His responses did not satisfy several members of the subcommittee; they pressed him to explain how, in the absence of a valid probability study, N.R.C. knew that the risk really was so small. The general difficulty of providing such an explanation had been noted years before in an internal A.E.C. memo written by Hanauer, in March 1972, just as the Reactor Safety Study was getting under way. "What are we going to do . . . in licensing facilities while this study is perking along?" Hanauer wrote. "$64 for the answer—wave arms and talk loud."

PART FOUR

LOSS OF FAITH

STEPHEN HANAUER writes some of the zippiest memos in the federal bureaucracy—short, brisk reports that get right to the essence of complex issues. A plump, bespectacled and highly qualified nuclear engineer, he has served for almost two decades as one of the government's chief nuclear-safety experts. His principal job has been to advise the top management of the Atomic Energy Commission and its successor, the Nuclear Regulatory Commission, on how the commercial nuclear power industry should be regulated.

Hanauer's views are routinely solicited on a wide range of topics, and on many occasions they are simply volunteered. His missives, which some of his associates refer to as "Hanauergrams," offer frank opinions that sometimes rebuke the safety efforts of both the industry and his own agency. His blunt reproaches are stated with such playful good humor, however, that his superiors are more often amused than offended. Since they can easily deflect the unwelcome advice he gives them—they have frequently just ignored it—he has remained in the agency's good graces. His discretion in not giving his candid opinions in public is also appreciated. Hanauer is apparently unperturbed when his safety recommendations are brushed aside. He can take consolation in his enviable record of being later proved right.

A native of Knoxville, Tennessee, Hanauer began his career thirty miles from there, at the A.E.C.'s Oak Ridge National Laboratory. "I hired Steve because his father was a good friend of my cousin," former laboratory director Alvin Weinberg said in a recent interview. "The only case of nepotism in my whole life! My cousin called me up one day and said, 'Look my friend Morris Hanauer has a very bright son from Purdue University'—this is all of thirty years ago almost—'who's looking for a job. Would you be willing to talk to him?' I said yes, I'd be willing to talk to him. So he showed up one day. He was a very, very bright guy."

At Oak Ridge, Hanauer became the protégé of E. P. Eppler, a leading expert on the problem of common-mode failures. He also co-authored a report on nuclear-plant instrumentation and control systems that became one of the standard reference works on the subject. He was appointed a professor of nuclear engineering at the University of Tennessee, and in 1965 he was asked to join the A.E.C.'s prestigious Advisory Committee on Reactor Safeguards. He became chairman of this select group of part-time advisers, and in 1970 accepted a full-time position with the A.E.C. Along with everyone else on the agency's regulatory staff, he became a member of the N.R.C. staff when the A.E.C. was abolished in 1975.

In addition to his role as general technical adviser, Hanauer has headed several ad hoc task forces assigned to look into a variety of sensitive reactor-safety issues. He was in charge of the A.E.C.'s 1971 task force on emergency core cooling, the regulatory staff's 1974 review of the Reactor Safety Study (which he also helped to organize), N.R.C.'s special study group that investigated the Browns Ferry fire of March 1975, and the N.R.C. panel that studied the reliability of the devices that are used to shut off nuclear reactors in an emergency. He is currently heading the N.R.C. Division of Safety Technology.

Like the Duc de Saint-Simon, whose diaries provided an intimate account of life at the court of Louis XIV, Hanauer is a diligent observer and note taker. The hundreds of memos he has written over the years have been conveniently kept together, in order, in what he calls his "chron file." They provide a running commmentary on the development of key federal policies relating to nuclear-plant safety.

The industry takes issue with many of Hanauer's findings, as do other nuclear proponents, such as Alvin Weinberg. Hanauer would not make the kind of "tough statements" that he does, according to his former mentor, if he were writing as a decision maker instead of as a technical adviser. "Steve is given to a kind of posturing, actually," and readers of his internal reports should be cautioned that he likes to use "overstatement" for effect, Weinberg noted. "We finally rubbed off some of the sharp edges from Steve, but we never quite succeeded in rubbing them all off." Whether Hanauer speaks too strongly—or whether Weinberg and the industry tend to understate the risks—is, of course, what the reactor-safety debate is all about.

The A.E.C. and the N.R.C. have treated Hanauer's memos as confidential and have not routinely made them public. What the public has been allowed to see are the official "Safety Evaluation Reports" for each plant. They do not mention the dissenting opinions on the adequacy of plant-safety precautions that might be expressed by Hanauer or other government experts. My request that the N.R.C. make public Hanauer's entire "chron file," containing all the memos he wrote during his tenure as a government safety adviser, was not received with enthusiasm. It required several Freedom of Information Act petitions, a lawsuit in federal court, and demands from Congress to force the N.R.C. to release them.

WHEN STEPHEN HANAUER went to work for the A.E.C., in 1970, nuclear plants provided the nation with less energy than it derived from firewood. During the preceding decade a dozen or so reactors of modest size had gone into operation. They supplied less than 2 percent of the country's electric power, which came to about a half of 1 percent of total energy use. The nuclear power industry was relatively small, its problems manageable. In the middle and late sixties, however, the A.E.C. had authorized the building of nearly a hundred large reactors of advanced designs. A major construction boom had begun, practically overnight.

With the new generation of plants nearing completion in the early seventies, the A.E.C. was deluged with requests for licenses that would permit them to operate. To the lawyers who headed the A.E.C. regulatory staff, this was a simple matter of preparing the necessary papers. The agency's technical experts, as a preliminary to licensing, were asked to prepare a routine Safety Evaluation Report for each plant to certify that it met federal safety requirements. This part of the licensing formality proved to be more difficult than anyone had expected. There were a number of complex safety issues that no one seemed able to resolve.

The belated recognition that there were major, uncorrected reactor-safety problems was the result of policies adopted by the A.E.C. when the commercial nuclear power program began. Starting with the first set of federal nuclear-safety regulations, in 1955, the A.E.C. followed a laissez-faire regulatory philosophy. Utility companies that wanted nuclear plants were given permission to build them with minimal interference from the federal government. Safety was supposed to be a paramount consideration, but the A.E.C. decided to play a background role. It would simply set general safety objectives for plant designers to meet but would not dictate the specific safety features that had to be installed. Detailed safety decisions would be left in the companies' hands. Nor would the A.E.C. be a constant presence at plant construction sites. The companies building the plants were expected to supervise their own work. When they were done, the A.E.C. would review the plants and then issue federal operating licenses.

A.E.C. safety reviews were limited by the fact that the Commission staff usually knew very little in advance about the design of proposed plants. The A.E.C. did not require detailed designs to be submitted in order to receive a construction permit, and the builders often submitted very sketchy information. They themselves did not begin detailed design work until they had construction permits in hand. No one would really know what the plants would be like until after they were built. Moreover, since the A.E.C. had adopted few specific safety standards, the staff lacked a formal basis on which to judge the adequacy of plant designs. The approval of the construction permits and operating licenses by A.E.C. safety reviewers became a pro-forma exercise, the official safety "evaluations" being more a matter of impression than of technical analysis. "We were winging it," one member of the original A.E.C. regulatory staff said in a recent interview. In 1976, N.R.C.'s inspector general, Thomas McTiernan, prepared for the Commission a report that contained the confidential observations of several government safety experts on the safety-review process. "Requirements established for licensing older plants vary from one plant to the next and it is difficult for the reviewer to determine why requirements placed on one plant are not uniformly enforced," one official noted. Government safety policy, another agency safety expert commented, was often implemented "on an inconsistent case-by-case basis," with the government "vacillating from position to position." "It's not a question of overregulating or underregulating but rather of misregulating, a lack of rationale and whimsical direction of the regulatory process," another official privately observed.

Informal and unpredictable federal regulation led to a high degree of anarchy in nuclear-plant design and construction practices. The utilities started to build one-of-a-kind, custom designs that had different types of reactors, control systems, and safety apparatus—all of which incorporated whatever technical novelties appealed to the companies. Eager to build larger and more powerful reactors, the utilities did not wait for operating experience with one design before they started to build larger, more advanced reactors. No tests were made to check on the reliability of much of the equipment that was being installed.

By the late sixties, as a nuclear-plant construction boom got under way, utility companies, architect-engineering firms, construction companies, and other suppliers—few of which had a great deal of experience with nuclear technology—began introducing one technical innovation after another. They were proceeding so quickly that designers were often only a half step ahead of the welders and concrete pourers. With little independent supervision and few explicit safety standards, there were many opportunities to make mistakes.

United States electric utility companies were unprepared for their sudden entry into the nuclear power age. Conventional power-station engineering had become a technological backwater—not a glamorous, high-technology field. The top engineering talent had not flocked to the industry, and few utilities had sophisticated technical staffs. "We should recall that the early nuclear power projects, as is always true in pioneering new technologies, drew exceptional people," N.R.C. Commissioner Victor Gilinsky remarked recently. "But the rapid expansion of the 1960s and early 70s brought in less competent organizations. Even where experienced engineering and construction firms were involved, they were overextended, and design and construction was often no longer done by the first team."

As a relatively staid, regulated industry, moreover, the electric utilities had not traditionally attracted the most talented corporate managers. A.E.C. officials worried privately about the companies' "marginal management capabilities." Having little technical expertise in nuclear technology, the utilities were not knowledgeable purchasers of nuclear equipment. "The average utility knew as much about the nuclear plant it was buying as the average car-buyer knows about cars," a vice-president of one utility said privately. "They knew how big it was, and what it cost. We got into nuclear power because the president of my utility used to play golf with the president of another utility. They bought one, and so we bought one."

Most utility companies were painfully naïve about the very large difference between building a nuclear plant and building a fossil-fuel–burning power station. There is no risk of accidents at a coal- or oil-burning plant that could have catastrophic, off-site consequences. The builders of those do not have to take elaborate safety precautions. Utility companies, accordingly, lacked experience with the kind of stringent quality-control practices that were required in building nuclear plants. A study, in 1977, of the management practices at one utility that entered the nuclear business,

Florida Power Corporation, explained some of the problems it faced.

Decisions that are relatively simple in a fossil plant entail consideration of many more factors in a nuclear plant, the Emerson Consultants of New York explained in a confidential report for the company. The utilities got into trouble because senior management found itself far removed from and unfamiliar with the details of nuclear technology. The lack of federal safety standards amplified the problems caused by the utilities' inexperience. Lax rules permitted them to get into trouble, the consultants noted. The industry's greatest problems with nuclear power reflected its difficulty in recognizing how carefully and precisely everything had to be controlled, the consultants told their client.

Economic factors, according to Emerson Consultants, also caused utility managements to resist the kind of costly precautions that were needed in building nuclear plants. Lower-level managers, assigned to supervise day-to-day plant operations, found it necessary to continuously tighten operating procedures because mistakes or loose control that would be insignificant in a fossil plant could produce catastrophic results, the Emerson Consultants observed. The constant changes meant a constant increase in costs. Although this was inherent in the new business, it was hard for the top management of the utilities to accept. The net result was some estrangement between plant and corporate management.

At Florida Power Corporation's Crystal River Nuclear Station, management deficiencies were found to be widespread. Operator training was inadequate, maintenance practices were sloppy, personnel were chronically overworked, and there were many other problems that left the plant vulnerable to avoidable accidents, Emerson Consultants concluded.

Since the A.E.C. relied on the utility companies to make the basic decisions about plant safety, and did not know what the plants were really like until after they were built, design mistakes were often uncovered when it was too late to fix them. The flaws were already cast in steel and concrete. Portions of the plants could have been rebuilt, of course, but the enormous expense of doing so would have undermined, if not destroyed, the economic attractiveness of nuclear energy. The A.E.C., therefore, decided to adopt a forgiving attitude toward the safety deficiencies at plants that had already been built; it simply agreed to overlook many of their embarrassing design blunders.

The Commission's compromise with the industry was to let these plants operate without major modifications, while it required that future plants be designed differently. The official leniency toward specific safety defects grew over the years into a policy of granting wholesale exemptions to the nominal safety requirements. "How paper our tigers are!" Hanauer noted in a memo that reviewed an A.E.C. staff proposal for waiving one of the rules.

Despite the rapid and disorderly growth of the nuclear industry, the A.E.C. was slow to develop more formal regulatory arrangements. The agency persisted in issuing construction permits before seeing detailed designs—although there was pointed advice from the A.E.C. staff in the early seventies that this practice was at the root of many reactor-safety problems. Instead of submitting detailed designs, the utilities kept offering the regulatory authorities what Hanauer referred to in a 1975 memo as a "bunch of promises" that their proposed plants would be built in accordance with appropriate safety criteria. Even after the plants were built, A.E.C. safety analysts complained that they still had little idea what equipment had been installed in them. Hanauer noted in a 1972 internal memo, concerning the electrical systems of the Browns Ferry plant, in Alabama, that plant designers were still giving the A.E.C. "comic books instead of real information."

The A.E.C. made one ostensible attempt to impose overall controls on the burgeoning nuclear program. In 1965, it began to develop "General Design Criteria" for the builders of nuclear plants to follow. The criteria were first published in draft form in the summer of 1967 but were then revised and were not finally adopted as A.E.C. regulations until 1971. These guidelines for plant designers proved to be of minimal value since they were so exceedingly vague. They might more descriptively have been called "very general" design criteria.

"The criteria were left flexible, quite deliberately, thereby allowing many individuals holding a wide range of opinions to agree to them. The same flexibility was necessary in their application," David Okrent, of the A.C.R.S., said recently. "Quite consciously, the general design criteria left most matters up to 'engineering judgment.' " Hanauer, in a 1972 memo, had noted that until the Reactor Safety Study, begun that year, was completed, the A.E.C. staff would have to bluff its way through the licensing process. When asked to justify A.E.C. safety claims, he said, the staff would just have to "wave arms and talk loud." Several years later, asked what this meant, Hanauer said that the staff was supposed to cite its "engineering judgment."

The General Design Criteria required, for example, that "appropriate" protection be provided against "credible" accidents and "anticipated" difficulties that could threaten plant safety. The subjective terms "appropriate," "credible," and "anticipated" were left undefined. Designers were told that "in each plant a main control room shall be provided," an obvious general requirement, but there was no specific guidance on what controls and instruments should be in it. Other A.E.C. rules, such as the reactor-siting criteria it published in 1962, were similarly "so general as to be of little use," Okrent states. "Our population siting criteria are indefinite at best," Hanauer wrote in a concurring memo.

Abortive attempts were made by the regulatory staff to develop more explicit criteria. In 1969, Edson Case, a senior member of the A.E.C. staff, held a private meeting to discuss new siting criteria with the staff of the Congressional Joint Committee on Atomic Energy. Case explained that "judgment will be used in applying" the site-selection criteria that were under development. "Literally interpreted, this could mean that 'We should make up the rules as we go along,' " one Joint Committee staff member noted. This was, essentially, what the A.E.C. did with most of the safety issues that arose.

No systematic revision has been made of the ambiguous General Design Criteria of 1971. A tightening of the safety requirements did come about, though, on an informal basis. As the A.E.C. staff reviewed individual nuclear plants, it would negotiate the resolution of difficult safety issues with the owners. Various "gentlemen's agreements" were made, and A.E.C. staff "positions" gradually emerged on how certain safety questions should be handled. The staff's preferences took on the force of regulations. In 1970, the staff began to publish occasional "Regulatory Guides" that clarified the position it would take in licensing further plants. The "Reg Guides," as they were called, were not regulations, per se, since their advice to the designers was nonbinding, but they tended to become de facto rules. They were not always very specific, however, for the "golden words" they contained were sometimes pious platitudes rather than clear technical instructions, according to Hanauer. The "implementation" section of some of them, he said, was "a joke."

In preparing the Reg Guides, the A.E.C. staff fell into the habit of delegating the work of writing needed safety rules to industry committees. Industry representatives, that is, working under the auspices of organizations such as the Institute of Electrical and Electronics Engineers (I.E.E.E.), got together and prepared a "standard" governing a certain aspect of plant design. The Commission staff would then write a Regulatory Guide that adopted the standard, in whole or in part. The guide subsequently became the basis that the staff used for approving plant designs. Industry committees, in effect, were allowed a major role in writing the rules that the industry would have to follow.

The conflict of interest that this arrangement involves became apparent. The typical industry standard was written to reflect the "state of the art"—that is, current industry practices—rather than the more stringent requirements that might be needed to protect the public safety. The industry standards simply authorized the industry to continue doing what it had been doing and were vague enough to allow plant designers and builders to adopt a variety of practices.

An example of the kind of standard prepared by the industry is one written in 1971 by I.E.E.E. relating to the "environmental qualification" of nuclear-plant electrical equipment. Since some of the electrical equipment in the plant is needed to control the reactor in an emergency, it is very important that such apparatus be able to operate properly in the accident "environment." Electrical equipment near the reactor might be exposed to high temperatures and humidity, and to intense radiation, if the reactor springs a cooling-water leak. This equipment must be able to withstand these adverse conditions. I.E.E.E.-323-71 was the industry's standard for the "environmental qualification" of electrical equipment.

"I cannot find a single redeeming feature in this worthless document," Hanauer wrote, in a note to Jay Forster of General Electric, the head of the I.E.E.E. committee that wrote it. "Far from being what its title suggests, it contains only the most general kind of stuff on how to qualify something—anything. The body of the document is not even specific enough to be related to electrical equipment. Furthermore, the various clauses are so general that it's essentially impossible to determine compliance. For these reasons the referenced document in its present form is . . . without value."

Utility companies proceeded, nevertheless, to cite their compliance with I.E.E.E.-323-71 as proof that their electrical systems were "environmentally qualified." The A.E.C. licensed the plants and allowed them to operate, although Hanauer continued to tell senior agency officials that the ability of electrical systems to work under accident conditions was still a "real safety concern" that was "important and not well in hand."

THE COMPLEX SAFETY PROBLEMS that developed during the nuclear-plant construction boom of the sixties did not prove to be an impediment to the issuance of operating licenses when the plants were completed. With Hanauer's help, an A.E.C. task force expeditiously disposed of the backlog of license applications. Hanauer, the head of the group, prepared the internal A.E.C. memos that summarized its deliberations. He used a standard format for these reports: in the left-hand column of the page he noted the subject and the highlights of the group's discussion, and in the right-hand column he recorded the decisions that were reached. The task force was able—administratively if not technically—to "resolve" all safety issues and approve the licensing of the plants.

The task force's standard practice was to take any question about safety that it found too difficult to answer and to consider how many plants were affected by it. If several plants were, then the matter would no longer be regarded as an issue that had to be decided in individual licensing cases. It would be set aside and put into a new category in which it would be treated as a "generic unresolved issue." The answer to such questions would be sought in the general safety-research programs of the Commission and the industry.

In the meantime, permits to build and operate plants, even though they might suffer from suspected safety flaws, would be issued. Thus, the bigger the problem, the less attention that had to be paid to it in approving individual plants. The task force therefore approved one plant after another by deciding that it did not have *special* safety problems and that—for the time being—the "generic" ones that might affect it could simply be ignored.

According to the Atomic Energy Act, the A.E.C. was supposed to be licensing plants on the basis of a positive finding that it was safe to do so. Using the weaker standard invented by the A.E.C. staff, they would license a plant if they were satisfied that it was not *uniquely* unsafe. The "labeling" of a problem as "generic" was "a convenient way of postponing decision on a difficult question," the presidential commission that investigated the Three Mile Island accident concluded.

Thus, when the task force was informed, in 1971, of a problem with certain components that would be installed on the reactor-cooling system at a proposed plant in Michigan—the Fermi plant, Unit 2—it decided that other plants by the same manufacturer were affected by the same difficulty. The task force wanted to ask the manufacturer for more information about these components but decided, nevertheless, that it would treat the matter "as a continuing problem. Will not hold up the C.P. [construction permit] for this even if the answers are unsatisfactory."

Apprised that one of the basic safety systems in the plant might not be able to shut off the reactor quickly enough in an emergency, the task force simply recorded its "decision" that this was "a generic problem—no further discussion on this case." The A.E.C. staff informed the task force that the motors for important reactor-coolant pumps might fail under certain conditions. This problem was "a complicated thing to analyze," the task force noted. "Should drop it for this plant." There was also a "potential for control rod guide tube collapse," the staff had reported, which could prevent the control rods, which regulate the chain reaction, from going into the reactor in an emergency. "Treat it as a generic problem. Do not hold up Fermi for this," the task force decided.

The technical issues that the task force formally decided to ignore included a number of problems with major safety implications. One of the foremost of these concerned "turbine missiles." Each nuclear plant has an immense turbine generator, the device that all steam-electric power plants use to produce electricity. The steam created as the reactor operates is used to spin the large turbine blades, the way the wind turns a windmill. The turbine, which is almost as long as a football field and weighs hundreds of tons, is housed in a building adjacent to the reactor. The safety problem is that turbines, which spin at some 1,800 revolutions per minute, sometimes explode. The blades of the turbine can fly off or, worse, the giant turbine rotors—the hubs from which the blades emanate—can crack. The fragments of a ruptured turbine rotor, weighing many tons, become high-velocity "missiles" that can go crashing through the plant damaging other equipment.

Turbines have exploded at a number of conventional power plants, causing massive destruction of nearby equipment and structures. There is ample reason to take precautions against the risk of similar accidents at nuclear plants. Designers, however, had overlooked even the elementary precaution of installing the turbines so that the direction of spin was *away* from the reactor. Instead, in most nuclear plants, the turbines were placed parallel to the reactor; the missiles that might result from an explosion would be aimed *at* the reactor. The building around each reactor has thick concrete walls, but they were never designed to withstand massive turbine missiles. Special missile shields to protect reactors and other critical components had not been installed. A shower of turbine missiles, therefore, could conceivably break one or more pipes in the reactor's cooling system and damage the emergency cooling equipment as well. This could set the stage for an uncontrolled meltdown that would be all the worse since the building around the reactor would be punctured by the missiles. Radioactive debris from the molten fuel could promptly escape and be spread over the surrounding area by the wind.

On new plants, of course, there were some steps that could be taken to mitigate the problem. Turbines could be "oriented" properly—installed perpendicular to the reactor—so that the direction of spin was away from it. (This would help to protect against "low trajectory missiles" but not against "high lobs"—chunks of the turbine rotor that were lofted into the air by an explosion and then rained down on the plant.) Missile shields and other features might be installed to provide further protection. But in plants already built, these steps were not feasible. One cannot move a massive turbine around like a piece of furniture. Nor would it be easy to install missile shields without rebuilding the plants, since space and structural support for them had not been provided. "It is likely that erecting such barriers would be very expensive or even virtually impossible," the Commission's structural analysts concluded in an internal report.

"Turbine missiles," Hanauer told the commissioners in 1975, were a "bad example" of the staff's failure to resolve generic safety problems. "We seem not to be able to make up our minds." One thing was clear to the staff, however, and that was the priority attached to the licensing of additional nuclear plants. They would continue to be licensed even though their reactors were known to be unprotected against the "generic" problem of turbine missiles. The "decision" column in the minutes that Hanauer kept of the task-force meetings noted that the turbine-missile problem "should be ignored."

The reassuring assumption that A.E.C. officials made when they deferred difficult safety questions was that subsequent safety research programs would be able to resolve them satisfactorily. "We have licensed many plants in view of, if not contingent upon, safety research to be performed by someone in the future," Hanauer wrote in a note to his colleagues. When construction permits were issued, the builders of plants were asked to make "commitments" to sponsor "appropriate" research to find the solutions to outstanding safety problems. They all promised to do so. They seldom made clear the specific studies or experiments they would perform, the budget they would allocate for this research, or the timetable they would agree to meet. The A.E.C. did not press them for the details.

As the years passed, there was little evident progress in the resolution of generic safety problems. The industry's lack of good faith in performing required safety research was especially obvious in connection with its failure to resolve the emergency-cooling problem that had been amply documented in the middle sixties. The A.E.C. authorized construction on the assumption that research on this critical issue would be completed by the time the plants were ready to operate. Instead, the A.E.C. had a "six-year experience of vendor nonfeasance and malfeasance with respect to E.C.C.S.," Hanauer noted, in 1972.

The E.C.C.S. problem remained on the listing that Hanauer gave to A.E.C. regulatory staff officials, in 1972 and 1973, of "real reactor safety problems" that were "important and not well in hand." A "real improvement in E.C.C.S." for pressurized-water reactors was required, he wrote in a 1973 memo. The E.C.C.S. issue was "about right for reopening," he wrote in 1975. (His series of private memos on the subject are all the more surprising, of course, since he headed the A.E.C. task force that publicly defended the adequacy of the industry's E.C.C.S. designs in the 1972–1973 A.E.C. hearings on the subject.) The A.E.C. could have held up plant operating licenses until it was satisfied that adequate E.C.C.S. equipment had been installed. It did not do so, forfeiting much of its power to make the industry fulfill its safety obligations. The A.E.C. staff, Hanauer noted in one internal report to his colleagues, lacked "the guts to turn down reactors for which inadequate safety research has been performed."

WHILE ASSENTING to the licensing of the plants that had already been built, senior A.E.C. safety analysts proposed major changes in the safety requirements for future ones. They did not want the design flaws of the first generation of large reactors repeated as several hundred more of them were built. (They justified allowing the early plants to operate, despite safety defects, on the grounds that there were only a few plants involved.) Hanauer's views on needed safety improvements were set forth in a number of memos, most notably the ones that he sent to the A.E.C. management on how to correct the "various bad design choices" that General Electric had made on its boiling-water reactors.

The A.E.C. required that every reactor be housed inside a large superstructure called a "containment." Its thick walls were supposed to serve as a leak-tight barrier against the accidental release of radioactive materials from the plant. In the event of a pipe rupture in the reactor's cooling system, steam and hot water from the reactor would be dumped into the containment chamber. Radioactive gases that were released from the reactor were also supposed to remain safely confined there. G.E.'s problem was that its reactors were larger than those of the other manufacturers. (This was so because G.E.'s "boiling-water" reactors were designed to hold a large volume of steam; in its competitors' designs, steam was made not in the reactor but in auxiliary tanks called "steam generators.") Plants with G.E. reactors would therefore need a larger containment building. The extra cost of this would be a major competitive disadvantage for the company.

G.E. engineers found a solution. They designed a scheme in which the hot, high-pressure steam that would escape from a leaky reactor would be diverted into a large *torus*—a doughnut-shaped chamber that would be half filled with water. The cold water in the torus would condense the steam and lower its pressure. With the volume and pressure of the steam reduced, G.E. would have to build only a small containment chamber, and this auxiliary torus, rather than a mammoth strong box around each reactor. G.E. included its "pressure-suppression" containment design in every plant it proposed to build. The A.E.C., without detailed checking, was quick to approve it. G.E. proceeded to build fifty-four plants incorporating this design feature.

In November 1971, Hanauer received a copy of a memo written by Gus Lainas, an A.E.C. safety analyst, that described a possible defect in G.E.'s pressure-suppresion design. In order for this system to work, the steam that was leaking out of the reactor had to go *into* the water in the torus. The plumbing arrangement that made this possible involved a number of valves. Unfortunately, the malfunction of a few of them would permit the steam coming out of the reactor to "bypass" the pool of water. Instead, the high-pressure steam could accumulate in the small containment chamber around the reactor and cause it to rupture, which could set the stage for a large release of radioactive materials from the plant. "G.E. wants us and A.C.R.S. not to mention the problem publicly," Hanauer wrote in a memo that summarized an internal meeting on the issue. "They are afraid of delaying [reactor licensing] hearings in progress."

In the following months, Hanauer looked into the possible problems with G.E. containments, and he noted that a few Westinghouse plants also had a pressure-suppression system. (They used ice, rather than water, to cool the steam that might leak out of the reactor.) Hanauer concluded that the pressure-suppression containments should be banned. "Here's an idea to kick around," he said in a light-hearted note that he sent to senior A.E.C. officials. Attached to the one-line note was a three-page technical report that he had prepared. Its conclusion:

> Recent events have highlighted the safety disadvantages of pressure-suppression containments. While they also have some safety advantages, on balance I believe the disadvantages are preponderant. I recommend that the A.E.C. adopt a policy of dis-

> couraging further use of pressure-suppression containments, and that such designs not be accepted for construction permits filed after a date to be decided (say two years after the policy is adopted).

G.E. plants already in operation would be allowed to remain in operation, and G.E. plants under construction could be completed, all with pressure-suppression containments. But no more would be allowed after that.

In response to Hanauer's memo, Dr. Joseph Hendrie, a senior A.E.C. official, sent a short note on the subject to Dr. John F. O'Leary, the Director of Licensing. Hendrie was in charge of the A.E.C. branch that carried out the official safety review before each plant was licensed. "Steve's idea to ban pressure-suppression containment schemes is an attractive one in some ways," Hendrie wrote. Ordinary large containment buildings, he said, "have the notable advantage of brute simplicity in dealing with a primary blowdown [leak of water from the reactor]." He challenged none of the technical analysis in Hanauer's report, and raised no objections, on any scientific grounds, to the proposed ban on this type of apparatus.

"However," Hendrie continued, "the acceptance of pressure-suppression containment concepts by all elements of the nuclear field, including Regulatory and the A.C.R.S., is firmly embedded in the conventional wisdom. Reversal of this hallowed policy, particularly at this time"—the E.C.C.S. hearings then in progress were proving a major embarrassment to the A.E.C.—"could well be the end of nuclear power. It would throw into question the continued operation of licensed plants, would make unlicensable the G.E. and Westinghouse ice-condenser plants now in review and would generally create more turmoil than I can stand thinking about." Hendrie proposed no corrective actions to deal with the safety problem Hanauer had raised.

Hanauer got no reply to his memo, and the matter was resolved by being ignored. Politically, his recommendation put the A.E.C. in an impossible position, since to adopt it would have been to acknowledge that the A.E.C. had blundered in authorizing fifty-four plants with pressure-suppression containments. No bureaucracy is inclined to make admissions of this scope. The admission, moreover, would have immediately provided grounds for lawsuits aimed at shutting down existing G.E. reactors. If their containments—one of the most important required safety features—were defective, how could the A.E.C. justify allowing them to remain in operation?

Robert Pollard, a former A.E.C. and N.R.C. nuclear-safety engineer, has said that once the regulatory staff approved nuclear equipment of a given type, it found itself "blackmailed" by this fact: to acknowledge defects that had to be corrected in future plants was to admit to a lack of safety at existing ones. Major changes intended to bring about long-term safety improvements, therefore, sharply conflicted with the short-run political and economic interests of the industry and the Commission. Hendrie's refusal to adopt Hanauer's proposed ban on pressure-suppression containments was not a capricious rebuff. It represented the A.E.C. management's balancing of the agency's safety and promotional responsibilities.

Hanauer's memos urging correction of other "bad design choices" by G.E. were similarly brushed aside. Intead of installing a full emergency cooling system on each reactor, G.E. had attempted to cut costs by installing only two sets of emergency cooling pumps. One set was designed to pump a small amount of water into the reactor to make up for small leaks of cooling water. The other set of pumps, which had much greater capacity, was designed to refill the reactor in the event of a large loss of cooling water. The large-capacity pumps, however, worked only when the pressure inside the reactor was low. There were no pumps that could supply a large volume of water at high pressure.

Instead of providing them, G.E. simply installed an extra set of pressure-relief valves on each reactor. If there was a leak of cooling water that could not be controlled by the small, high-pressure pumps, the valves could be opened. They would drain cooling water out of the reactor, and lower the pressure inside, so that the high-capacity pumps could be turned on. In other words, in order to control a modest leak of cooling water, G.E. designers installed valves that would intentionally create a large leak, like that caused by a major pipe rupture. It was as if a doctor decided to induce pneumonia so that somebody's common cold could be cured with antibiotics.

Deliberately worsening an accident in order to control it was preposterous, and there was the further problem, Hanauer noted, that valves, such as the extra ones that G.E. had installed, sometimes malfunctioned. These valves, then, which were supposed to help control loss-of-coolant accidents, could themselves be the *cause* of such accidents if they opened when they shouldn't or stuck open when they were supposed to close. "I know of no present safety-system design that has adequate reliability (assurance of operation) in both directions," Hanauer noted. His advice: "eliminate" these valves and put in the additional emergency cooling pumps that were required. The A.E.C. management's response was: Leave G.E. plants as they are.

A final major worry of Hanauer's about the G.E. plants related to the system installed for shutting them off in an emergency. All nuclear plants are required to have a SCRAM system that quickly inserts control rods into the reactor. They are the emergency brakes that stop the uranium chain reaction. In pressurized-water reactors, the SCRAM system has an elegant simplicity. The control rods are held above the reactor by magnets. In a serious crisis, the power to the magnets is cut off and the control rods automatically drop into the reactor. Even if everything else fails, gravity will always be there, a fact that led designers to consider such a SCRAM system "fail safe." G.E.'s SCRAM features, in contrast, involve exceedingly complex engineering, almost a Rube Goldberg arrangement.

In the G.E. design, the control rods do not fall in from above but have to be driven into the reactor from below. Gravity is obviously no help, and a complicated hydraulic system was designed by G.E. to force the rods up into the reactor. This hydraulic system uses high-pressure water acting on a piston to push the rods into the reactor. The water that drives the piston comes from the reactor itself. To SCRAM the rods, one side of the piston is vented and the water is allowed to escape.

The plumbing system that diverts water from the reactor for this purpose has a number of awkward features. For one thing, the water that is expelled to let the piston move has to go somewhere. An elaborate piping system, and a set of empty tanks, has to be provided to handle this discharge. One problem is that leaky valves can allow the supposedly empty receiving tanks to fill up with water. If this happens, the hydraulic system fails and the rods do not go into the reactor. It is necessary to provide instruments to make sure that the receiving tanks remain empty, and G.E. installed "float switches" for this purpose. Floats, that is, were put into the tanks, and they were supposed to rise up, like a cork, to indicate the presence of water. Instruments would report this to the control room, and engineers could then correct the problem so that the SCRAM system would not be compromised.

Unfortunately, G.E. reported to the A.E.C. in 1974, the floats used in six plants did "not perform as desired." They became waterlogged, and sank. The G.E. design had many other weaknesses.

G.E. responded to criticism of its SCRAM system by citing its estimates that there was less than one chance in a hundred million that it would fail to work. Hanauer dismissed this as "nonsense" and told the A.E.C. management that, in his judgment, G.E. was using "fake probabilities" to justify an obviously unsatisfactory design. He urged the A.E.C. to require G.E. and the other reactor manufacturers to install alternative SCRAM systems to provide more reliable means for rapidly shutting off their reactors. (Even the seemingly foolproof SCRAM system on pressurized-water reactors had problems.) Instead of taking prompt action to require new SCRAM systems, the A.E.C. management decided to put the issue on the back burner. "No further discussion on this case," they concluded in 1971, when the subject was raised in connection with the licensing of the Fermi plant, Unit 2. The problem could be treated as just another "generic" issue that it hoped to resolve in the future.

The rejection of Hanauer's proposals for repairing G.E. designs fitted into a larger pattern. As more plants were reviewed, Hanauer and other experts continued to discover more problems.

They were just doing their job. The A.E.C. management, which was also trying to fulfill its mission, acted decisively to protect the industry from costly additional safety requirements. Problems that could be fixed easily, with little cost to the industry, were ordered fixed. Many others, which were more difficult and more expensive to repair, or which might cause inordinate licensing delays, were deferred or simply ignored.

Senior management officials left little doubt about how they resolved the conflict between the agency's promotional and regulatory responsibilities. The report to N.R.C. by Thomas McTiernan included numerous statements by Commission safety reviewers on how they were thwarted in their work. "If a person mentions a safety problem, management pressures such a person to forget the safety problem," José Calvo, an expert on plant electrical systems, said. Don Lasher, who was also an N.R.C. expert in this field, said that he had been told to keep "hands off" certain issues because of the management's "political decision." Raymond Scholl, another Commission technical reviewer, told the inspector general's office that management officials were "reluctant to raise new safety issues which delay the licensing process." He said that he felt this attitude was "typified by Joseph Hendrie's statement, 'Don't turn over new rocks.' "

WHEN A PROPOSED PLANT WAS REVIEWED, the A.E.C. staff looked at schematic drawings of the plant, speculated about the kind of hypothetical accidents that might occur, and tried to determine whether plant safety equipment would be able to bring them under control. A.E.C. safety analysts functioned, essentially, as armchair critics of plant designers and looked at equipment diagrams, that is, not at actual pieces of machinery. Few of them had any practical experience in nuclear-plant construction or operation, and they seldom paid any attention to the day-to-day problems that can occur with such apparatus.

No matter how well it is designed, equipment will not work as intended unless it is installed, maintained and operated correctly.

A perfect design, neatly detailed on the engineer's blueprints, is not enough to ensure safety. The care and diligence practiced by welders, maintenance crews, quality-control auditors, reactor operators, and many hundreds of others will determine the degree of safety achieved. The A.E.C. did not customarily study or closely regulate these aspects of plant safety. They were mundane details entrusted to the utilities. The companies were supposed to adopt sensible procedures governing plant construction and operation, and plant personnel were expected to follow them meticulously. As it happened, the complexity of the plants, and the utilities' unfamiliarity with quality control, led to endemic shortcomings in many routine chores important to safety. The "fuzzy-gloved mechanics," as the Emerson Consultants described the members of the plant work crews, did not always do what was expected of them.

At Florida Power Corporation's Crystal River plant, for example, the Emerson Consultants' confidential report to the company noted many lapses in the required safety precautions. To begin with, operating personnel lacked detailed knowledge of what equipment had been installed in the plant when it was built. The quality of the records was poor, Emerson's report noted. Many basic technical drawings were missing. Even when the manufacturer's drawings were available, reading them was difficult because Gilbert Associates, the architect-engineering firm employed to supervise overall design of the unit, did not use the same numbering system as the reactor manufacturer, Babcock & Wilcox.

Confusion at the plant on how to maintain key pieces of equipment was compounded by an inadequately trained work force, a high turnover rate on the plant staff, and a morass of procedures. Detailed record keeping was required to show that proper quality control was being practiced, but maintenance supervisors had been overwhelmed by the enormous and ever-increasing administrative and documentation workload, Emerson Consultants found. Consequently, they are doing very little work supervision and doing an inadequate job of maintaining the required documentation. The resulting errors were potentially expensive to Florida Power, the report concluded. Some believe that errors are no more frequent than in a fossil plant; however, in the nuclear environment minor mistakes can have disastrous results, the consultants added.

As more plants went into operation, a stream of reports started coming back to A.E.C. headquarters on the equipment breakdowns and operator errors they were experiencing. "Not a day goes by without one or more mishaps at an operating reactor," Hanauer noted in a 1971 memo. Many of the reported malfunctions were trivial, of course, but others were more serious. A systematic program was needed to analyze the thousands of reports and to separate one from another. None was established. A problem would occasionally receive official attention, but this occurred on a hit-or-miss basis. No office within the agency was responsible for monitoring the reports, evaluating their safety implications, and then overseeing needed corrective actions. The A.E.C. management's priority was licensing more plants, not supervising the safety of existing ones. This bothered Hanauer.

On his own initiative, he began collecting data on the mishaps at the operating plants. He kept himself on distribution lists so that he would get copies of "incident" and "abnormal occurrence" reports that described what had happened. When he came across a significant equipment malfunction or operator error, he put the report on it into a special private file, his "Nugget File." The wide gap between theory and practice in nuclear-plant operation is evident in even a cursory review of the entries in the file.

At an unidentified reactor—names were sometimes deleted from A.E.C. accident records—a modification was being made in the reactor-cooling system. At the beginning of this work a "regulation basketball," wrapped in electrical tape to make it bigger, was inserted into a ten-inch pipe in order to prevent leakage when the line was opened up. In the middle of the work, the basketball suddenly slid through the pipe and fourteen thousand gallons of radioactive water spilled out in the next five minutes, flooding the basement to the point where it nearly caused short circuits in the power supply to emergency recirculation pumps. The A.E.C. admonished the operators that "where the risk of fuel melting and personnel safety are involved, consultation with knowledgeable people should be made prior to questionable operation."

At a boiling-water reactor in Lacrosse, Michigan, samples of water taken from taps in a laboratory sink showed high radiation levels. Additional checking confirmed the presence of radioactivity in one of the plant's drinking-water fountains. Investigation of the problem led to the discovery that a 3,000-gallon radioactive-waste tank had been inadvertently connected to the plant's drinking-water system. "The coupling of a contaminated system with a potable water system is considered poor practice in general," the A.E.C. told plant operators.

At another unidentified reactor a design mistake in the electrical control system was discovered. Under certain circumstances, the control rods would unintentionally go *out* of the reactor when the operators pushed the buttons that supposedly signaled them to go *in.* Of the twenty-one control-rod drive motors at the plant, thirteen were found to have this propensity to work backward. The A.E.C. cautioned designers to be more careful in their evaluation of such equipment.

At the Quad Cities Nuclear Plant, Unit 2, in Cordova, Illinois, an "obstruction" was found that was affecting the flow of cooling water inside the reactor. An investigation revealed that an entire welding outfit—tanks, hoses, welder's gloves, etc.—had been left inside the reactor.

Repeated instances of "sloppy" operating procedures and "poor workmanship" were undermining safety at the operating plants, Hanauer noted as he tried to bring these problems to the attention of senior A.E.C. officials. He frequently came across a reported incident at one plant, he told his colleagues, that appeared to have major safety implications. In such cases, he would staple a copy of such a report to a "buck slip" and send it the officials who should be doing something about it. (Buck slips are the transmittal forms used for moving documents from one office to another.) He often scrawled a puckish comment on the buck slip to try to stimulate corrective action.

One of the most common problems that Hanauer observed involved valve malfunctions. Valves perform many key roles in nuclear plants, which have complex plumbing systems to provide vital cooling water for the hot uranium fuel. Plant safety is therefore dependent on valve reliability, and a valve that stays shut when it should open, or sticks open when it should close, can create a serious problem. Certain key parts of valves were "still failing too often, for the same reasons over and over," he noted in a 1972 buck slip.

On G.E. boiling-water reactors, for example, valves had opened unexpectedly and begun to drain cooling water out of the reactor on at least a dozen occasions. Safety apparatus, such as emergency cooling systems, had been found inoperative in a number of plants because valves were mistakenly closed. At the Indian Point plant in New York, the operators accidentally destroyed emergency cooling pumps during a test—because they turned them on but forgot to open the valves that supplied the pumps with water.

"If only valves could read!" Hanauer wrote in a memo on these problems, then they could follow the instructions and "go when they are told to go." The "operating record with valves," he noted on a further occasion, "is bad." The problem with these devices—thousands of which are used in every nuclear plant—went uncorrected despite his frequent admonitions.

Another widespread problem that Hanauer noted concerned the electrical control systems in nuclear plants. By means of a buck slip, in July 1973 Hanauer tried to bring to the attention of his colleagues a report on a potential defect at the Maine Yankee nuclear plant, in Wiscasset, Maine. Nuclear plants need an electrical system to control the plant during normal operation. They also have to have an electrical system to control the plant in an emergency—that is, to run the plant safety apparatus.

Hanauer noted that designers often cut corners—instead of installing a completely separate electrical system for use in emergencies they mixed the two plant electrical systems together. Normal control and instrument cables, that is, sometimes also performed safety functions. The problem with this was that an accident that destroyed or disabled the normal control system could then also disable the controls for plant safety systems. He thought that such a potential problem could arise at Maine Yankee, but that it also had much broader implications. Hanauer sent a copy of the report on Maine Yankee to the agency's electrical-systems branch. No action was taken. Three years later, at the Zion plant in Illinois, the same kind of electrical-system problem occurred again, evidence of what Hanauer called an "unsafe" Westinghouse design—although the problem, he noted, also affected the reactors of other manufacturers. The deficiency had not been corrected in the intervening years and still has not been. Hanauer has advised the agency repeatedly that this electrical-system problem could "start the ball rolling" on an accident that plant safety devices might be unable to stop.

Among the omens of possible future difficulties that the A.E.C. had not taken seriously enough, according to Hanauer, was an accident that occurred on January 3, 1961, at the A.E.C.'s reactor-testing station in Idaho. At 9:03 P.M., a small prototype reactor known as the SL-1 exploded. Three technicians were working on it, during a late-night maintenance shift. The reactor was shut down when they began their work, and the control rods that curb the chain reaction were fully inserted. In the process of performing maintenance on the central control rod, however, they were required to partially withdraw it—far enough to do the necessary work on it but not so far that the reactor would start to operate.

According to the subsequent A.E.C. investigation, one of the technicians apparently jerked the rod very hard and pulled it too far out of the reactor. The chain reaction suddenly started up. The reactor's power level increased rapidly, the pressure of the cooling water inside it surged, and the reactor exploded. One of the technicians was found on the ceiling of the reactor building, impaled on a control rod. It had been ejected by the force of the explosion. The other two were found on the floor. All died, almost instantaneously, of massive nuclear-radiation injuries. The reactor was completely destroyed. There was no off-site injury, since the reactor was located in a remote Idaho desert.

The A.E.C. attributed the SL-1 accident to human error, worsened by a design defect that allowed the withdrawal of a single control rod to cause such a rapid "power excursion." Reactor designers were told to make sure that control-rod systems were installed in the future so that such an accident could not happen again. This done, the A.E.C. considered the case closed. The episode was a tragic technical lesson about control-rod design, officials explained, but one that could be corrected at other reactors and which therefore did not raise any lingering questions about public safety.

There was, however, an ominous aspect of the SL-1 explosion that Hanauer discussed in an internal A.E.C. memo, dated September 10, 1971, but which the A.E.C. had not disclosed publicly: the SL-1 explosion was probably not an accident. The "accident," Hanauer noted, "is now known to have been initiated on purpose by one of the operators, bent on murder-suicide." A mentally unstable operator, according to the A.E.C.'s private speculations about the incident, had deliberately withdrawn the reactor's central control rod in order to cause a runaway chain reaction. He was overwrought, officials believed, because he thought that his wife was having an affair with one of his fellow operators.

The SL-1 explosion, according to Hanauer, raised "real concerns" about the risk of sabotage at nuclear plants—a malevolent act intended to disperse the contents of the reactor to harm the surrounding population. "I worry a good deal about an 'inside job' by a disgruntled or psychotic utility employee. Some attempts are buried in obscure reports. These employees have the knowledge, the means, and opportunity galore. Add a motive and you concoct trouble," Hanauer wrote in a memo addressed to the A.E.C. official in charge of plant security. "Maybe next time such a guy will contact his nearest friendly Weatherman chapter."

Sabotage attempts have subsequently been reported at a number of nuclear plants, including several attempts that were attributed to plant employees. Hanauer has urged that psychiatric screening be required of reactor operators, before they receive their N.R.C. licenses. He also believes that security steps ought to be taken—to restrict access, for example, to certain parts of the plant. These recommendations have not been carried out. No such screening is attempted, and security at United States nuclear plants, according to a study a few years ago by the Congressional General Accounting Office, remains "at best, inadequate."

A "special management review" of the operating plants, which the A.E.C. undertook in 1973, documented the extent to which the program of "industry self-regulation" had broken down. At *all* the operating plants the "reactor safety committees" that supposedly oversaw compliance with federal regulations were found not to be doing the work expected of them. (They were not bothering to investigate some of the accidents at the plants, for example.) At *all* the plants the owners had failed to prepare comprehensive written instructions so that the reactor operators would know what they had to do to keep the reactor running within safe limits.

At *most* of the plants the companies were failing to do some of the required equipment testing and maintenance. At approximately *one half* of the plants, the companies had violated explicit safety conditions written into their federal operating licenses. At *none* of the plants had the companies "fully implemented" the "quality-assurance program" that the A.E.C. looked upon as the key to safe operation.

IN RESPONDING to the reported safety deficiencies, the A.E.C. had several options. Under the Atomic Energy Act of 1954, it had full legal authority to order needed safety improvements. It also had the power to impose fines on the companies and to "suspend, modify, or revoke" the operating license of any plant that did not meet its safety requirements. It could keep any unit off line until it was satisfied that the problem was corrected. Across-the-board sanctions, however, would have embarrassed the companies, fueled the growing nuclear-safety controversy, and caused the utilities to rethink plans for building additional nuclear plants.

Short of draconian actions, there were still many other possible steps to improve plant safety. The A.E.C. could direct the utilities to install specific new safety features or to make needed changes in procedures. It could send its own inspectors to the plants to ensure strict quality control or require the utilities to hire independent quality-control auditors. Instead of letting the I.E.E.E. or other industry organizations write the key safety standards, the A.E.C. could do the job itself and insist on strict conformity to the rules it established.

None of these basic regulatory reforms was instituted. To begin with, the problems at the operating plants had not resulted in deaths or public injuries. A.E.C. advisers warned that if these problems went uncorrected, this record would not continue, but there was no sense of urgency about correcting problems that had not yet hurt anyone. The A.E.C. management took what John Gofman and Arthur Tamplin, two former A.E.C. scientists, once called the "body-in-the-morgue" approach: only after people were hurt would it attach a high priority to making necessary safety reforms.

Abandoning industry self-regulation, moreover, would have imposed a tremendous burden on the A.E.C. staff. The agency had never recruited a technical staff with the competence to do original engineering work. The small A.E.C. regulatory staff consisted of a few hundred engineers who reviewed the work of industry designers. They sat in a dinghy, as it were, towed along by the industry, and were not prepared to board the flagship and take command. For the A.E.C. to start issuing specific new safety standards, moreover, a great deal of research—especially on the long list of "generic unresolved problems"—would have to be done first. Even if they had wanted to take responsibility for prescribing the necessary cures, A.E.C. engineers had no ready solutions. Like permissive parents who belatedly saw the need to impose discipline on an unruly adolescent, they did not really know what to do.

The A.E.C.'s primary response to reported safety lapses was to exhort the companies to do better in the future. In a case where a reported incident at one plant might also affect others, the A.E.C.—if it happened to appreciate the generic significance of the difficulty—would ask other utilities (a) to check whether their plant used the identical component (the A.E.C. itself having no central records of its own on what equipment was installed in the plants); and (b) to take "appropriate" corrective action.

The reluctance of the A.E.C. to take charge was conveyed at a series of regional seminars for utility executives, in 1973, held by the A.E.C.'s director of regulation, L. Manning Muntzing. He presented the results of the A.E.C.'s survey on quality-assurance deficiencies but announced no major A.E.C. initiative to deal with this problem. Instead, A.E.C. officials at the seminars urged the executives to practice better "housekeeping in your operating power reactors."

General admonitions—which were not backed up by strong A.E.C. enforcement actions—had little impact on the industry. As thousands of reports continued to come into the agency on equipment breakdowns, quality-control lapses, and the like, the A.E.C. staff gradually began to issue more specific demands for safety improvements. More Regulatory Guides were issued. Other "notices," "bulletins," and "circulars" were sent to the plants to warn them of newly discovered problems. As the years went by and the problems continued, the A.E.C. staff began to call for additional reforms. In 1970, three general bulletins prescribing mandatory safety improvements were issued by the staff. By 1974 the number had jumped to sixteen. By the late seventies they were being issued at a rate of several per month.

Although the A.E.C. tried to avoid sweeping new safety requirements that would impose large costs on the industry, even the narrower demands it made began to undermine the economics of nuclear power. In many cases it was not so much brand-new safety requirements that were driving up costs as it was the belated recognition that the plants did not meet the "old" safety requirements, such as the ambiguous "General Design Criteria" developed in the late sixties. The vagueness of these criteria had initially seemed to be an advantage to the industry. It would allow the companies broad discretion in building the plants according to their own best "engineering judgment."

The looseness of the criteria ultimately worked out to the industry's detriment, however. Building plants under very hazy rules subjected the industry to the vagaries of subsequent interpretations and reinterpretations of the requirements by the A.E.C. staff. Midway in the building of a plant, the company might learn that a new A.E.C. staff "position" had been adopted. The builders would have to stop, redesign some component, take out or tear down what they had already installed, and start again.

A 1974 study by the General Accounting Office of one plant—the Sequoyah Nuclear Power Station that the T.V.A. started building in 1968—noted that twenty-three design changes had been required "where a structure or component had to be torn out and rebuilt or added because of required changes." Eleven of these changes had a major impact on construction costs, which the G.A.O. defined as a cost increase of more than two million dollars. One of the major changes involved stemmed from the fact that the plant incorporated a new containment design—a Westinghouse pressure-suppression system—that "had not been tested" when construction began, the office said.

While construction was in progress, design weaknesses were discovered. Subsequent repairs were made to the system in February 1972, but later that year tests showed further design weaknesses. Not until September 1974 was the pressure-suppression system redesigned, and still more testing of it had to be done. (The cost of rebuilding the plant's containment would have been even greater, of course, if Hanauer's recommendation for banning these designs had been adopted.) The Sequoyah plant had been scheduled to be finished in 1973, at a cost of $300 million. It was not completed until almost a decade later, and until $1.7 billion had been spent on it.

Cost escalation of this magnitude proved to be an endemic problem. Nuclear plants that were built during the construction boom of the sixties ended up costing twice as much as originally estimated, on the average, and taking far longer to build than the companies had expected. For newer plants, the cost increases have been even more spectacular. Lacking experience with elaborate quality-control and safety requirements, the utilities were dumbfounded by the complications and costs they involved.

The Pacific Gas and Electric Company, for example, began construction of its Diablo Canyon nuclear plant in 1966. "We did not . . . anticipate the detail in documentation and independent inspection of workmanship which would be required," Donald Brand, the company's vice-president for construction, has explained.

> For instance, simple field changes to avoid physical interference between components (which would be made in a conventional plant in the normal course of work) had to be documented as an interference, referred to the engineer for evaluation, prepared on a drawing, approved, and then released to the field before the change could be made. Furthermore, the conflict had to be tagged, identified, and records maintained during the change process. These change processes took time (days or weeks) and there were thousands of them. In the interim the construction crew must move off of this piece of work, set up on another, and then move back and set up the original piece of work again when the nonconformance was resolved.

In contrast to conventional plants, where electrical cables could be installed with relative ease, the job of laying cables in a nuclear plant involved many extra requirements.

> Installation of wire must be done according to written procedure and must be documented [Brand continued]. Every foot of nuclear safety-related wire purchased is accounted for and its exact location in the plant is recorded. For each circuit we can tell you what kind of wire was used, the names of the installing crew, the reel from which it came, the manufacturing test, and production history. The tension on the wire when it is pulled is recorded and the tensioning device is calibrated on a periodic basis.

Mr. Brand added, with exasperation, that "none of these requirements were in existence when Diablo Canyon was planned."

The plant was not finished until 1975, but by then another problem had been discovered: an earthquake fault some two and a half miles from the plant. (The company had thought the nearest fault to be twenty miles away.) Reanalysis of plant-safety precautions, rebuilding of parts of it, and further licensing proceedings followed. By 1981, when all of this was completed, further problems developed: engineers were found to have used the wrong technical drawings when they were attempting to shore up the plant to provide increased protection against earthquakes. More safety reviews and licensing delays followed. Some fifteen years after construction started, the plant was still not operational. Projected cost of Diablo Canyon: $320 million; actual cost: $2.6 billion.

By the summer of 1974, the cost increases in nuclear plants had begun to force the utilities to make a wholesale reevaluation of their plans for further construction. Two additional factors added to the doubts about the economics of nuclear power. One was the record interest rates that the utilities had to pay for money. They are a major element in nuclear-plant financing, since most plants are built with borrowed funds raised by the issuance of bonds. Moreover, with long construction schedules, the interest charges built up over the duration of the project become one of the dominant elements in the ultimate cost of the plant.

Escalating safety requirements, lengthening construction schedules, and high interest rates would all combine to produce a tenfold increase in the projected cost of nuclear plants. Plants that in the sixties were expected to cost a few hundred million dollars would require billions of dollars by the late seventies and early eighties. Nuclear electric power, which A.E.C. Chairman Lewis Strauss had forecast would become "too cheap to meter," became, instead, an extremely expensive commodity.

The second factor affecting plans for additional nuclear plants was the worry that there would be no market for the expensive power they produced. The Arab oil embargo of October 1973, the quadrupling of oil prices in the following months, and the consequent "energy crisis" greatly altered previous energy-demand forecasts. It appeared to the nuclear industry, at first, that the energy crisis was a godsend. Here was definitive proof, they noted in advertisements, of the need for nuclear power to supplant dependence on "unreliable" Arab oil.*

* They made this argument even though most of the electricity in the United States was generated by coal, not by oil.

One of the side effects of the "energy crisis," however, was a dramatic slowdown in the growth in electric-power demand. For almost seventy years, the use of electric power had grown at a remarkably steady rate of about 7 percent per year—which meant that electric-power consumption doubled every ten years. Falling costs of electric power during much of this period encouraged the continuing growth in demand. The utilities had become accustomed to forecasting future demand simply by assuming that the 7 percent growth would continue. The assumption was patently invalid once prices began to rise sharply. Consumers found it economical to cut back on electric-power usage, and previous trends, such as the building of all-electric homes, were suddenly reversed. Instead of discussing the rapid growth in electric-power demand, analysts began to debate whether there would be any growth at all.

To meet their rising costs, both of construction and of operation, the utilities appealed to state public-utilities commissions for permission to charge higher rates. Given the consumer protests against this, the rate relief they requested was not readily forthcoming. Squeezed for cash, and unable to cut the costs of operating their existing power plants, one of the obvious solutions to the utilities' financial woes was to curtail their construction programs. The soaring costs of nuclear plants, and the doubtful need for many of them given the slowdown in electric-power growth, made them the targets for worried financial officers. A good prime minister, it has been said, has to be a good butcher, an axiom that corporate executives did not need to be reminded of.

To the dismay of the A.E.C. and the reactor manufacturers, the utilities started tearing up plans to build the nuclear plants that they had ordered in the early seventies, delaying work on several already under construction, and rethinking further commitments to nuclear power. In 1974, the Southern California Edison Company canceled its Eastern Desert plant. The Northern States Power Company scrapped plans for the Tyrone-2 plant. Consumers Power, Georgia Power, and Carolina Power and Light also abandoned projects. Others followed suit over the next few years. Only recently accepted by the utilities as the wave of the future, nuclear power suddenly appeared to be a technology whose time had passed.

THE DIFFICULTIES FACING the nuclear program were aptly summarized by a headline in the industry newsletter *Nucleonics Week*—"Nuclear Power in the U.S.: Chaos Reigns Supreme as 1975 Opens." The growing safety controversy, as well as the economic Class 9 accident of the previous year, were making a shambles of the plans for nuclear power expansion. It was clear to many observers that decisive action needed to be taken to "revive the nuclear option."

On January 19, 1975, the U.S. Atomic Energy Commission, which had led the program since its inception, was abolished. The controversy over nuclear power had been growing for several years, and it had become evident to the Nixon and Ford Administrations, and to Congress, that the A.E.C. had to go. The nuclear program would not be able to expand in the long run if the public lacked confidence, as it increasingly did, in the A.E.C.'s safety assurances. The Commission's obvious conflict of interest—as both promoter and regulator of the nuclear industry—could no longer be tolerated.

Even the A.E.C. management privately recognized some of the agency's shortcomings. In an internal memo entitled "Credibility," written in May 1974, Dr. Edwin Triner, the director of the A.E.C.'s Office of Program Analysis, noted that "many of the criticisms being leveled at the A.E.C.'s regulatory program by small but intensely interested and sincere groups of individuals are of such sufficient or potential validity that under the proper circumstances, they could attract a broad base of subscribers. . . . [It] is a prospect that should never be far from our minds." The memo was written at the request of L. Manning Muntzing, the A.E.C.'s director of regulation.

To improve the agency's public image as a "tough regulator" of the nuclear industry, Triner suggested the A.E.C. should simply begin to enforce its basic safety regulations aggressively. "Quite frankly, our performance in this regard is not very distinguished," he explained, referring to the A.E.C.'s reluctance to penalize licensees even when they "systematically or flagrantly abuse the privilege of limited self-regulation." The A.E.C. had to end its "excessive tolerance" of safety infractions, he said, and "impose penalties on the large utilities . . . in a much more vigorous manner than we are doing at present."

The Nixon Administration had an alternative solution to the A.E.C.'s image problem. It did not want expanded safety inspections or the imposition of further controls on the industry. Instead of improving the performance of the federal government in regulating the industry, the Administration's strategy was simply to remove the *appearance* of pro-industry bias that resulted from the A.E.C.'s dual mandate as a promoter and regulator. The Nixon Administration, with A.E.C. support, proposed an "energy reorganization act" in 1973 that would abolish the A.E.C. and replace it with a "new," "independent" agency that was responsible only for nuclear regulation. Public confidence in federal supervision of the industry could then be restored. The new law that the Administration asked for was passed by Congress in November 1974, and the new agency—the U.S. Nuclear Regulatory Commission—came into being the following January.

According to the terms of the reorganization act, the N.R.C. would be something less than a completely new agency. It would actually be nothing more than the regulatory staff of the old A.E.C. camouflaged by a different name. A new set of five commissioners was appointed to head the N.R.C., and there were some new senior management appointees as well. With few exceptions, all the posts were filled by former A.E.C. officials.

The first chairman of the N.R.C. was former A.E.C. Commissioner William Anders, the former astronaut. The other N.R.C. commissioners were Victor Gilinsky, a physicist who had been on the A.E.C. regulatory staff; Edward Mason, an engineer from M.I.T. who had been a member of the A.C.R.S.; Marcus Rowden, former general counsel of the A.E.C.; and Richard Kennedy, who had been a member of Henry Kissinger's National Security Council staff. As one of its first official acts of business, the N.R.C. commissioners adopted, without review or substantive modification, all the safety and licensing regulations of the A.E.C. The N.R.C. had full legal authority to rewrite the basic safety rules governing the nuclear industry. It chose not to do so.

As nuclear safety issues became more complicated, the licensing process grew longer, although the A.E.C. tried to find ways to shorten it. The N.R.C. promptly set out to complete this work and to reform A.E.C. procedures so that nuclear plants would be licensed faster. "Faster is better" had practically become the A.E.C.'s theme song, Edwin Triner wrote in one of his internal memos, although Triner had urged a "healthy skepticism" about such a goal.

The new agency's highest priority was to curtail the safety-review process, and it "rated" its safety reviewers "on speed rather than on the depth of review," Raymond Scholl, of the N.R.C. staff, observed. Instead of affording its experts the time and freedom to investigate new safety problems, N.R.C. adopted a "standard review plan" to keep them focused on a narrow set of preselected issues. (The plan had been under development at the A.E.C. since 1972.)

"N.R.C. exists to license safe plants, and reviewers should be free to ascertain safety issues and resolve them," one safety reviewer, Howard Daniels, told the N.R.C. inspector general in 1976. "A reviewer should not feel that he has to either pull punches one way or the other." His own experience, Daniels added, "has been that this is often done, and that the reviewer is not really free to objectively assess a problem and come up with findings." José Calvo told the inspector general some reviewers kept pressing safety concerns that N.R.C. management did not want to deal with. They would get a "black mark" on their records. He was amazed, Calvo added, "at the fact that reviewers come under attack when they raise a safety issue, even though that is their job. Just as amazing is the fact that, if the reviewer does not raise a safety issue, everyone just accepts it, even though it may mean that the reviewer was not doing his job."

N.R.C. management disregarded all such complaints from the agency staff and was satisfied when optimistic "Safety Evaluation

Reports" for new plants were prepared simply by cutting out and pasting together sections of the reports on previous plants. The "standard review plan" adopted by N.R.C. was the formal version of Joseph Hendrie's private instruction to A.E.C. staff safety reviewers not to look under new rocks. In 1977, the N.R.C.'s inclination to expedite licensing by limiting safety reviews was further enhanced when Hendrie himself was appointed chairman of the agency by President Carter.

Although it chose to ignore it, the N.R.C. received cogent advice on the need to make basic reforms in the regulatory program it had inherited from the A.E.C. Shortly after the N.R.C. was formed, Stephen Hanauer prepared a general report for the new Commission at the request of Commissioner Victor Gilinsky. He asked Hanauer to identify the key safety problems that the commissioners ought to be thinking about. Hanauer wrote a four-page memo entitled "Important Technical Reactor Safety Issues Facing the Commission Now or in the Near Future." It was dated March 13, 1975, and it focused on nine issues, the first and foremost of which was the need to revise the dangerously oversimplified safety regulations that had been developed by the A.E.C.

"Although your mother-in-law and your Congressman will tell you that the safety goal is zero risk, we know that this is unattainable and that some non-zero risk must be accepted in all activities," Hanauer wrote to the Commission. A "realistic" approach for the regulators to take would be to insist that the designers of each nuclear plant provide protection against a broad "spectrum" of possible accidents, he said.

The A.E.C., however, had taken a more limited approach. It required the industry to provide safeguards only against a certain narrow set of hypothetical accidents. "No safeguards" were required against other types of contingencies. The A.E.C. had been quite cavalier about where it drew the line, and it was willing to accept the risk of certain types of accidents, especially when the cost of protecting against them was high. "Serious consideration should be given to modifying the present all-or-nothing approach in the light of reality," he advised.

As an example of the kind of risk that had been arbitrarily dismissed by the A.E.C. Hanauer cited the problem of human errors that could lead to major accidents. "Present designs do not make adequate provision for the limitations of people," he wrote. The A.E.C. had written regulations for the kind of hardware that had to be installed at each plant. It had not issued detailed regulations on how the equipment should be operated. It left that up to the individual utility companies.

Such basic considerations as how the reactor was to be controlled during emergencies—by human operators or by automated equipment—were not covered by any explicit A.E.C. regulation, Hanauer noted. In fact, since there was no requirement mandating that expensive, automated control systems be used, designers opted for less costly control rooms in which the small crew of operators would be responsible for most aspects of crisis management. This put a great burden on the operators—especially since most of them were only high-school graduates with little understanding of the complex phenomena that can take place during major accidents. "Means must be found to improve the performance of the people on whom we depend and to improve the design of equipment so that it is less dependent on human performance," Hanauer advised.

His memo summarized many of the other points that he had made over the years. He noted his concerns about sabotage, turbine missiles, inadequate reactor-siting criteria, and the accumulation of generic unresolved safety problems. He also mentioned the disturbing implications of the reports that kept coming in from the operating plants showing the unreliability of key pieces of safety apparatus. The operating plants, he said, "are one of our chief sources of information" about safety-system reliability, and the reports from them showed too many unpleasant "surprises" about "safety problems we thought were put to bed."

Implementing Hanauer's recommendations would have necessitated sweeping changes in federal nuclear-safety regulations, as well as new costs for the hard-pressed utilities. Abandoning the A.E.C.'s simplified safety-review process, setting new requirements for operator training, ordering the installation of new automated control systems for handling emergencies, and many of the other steps he called for would have greatly complicated the reactor-licensing process. The N.R.C. took no steps to implement Hanauer's recommendations. It was satisfied that there was a "negligible probability" of serious reactor accidents.

The safety of nuclear plants had already been demonstrated, officials said, by the A.E.C.'s Reactor Safety Study and was ensured by the program of "defense in depth" that was followed during plant design and construction. Several "levels" of safety, that is, were required by the N.R.C. so that if one proved inadequate, this single failing would still not lead to major accidents, other forms of protection being available. Thus, although quality control was important and should be practiced at the plants, should a deficiency occur—the installation of a bad section of piping, let us say—this would not be expected to have serious consequences. The "backup" safety devices that were installed, such as the emergency cooling equipment, would handle the mishaps that might occur, such as pipe ruptures.

This safety equipment, moreover, was installed in duplicate, so that even if some of it failed, enough extra equipment would be available to keep the reactor under control. A defect in one of the "levels" of defense would be compensated for by other precautions, that is. In theory, this was exemplary common sense. In practice, however, with all of the malfunctions at nuclear plants, there was some question whether the plants' multiple defenses were anything more than a series of Maginot Lines.

THE N.R.C. COMMISSIONERS did not have to wait long to see Hanauer's warnings vindicated. On March 22, 1975, the week after he submitted his memo on major reactor-safety problems, the worst accident that had yet occurred at an operating nuclear plant took place. "Present designs," indeed, did not make "adequate provisions for the limitations of people," such as the management and staff of the Tennessee Valley Authority's Browns Ferry Nuclear Power Station.

A prototype for the giant atomic-electric power plants of the future, Browns Ferry had been under construction since 1966 near Decatur, Alabama. The plant had three large General Electric boiling-water reactors. Their combined output would supply enough electricity to meet the needs of two million T.V.A. customers. Two of the Browns Ferry reactors were operating at full power when the accident began.

Under the A.E.C. program of industry self-regulation, the management of the plant was responsible for controlling all activities at Browns Ferry that could affect public safety. Workers at the plant were not supposed to be able to walk up to a piece of equipment, randomly turn it on or off, move it around, make modifications to it, et cetera. To prevent mistakes that could disrupt the normal operation of the reactor, plant managers were told to adopt detailed written procedures for all personnel to follow. Among other things, the management was instructed to carefully monitor all "changes, tests, and experiments" that were performed while the reactor was in operation.

On Saturday afternoon, March 22, 1975, electricians were working on a postconstruction modification of the plant's electrical system. The work, which was not closely supervised by plant management, was being performed in the "cable spreading room"—where electrical cables from all over the plant converged—located directly below the control room for Browns Ferry Units 1 and 2. It was densely packed up to the ceiling with cable trays, open metal shelves that supported thousands of heavy black electrical cables. To get to the point where they were working, the crew had to crawl on hands and knees for several feet under the lowest cable trays. Part of their work involved checking for air leaks at a point where a set of cables passed through a wall. (On the other side of the wall was Browns Ferry Unit 1, with its reactor running at full power.)

To detect possible air leaks, workers held a lighted candle next to the cables and watched if the flame flickered. In violation of specific conditions in the plant's federal operating license, no detailed written procedure governing this work had been prepared. Nor had the plant's management bothered to review the hazards involved in the use of an open flame in the presence of combustible materials, which in the preceding days had already caused some small fires.

A twenty-year-old engineering aide, an untrained worker who had been on the job in the cable spreading room only since the day before, was helping an electrician check for air leaks. He happened to have longer arms than the electrician, so shortly after noon, he squeezed himself into the narrow space between the cable trays and the reactor-building wall, stepped into an air duct, and reached up next to a mass of cables with a lighted candle. He found an air leak—and he also set fire to the polyurethane insulation around the cables. He tried to beat out the fire with a flashlight and to smother it with rags. He then tried a CO_2 extinguisher and, when that failed, two dry-chemical extinguishers.

But the fire, sucked along by the air draft, spread along the cables and through the wall into the cable trays in the Unit 1 reactor building. Automatic sprinklers had not been installed, nor had plant personnel received adequate training on how to fight electrical-cable fires. The fire burned uncontrolled for seven and a half hours. It could have been put out quickly, N.R.C. investigators concluded, but the plant manager, against the advice of the fire department, refused to allow water to be sprayed onto the burning cables. He mistakenly believed that water should not be used on electrical-cable fires.

Some sixteen hundred electrical cables, including six hundred and eighteen that related to plant safety systems, were destroyed or badly damaged by the fire. The Unit 2 reactor, in the adjacent building, was safely shut down, but the Unit 1 reactor, with its electrical control cables—the plant's central nervous system—on fire, went perilously out of control. Theoretically, the plant had an ample array of duplicate safety devices to keep the reactor adequately cooled in any emergency. (It needed a copious supply of cooling water so that its hot uranium fuel would not overheat, and melt.)

The fire, however, burned through so many electrical control cables that *all* of the safety equipment installed to provide cooling water to the reactor was rendered inoperative. Browns Ferry "had lost so much control equipment and we didn't understand at the time the mechanism whereby we had lost so much," plant manager Harry Green later commented. "We had lost redundant components that we didn't think you could lose."

Under what Hanauer termed the A.E.C.'s "all-or-nothing approach" to plant safety, there were definite limits to the plant's "defense in depth." It was not required that a plant be protected from accidents that were thought to be extremely unlikely, such as the loss of all of cooling equipment as a result of a fire. Browns Ferry, accordingly, wasn't, and it had no special safety equipment for cooling the reactor in this circumstance. Plant operators had to set up makeshift arrangements to cool the reactor's fuel, and in the critical early phase of the accident were able to provide only a small trickle of water into the reactor to keep it under control. T.V.A. nuclear engineers said privately that a meltdown was avoided "by sheer luck."

Browns Ferry was supposed to have been designed so that cable fires could not have dire safety consequences. The A.E.C. had required duplicate electrical control cables to run the duplicate plant safety systems, to minimize this risk, but there was the danger that a fire could spread and destroy all the cables. The A.E.C., accordingly, had added the further stipulation that the duplicate cables be physically "separated," so that a fire involving one set of cables would not be able to touch the others. The A.E.C. did not take the further step, however, of specifying exactly how much separation was enough. It left this up to the industry.

In 1971, an I.E.E.E. committee headed by John Russ of General Electric—the company that was manufacturing the reactors for Browns Ferry—was established to write a "cable separation" standard. The group was not inclined to impose costly new requirements on the industry. Lester Rogers, the A.E.C.'s Director of Regulatory Standards, complained to the I.E.E.E. committee that it was "watering down" the rules it was writing. "I am seriously disturbed," Rogers explained in a May 1973 letter to Russ, since "there have been several fires which, had they occurred under different circumstances, might have resulted in grave safety problems due to loss of redundant equipment." He was referring to electrical-cable fires that had occurred in 1965, at the Peach Bottom nuclear plant in Pennsylvania; in 1968, at the San Onofre nuclear plant in California; and in 1971, at Indian Point Unit 2, in New York.

The A.E.C. itself, given weak I.E.E.E. standards, could have written the needed cable-separation criteria, but it did not do so. Its approach to fire prevention, like its handling of other reactor-safety difficulties, was to exhort the companies to be careful. It issued bulletins—in 1963, 1967 and 1974, for example—on the dangers of polyurethane fires. It held seminars for the utilities, such as one in 1973 at which Muntzing and other officials urged attention to proper "housekeeping" at the plants. A.E.C. officials told the company representatives at these sessions—which T.V.A. personnel attended—that this included "fire prevention and control."

A.E.C. inspectors informed the Commission that its Dutch Uncle talks with the industry on fire-prevention requirements were not working. In 1969, F. U. Bower, an A.E.C. inspector assigned to its Atlanta, Georgia, regional office, which inspected Browns Ferry a few times a year, sent a memo to his supervisors in which he protested the vagueness in the A.E.C.'s regulations about cable separation. Despite lip service to the need for cable separation, Bower wrote, there was a "complete lack of any governing set of requirements that must be met by the field [cable] installers." He added, "It seems incongruous to require the expenditure of immense sums of money to supply specific safety systems . . . without providing equivalent standards for controlling the [electrical-cable] installation that . . . control[s] . . . these same systems." As a result of inadequate standards, Bower observed, there were "widespread" deficiencies in electrical-cable separation.

As construction of Browns Ferry had proceeded, other inspectors from the A.E.C.'s Atlanta office had noted T.V.A.'s failure to take elementary precautions against electrical-cable fires. "T.V.A. lacked an organized and documented program to assure that installation of critical systems control, power, and sensing cable is consistent with their safety function," a 1970 A.E.C. inspection report on the plant noted. "In the critical areas of separation of redundant circuits," it said, T.V.A.'s efforts appear to be "superficial" or "nonexistent."

On January 19, 1973, while the operating license for Browns Ferry was under review, the A.C.R.S. held a special meeting of its "Ad Hoc Working Group on Fire Protection." A.E.C., A.C.R.S. and T.V.A. officials attended the meeting, as well as nuclear-industry fire-insurance inspectors.

Following a discussion of Browns Ferry's fire-protection "philosophy and practices," D. E. Patterson of the A.E.C. Division of Operational Safety warned that plant designers had failed to take the "special preventive measures" that were needed to protect the plant against the risk of "a catastrophic fire." The probability of such a fire, he said, was "apparently much higher than the probability of other events for which A.E.C./A.C.R.S. requires special preventive measures." Yet obvious precautions—such as the installation of fire barriers to prevent the spread of fire between sets of duplicate cables—had not been taken at Browns Ferry and other plants.

To install fire barriers and to make other needed changes in the plant—such as replacing highly combustible materials (like polyurethane cable insulation) with fire-resistant ones, and improving the general layout of cables—would have meant major expense and delays for Browns Ferry Units 1 and 2, which were then nearing completion. This would have been a setback for T.V.A.'s ambitious construction program, as the authority was quick to point out. "Any delay in a leading unit will cause delays in the following units," Jack Gilleland of T.V.A. told the A.C.R.S. "T.V.A. is attempting to confine any changes to [Browns Ferry] Unit 3 in order to keep Units 1 and 2 on schedule." When visiting A.E.C. safety reviewers criticized the electrical-cable separation at Browns Ferry in December 1972, T.V.A. promised to "better implement the electrical separation requirements" on their next plant, Browns Ferry Unit 3.

On June 26, 1973, the A.E.C. had issued Browns Ferry Unit 1 a license to operate. After licensing, the plant went through several months of preoperational testing. The senior A.E.C. inspector who was reviewing the planned start-up of the reactor, Charles E. Murphy, sent a memo to A.E.C. headquarters, in March 1974, warning about the electrical-cable installation at the plant. "I didn't expect a fast response to this memo," Murphy said in an interview. He did not get any response at all.

A year later, on March 22, 1975, Murphy did receive a telephone call at his home. A T.V.A. official told him that the electrical control cables at Browns Ferry were on fire. Murphy, who was the first N.R.C. official to be notified, turned to his wife and said, "Oh my god!"

THE TELEVISION NETWORKS and the national news media gave extensive coverage to the Browns Ferry accident. It was a major embarrassment to the industry and to the new regulatory agency, which hurriedly began to investigate what had happened.

For a few months, the effort received N.R.C.'s highest priority, but as the headlines faded, the urgency attached to this work diminished. N.R.C. and other federal agencies prefer to work at a slow-paced "bureaucratic shuffle." Officials do not run, that is, when they can walk, and do not rush to do today what they could just as well put off until tomorrow. As other problems arose, the N.R.C. staff quickly became preoccupied with them; the Browns Ferry fire soon came to be treated more as a historical curiosity than as reason to take action to improve the safety of United States nuclear plants.

There were two general ways in which the Browns Ferry accident could be interpreted. In the narrowest sense, it was evidence of the safety problems that can be created by electrical-cable fires. The obvious lesson was to take more aggressive steps to protect against such fires. Looked at more broadly, however, the fire was an indication of much larger safety problems, such as the vulnerability of the plants to common-mode failures and the failure of plant managements to supervise their units properly.

If fire, one type of common-mode failure, could occur, what other potential sources of such accidents had been overlooked? If managers at Browns Ferry were allowing workers to do something as imprudent as using a lighted candle in the presence of highly combustible materials, what other breakdowns in industry self-regulation were taking place? To answer these pertinent, larger questions, N.R.C. would need to undertake a broad review of the way in which nuclear plants were being run.

N.R.C. chose to look at the Browns Ferry accident, and at other reported incidents, very narrowly. It focused almost exclusively on the particular symptoms associated with a given safety difficulty—such as inadequate fire prevention in the cable spreading room—not at what caused them. N.R.C. concluded its investigation of the Browns Ferry fire by asking the owners of other plants to review their fire-protection programs and to develop plans for improving them. (No firm deadlines were set for this work, and all the existing plants, in the meantime, were allowed to remain in operation.) It did not order a general review, or upgrading, of the plant-management practices so that other breakdowns in industry self-regulation might be prevented in the future. Senior N.R.C. officials, following the principle enunciated several years before by Dr. Joseph Hendrie, knew what questions *not* to ask.

A succession of other crises during the next few years made it all the easier for N.R.C. to forget the Browns Ferry fire. Pipe cracks were found in a number of G.E. boiling-water reactors. More deficiencies were found in their pressure-suppression containments. Earthquake faults were belatedly discovered close to some nuclear-plant sites. Mistakes were found in the computer predictions that had been used to analyze earthquake effects on other plants. Cracks in turbine rotors were found, raising the old and still unresolved problem of turbine missiles. New "generic" problems were discovered, such as electrical-system flaws that could disrupt all power supplies to plant safety systems. On top of these particular difficulties, there was the general economic crisis in the industry.

The cancellations of nuclear-plant construction projects that began in the summer of 1974 proved to be more than a temporary setback for the industry. Nuclear-plant construction-cost overruns continued to plague the utilities, and they were refusing to buy any more. With the industry already fighting for economic survival, N.R.C. was reluctant to order needed changes, which might be expensive, to solve the growing number of reactor-safety problems. "There is an apparent management attitude that T.R.s"—N.R.C. technical reviewers—"should not raise new safety issues," Raymond Scholl, of the N.R.C. staff, said in an internal report, in 1976. "[The] nuclear steam suppliers are going broke (only four left) and T.R.s shouldn't kill the industry."

Official inaction on needed safety improvements led to a continuing struggle between senior management officials and the agency's technical staff. In February 1976, Robert Pollard, the N.R.C. official in charge of safety reviews for Indian Point 3 and six other plants, resigned in protest. His views on N.R.C.'s failure to enforce its basic safety regulations were aired on the CBS program 60 *Minutes,* in congressional hearings, and in subsequent lawsuits brought against the agency. Three nuclear engineers from General Electric also resigned that month and criticized the adequacy of N.R.C.'s regulation of the industry.

In September of that year, Ronald Fluegge, another N.R.C. safety expert, resigned and publicly expressed his concern about accidents in which the reactor itself might overpressurize and rupture catastrophically. To end an already trying year, five N.R.C. electrical-system experts testified before Congress in December that the agency was "covering up" safety problems that they believed to be very serious.

The protests from N.R.C. scientists fueled the growing political controversy over nuclear power. Citizens' protests against nuclear power policies led to mass demonstrations, sit-ins, and "occupations"—such as ones at the construction site of the Seabrook plant in New Hampshire in 1976 and 1977, at which more than fourteen hundred people were arrested. Signature-gathering campaigns were also organized that placed antinuclear "initiatives" on the ballots in thirteen states in 1976 and 1977. All but one failed at the polls—the industry campaign expenditures were much larger than those of the opposition—but the mere fact that these large-scale protests had occurred posed grave problems for the planned expansion of the nuclear industry.

While the opposition was not powerful enough to get Congress to adopt a "nuclear moratorium," it gained enough clout to block legislation designed to speed up licensing and to get federal help in nuclear-plant financing, which the industry urgently needed. One legislative battle after another ended in a stalemate.

With the nuclear issue strongly polarized, Congress was unable to play a major role in settling basic policy questions. The highly partisan Joint Committee on Atomic Energy, which had championed the nuclear program and taken the lead on all legislation on the subject, was itself a victim of the controversy. It lost its exclusive jurisdiction over nuclear power in 1974 and was abolished in 1976. A senior Republican member of the committee and longtime nuclear proponent gave a private explanation for the problems that arose with its supervision of the nuclear program. "First, we didn't know what we were doing, didn't understand the technology. Second, we were too close to the industry. Third, we had bad P.R.," he said. The rest of Congress gave the committee broad powers over nuclear development, he added, with the understanding that the program "not get them into trouble. We got them into trouble and we were abolished."

As the nuclear controversy expanded, congressmen generally avoided the issue for fear of offending one side or the other. Occasionally, when a major safety problem arose, one of the seven congressional "oversight" committees or subcommittees that assumed the duties of the Joint Committee would hold a brief hearing. In some cases, the members and the staff probed the issues carefully, prepared detailed follow-up reports, and tried to bring about needed reforms. Congressman Morris Udall's Subcommittee on Energy and the Environment, for example, held extensive hearings on the validity of the Reactor Safety Study. His protests about the misleading manner in which the report's findings were presented to the public forced the N.R.C., in January 1979, to repudiate the results of the study.

In many cases, however, congressional hearings were simply used as an opportunity for members to make headlines. Senator Gary Hart of Colorado, who headed the Senate Subcommittee on Nuclear Regulation from 1976 until 1981, is widely regarded as a "master of the one-day hearing." In March 1979, N.R.C. announced that five plants would have to be shut down because a mistake had been made in analyzing their ability to withstand earthquakes. An aide to Senator Hart promptly started to search for background information on the problem, to determine whether the subcommittee should hold a hearing. He wanted to know, he said, if there were any N.R.C. internal documents on the problem that would be "good enough to get Gary on television."

WITH ONLY AN OCCASIONAL PROD from Congress, N.R.C. was left to its own devices to solve the complex problems besetting nuclear power. During their first few months in office, there was basic agreement among the five commissioners. Except for Victor Gilinsky—who was concerned that the A.E.C.'s encouragement of reactor exports might foster the spread of nuclear weapons around the world—they wanted the new agency to continue the policies established by its predecessor. The only major change they desired was to license plants faster.

The N.R.C.'s takeover from the A.E.C. went smoothly enough, but the calm period of transition was abruptly ended, after less than three months, by the Browns Ferry fire. Its brief honeymoon over, the agency was immediately put on the defensive. More controversy erupted a few months later, when N.R.C. released and endorsed the final version of the Rasmussen report, which the A.E.C. had begun in 1972.* The resignations of N.R.C. safety experts, and the political controversy of the following year, created additional short-term worries that further undermined the Commission's ability to focus in an orderly way on major policy issues.

The controversy over nuclear power, and public attacks on the N.R.C., took a toll on its senior officials. Chairman William Anders, who had been the leading spokesman defending the

* The Commission itself was privately divided on the validity of the report's optimistic estimates of reactor-accident risks, although it did not say so publicly.

agency against charges of a "reactor-safety cover-up," unexpectedly announced his resignation on April 20, 1976. Edward Mason, one of the original five commissioners, resigned later in the year to take a job with Exxon. The chairmanship of the agency changed hands another six times during the next six years.

In 1977, President Carter nominated a new "pro-nuclear" chairman, former A.E.C. management official Joseph Hendrie. He also nominated a like-minded M.I.T. professor of nuclear engineering and industry consultant, Kent Hansen, and, in an effort to balance the Commission, an "environmentalist," Peter Bradford.* Hendrie and Bradford were confirmed by the Senate, and joined the other two original Commission members, Victor Gilinsky and Richard Kennedy, whose terms continued for another few years. Hansen's nomination was blocked by critics of his ties to the industry.

With only four members, who customarily split two against two on most issues, N.R.C. was effectively deadlocked for more than a year. President Carter in 1978 finally appointed a physicist from the Department of Defense, John Ahearne, to be the fifth commissioner and the "swing vote." The spectrum of opinions on the Commission was still so broad that few collective judgments on how to regulate nuclear plants could be formed.

The meetings of the Commission regularly deteriorated into endless sparring sessions, which were not always cordial. No strong consensus on reactor-safety policy could be established. Few reform measures were even brought up for a vote, given the expectation that the Commission would be unable to reach a decision on whatever measures might be proposed.

The decision-making paralysis of the Commission meant that no sweeping changes in federal reactor-safety policies, such as the ones Hanauer had recommended when the agency was formed, could be made. It did not mean, though, that reactor licensing

* The Administration was searching, Bradford was told, for "an environmentalist who was in favor of nuclear power." The White House couldn't find one and decided to settle for a moderate environmentalist who was at least uncommitted on the issue. Bradford had been the Chairman of the Public Utilities Commission in Maine.

would be curtailed. That N.R.C. function ran essentially "on automatic." Following A.E.C. practice, the commissioners devoted themselves to broad policy making—the industry frequently referred to the commission as a "debating society"—and formally delegated all routine functions, such as the issuance of plant construction permits and operating licenses, to the agency's staff. Without waiting for Commission guidance on how to resolve the long list of safety issues, the staff simply proceeded to hand out one nuclear-plant approval after another.

BY THE LATE 1970s some six dozen nuclear plants were in regular if somewhat fitful operation around the country. (Equipment breakdowns kept them out of service much of the time, with the average plant working at less than two-thirds of its capacity.) The four years after the Browns Ferry fire were hardly trouble-free, but the most dramatic safety problems that arose were revealed in laboratory tests rather than by accidents at the operating plants.

In 1977, a pair of major findings were reported by N.R.C. researchers. In one set of experiments, they learned that even when electrical cables, unlike those at Browns Ferry, *met* all N.R.C. fire-protection requirements, they could still be destroyed by fire. The other tests showed that much of the electrical equipment around the reactor was not "environmentally qualified" and might short-circuit during serious accidents.

These findings, however, were less of a concern to N.R.C. than the continuing cost overruns and plant cancellations during the late seventies that were destroying the prospects for nuclear power expansion. There were, of course, many "incidents" and "abnormal occurrences"—three or four thousand "licensee event reports" were submitted to N.R.C. each year—but since none involved major radiation releases, they caused little official concern. N.R.C.'s attitude toward plant safety during this period has been described by the director of its Office of Nuclear Reactor Regulation, Harold Denton, as "complacent."

On Wednesday morning, March 28, 1979, Denton was notified

that senior N.R.C. officials were assembling at the "Incident Response Center," the agency's emergency communications room. He was going out of town and didn't rush over to join them. "I said, 'Ho, hum, I've got a more important meeting to go to,'" Denton recalled. He had to cancel his plans as the full dimensions of the problem—a "General Emergency" at a plant near Harrisburg, Pennsylvania—became known to the agency.

Technicians at Three Mile Island Unit 2, like those who brought about the accident at Browns Ferry, were working on a sensitive part of the plant while its reactor was running, in this case at 97 percent of full power. At 4:00 A.M., in the middle of what Hanauer calls the "graveyard shift," the maintenance crew inadvertently cut off one of the vital supplies of water needed to keep the T.M.I.-2 reactor adequately cooled. There were several safety systems capable of correcting the problem by providing emergency cooling water. Despite the mishap, the reactor should have been swiftly, routinely, automatically, and safely shut down. There were, however, some complications.

Three major difficulties—all of which Hanauer had warned N.R.C. about repeatedly—combined to turn the cooling-system problem at T.M.I.-2 into a near-catastrophe. First, a pressure-relief valve popped open and then stuck open. This caused the cooling water to start to drain out of the reactor. (The valve-reliability problem that Hanauer had noted, in dozens of memos, had never been corrected.)

Second, the control room had no reliable indicator that reported to the operators that the valve was open. It remained open, unbeknownst to them, for more than two hours. (Hanauer had warned in his handbook on control-room instrument design that instrument displays that "keep secrets" from the operators invited trouble.)

Finally, the operators, believing that the reactor was adequately supplied with cooling water, mistakenly shut off the emergency cooling pumps. (Their action was a classic example of the kind of "disastrous" common-mode failure that Hanauer had written about—a single event that can cause an across-the-board safety-system failure.)

The continuing, uncontrolled loss of cooling water caused the fuel in the T.M.I.-2 reactor to overheat spectacularly. It took several days to stabilize the reactor, with more than one hundred thousand people fleeing the surrounding area in the meantime. Later studies by the N.R.C. showed that the reactor, in the critical early phase of the accident, came within thirty to sixty minutes of a meltdown.

T.M.I.-2 experienced one of the worst industrial accidents in history, which also quickly became one of the most thoroughly investigated. A presidential commission, chaired by John Kemeny, the president of Dartmouth College, was established. Congress launched a number of separate investigations. The N.R.C. itself set up task forces, special review groups, and ad hoc committees to look into the event, as did the industry. What happened was reconstructed, second by second, and then analyzed in minute detail from every conceivable viewpoint. The critical early portions of the event were reenacted in a full-scale mock-up of the T.M.I.-2 control room. Investigators traced back through the voluminous records of the companies involved with T.M.I.-2 and probed every major aspect of its design and construction.

N.R.C.'s own licensing and safety-review process was scrutinized with similar care. At the end of all of this, multivolume reports, each the size of a big-city telephone book, summarized the official findings. Errors all the way from installing important instruments on the back side of the control panels—where the operators couldn't see them—up to N.R.C.'s lack of any systematic program for monitoring the safety of operating reactors were catalogued. Extensive recommendations for improving plant safety and N.R.C.'s regulatory program were made. The investigatory committees then disbanded.

Hundreds of reporters converged on the T.M.I.-2 site at the height of the accident. It was the lead story for five days on the television network-news programs. Considerable attention was also focused on the presidential commission hearings on the accident, portions of which were broadcast live. Today, the television cameras and klieg lights turned off, N.R.C.'s follow-up actions to implement the "lessons learned" at T.M.I.-2 attract hardly any attention at all. President Carter appointed a "Nuclear Oversight Committee" to watch over N.R.C.'s overhauling and upgrading of its safety programs, but President Reagan disbanded it. The only officials who closely monitor what N.R.C. is doing are the ones in charge of the agency—with few exceptions, the same senior management personnel who have been in charge of federal nuclear-safety regulations for the past decade.

N.R.C.'s planned program of safety reforms is contained in its "Action Plan Developed as a Result of the T.M.I. Accident," which it adopted in 1980. Before it went out of business, the President's Nuclear Safety Oversight Committee commented, in October 1980, that "For all its virtues, [the plan] represents a somewhat more intensive form of 'business as usual.' " The N.R.C. has a new inspector general, James Cummings, and his office, after an audit of N.R.C.'s "implementation of the Three Mile Island Action Plan," made a similar observation in a June 1981 internal report.

"Immediately following the accident at Three Mile Island and during the development of the Action Plan, N.R.C. put considerable time and effort into identifying changes needed in the regulatory process," the auditors concluded. "No other program within the agency had a higher priority. On the basis of our review, however, we do not believe the same commitment exists within the agency to implement the Action Plan as existed to prepare it. The agency seems to be implementing T.M.I. requirements through the normal business routine."

One problem in implementing the Action Plan—the same problem that has arisen over the years with the "General Design Criteria" and other regulations—is that it is frequently very vague. "Although the Action Plan contains both actions to be taken and schedules for their implementation, it is basically a conceptual document," Cummings and the N.R.C. auditing staff concluded. "It lays out for the industry and the staff the overall direction in which the Commission hopes to go and the timeframes in which it would like to get there. It is not a document which can be looked to for specific criteria on what needs to be done or how to do it." The auditors continued, "Based on the specific work we did and our discussions with officials throughout N.R.R. [the Office of Nuclear Reactor Regulation] we found that no one had a clear understanding of how things were supposed to have worked since the issuance of the Action Plan, how things were supposed to work now, or in the future. . . . In short, there was no system for managing implementation of the Action Plan."

Under different sections of the plan, the utilities were asked to report to the N.R.C. how they proposed to make various necessary safety improvements in their plants. N.R.C. had only an "embryonic system" for reviewing the adequacy of the proposals submitted by the companies, the auditors noted, and it was "not working." According to "Action Item I.A.2.1," for example, each utility was supposed to develop an improved program for training reactor operators—so they would not, like the ones at T.M.I.-2, mistakenly do things such as shutting off the emergency cooling pumps when they should be left running. The auditors found that when companies provided the N.R.C. with copies of their revised operator-training programs the "submittals were merely stacked in a corner," since different branches of N.R.C. "were still exchanging memorandums on who is to be responsible for the review of these programs."

Even some of the most obvious safety improvements suggested by the T.M.I.-2 accident have yet to be implemented. A pressure-relief valve, which stuck open, was responsible for turning an otherwise routine, albeit unscheduled, shutdown into a serious loss-of-coolant accident. There was a long record of previous valve malfunctions in the industry, and valves, of course, affect the performance of hundreds of plant systems. A program to make sure that such critically important components work better in the future is an obvious priority for the N.R.C. and the industry. The contrary appears to be the case, according to a report prepared for the President's Nuclear Oversight Committee in October 1981. "Little has been done to develop measures to minimize functional failure" of valves, it said, more than two and a half years after the accident.

The priority that N.R.C. attaches to various safety improvements required by the action plan is determined by adding up how many "points" it merits. Fewer than half the points in N.R.C.'s 210-point system, however, relate to the "safety significance" of the improvement. Safety considerations are subordinated to such other considerations as the amount of time and money that the industry and the N.R.C. would have to expend. Thus, if correcting a given safety problem will cost less than a million dollars, it gets twenty points; if the cost is greater, it gets no points. If fixing something can be done within a year, it gets thirty points; within three years, ten points; longer than that, no points. If it requires a "small" amount of N.R.C. staff time, it gets twenty points; a lot of staff time means that it gets no points.

Thus, when all the points are added up, inexpensive "quick fixes," rather than major, long-term safety improvements, are the major focus of N.R.C.'s "post-T.M.I." work. In 1973, Hanauer sent a buck slip to his colleagues in which he vented his frustration at the official reluctance to order the industry to make fundamental safety reforms. "Some day we all will wake up," he wrote. The day of enlightenment at the N.R.C. has not yet arrived.

EPILOGUE

FEDERAL PROGRAMS, like babies, are not always the result of careful planning. What the government wants to do and has the power to do, it will generally try to do—law, ethics and common sense frequently notwithstanding. Officials may pause at the outset of an undertaking for a nominal weighing of the pros and cons. This can involve elaborate cost–benefit analyses, hearing records, legal briefs, committee reports, environmental-impact statements, and the like. Still, it will be the enthusiasm of the proponents and their political power, rather than the merits, that will usually prove decisive.

Unlike the careful biological process of natural selection, decision makers do not always look at a broad range of alternatives before making a choice. Nature is the careful shopper; decision makers are often impulse purchasers. Once a major project is begun, moreover, it will grow and create a life of its own—once again, like a baby. If its rationale is disproved or forgotten, if it produces unwanted side effects, or even if it fails utterly, the momentum it achieves—its ineradicable, weedlike vitality—will be enough to sustain the program long past the point at which it should be curtailed or abandoned. Curiously, the more that is at stake the more this appears likely to be the case.

The nuclear power program in the United States, which has risked both public safety and billions of dollars over the last three decades, is an example of a government-sponsored enterprise that obeys the law of inertia. The Atomic Energy Commission was asked by Congress to promote the use of nuclear energy for peaceful purposes. It was a powerful, mission-oriented bureaucracy, and it set out to do its assigned task with single-minded fervor. There had been no debate in Congress about the desirability of a large nuclear power program—its virtues were unquestioned—and there was none within the A.E.C.

The Commission, of course, with its vast scientific resources, was in a much better position than Congress was in to review the potential hazards carefully, but it did not do so. It was not an era of self-doubt in the American technical community, and the A.E.C. had no reservations about its competence to develop a satisfactory nuclear power technology. To think otherwise was to reject the popular state religion, which the United States had all but formally adopted, that promised ever-expanding material progress from the exploitation of advanced technology.

The feasibility, necessity and safety of nuclear power were not propositions that the A.E.C. reviewed by the usual scientific means. They were dogmas promulgated by the agency and readily accepted by the nation's scientific, business and political hierarchy.

"Nuclear power proponents had something similar to a war mentality," Carroll Wilson, the first general manager of the Atomic Energy Commission, has remarked. "There was a whole set of forces moving in one direction with no one saying anything against it. The further it went, with all the commitments, and all the reputations, and all the investments at stake, you got an enormous snowballing of everybody defending the way it is."

Peter Bradford, a member of the N.R.C. from 1977 until 1982, observed that "much of the problem" with nuclear power resulted from "the commitments, pressures, and expectations spawned by the grave overestimates of nuclear needs and possibilities that once emanated from the A.E.C." He continued, "As bureaucratic and institutional prestige became committed—one almost rational step at a time—to stated and perceived national goals that had very little to do with real national interests, truth and other people's money were the first casualties. The truth took a beating in silenced concerns and rigged or suppressed studies."

The A.E.C. and the N.R.C., which was made from it, were able to ignore what they did not wish to believe and were inclined to cover up everything discreditable. "People can foresee the future only when it coincides with their own wishes, and the most grossly obvious facts can be ignored when they are unwelcome," George Orwell wrote. The agencies disregarded the warning signs—the numerous reports of trouble at the operating plants—as well as the advice from Hanauer and other experts who questioned the official safety assurances. Senior management officials had the power of zealots, as Orwell noted, to hug on to "quite manifest delusions."

The problems did not go away, of course, merely because they were ignored and have accumulated, uncorrected, in the plants now operating around the country. In many cases it was difficult to fix them even if anybody wanted to, since many of the most serious problems involve basic design mistakes. Other problems, which could have been corrected—and still could be—remain uncorrected because the cost of fixing them is more than the economically depressed nuclear industry thinks it can afford.

Past A.E.C. and N.R.C. estimates of accident probability—implying that there was more risk of being killed by meteorites than by nuclear accidents—have been withdrawn. (The so-called "Rasmussen Report," which contained these widely disseminated estimates and which N.R.C. enthusiastically endorsed in 1975, was unceremoniously repudiated by the agency in 1979.) No new official estimates on the likelihood of major accidents have been made, but a growing number of informed people have found good cause, especially after Three Mile Island, to think that it is far higher than anyone ever expected.

At Three Mile Island, where meltdown was narrowly avoided, the core was massively damaged. An accident capable of doing this had been previously dismissed as an "incredible event" since its probability was presumed to be less than one in a million per reactor-year. This tenet, which was a central one in federal licensing of nuclear plants, was obviously proved incorrect. "Core damage is credible," a Hanauergram, written a few days after the accident, noted.

What then is the risk to the American public from the six dozen nuclear plants now operating in their midst? Two members of N.R.C.'s Advisory Committee on Reactor Safeguards have recently published a study entitled "Implications for Reactor Safety of the Accident at Three Mile Island Unit 2." In it, David Okrent, of U.C.L.A., and Dade Moeller, of Harvard, present the most worrisome estimates that have ever been given of the likelihood of major nuclear accidents. "It appears to be difficult to demonstrate with a high degree of confidence that the frequency of severe core damage or core melt for reactors in operation or under construction is less than one in a thousand to one in two thousand per [reactor-] year," they concluded.

This is a very high estimate, and it is all the more disturbing since Okrent and Moeller express doubt that the risk could be lowered very much. "There are so many potential paths to a severe core damage or core melt accident that it will be difficult to make the frequency of such an accident significantly smaller, with a high degree of confidence."

What the Okrent-Moeller conclusion means is that with a hundred plants expected to be in operation in the United States during the next ten years, there is at least a 50 percent chance during this decade that one of them will have a meltdown or some other form of major accident. Worldwide, with some three or four hundred plants projected to be in operation in the coming decade, at least one near-meltdown, or worse, should be expected roughly every three years.

The consequences of these accidents will depend on a number of factors—the quantity of radioactive materials released, the atmospheric conditions at the time, local population density, the effectiveness of evacuation, and so forth. In July 1982, the N.R.C. staff made an elaborate series of calculations on the possible effects of major accidents at the Indian Point reactor. They found that under some circumstances only a small number of people who lived adjacent to the site would be harmed. Under other less fortunate "scenarios," many more people would be exposed to dangerous radioactive materials escaping from the reactor. In some of these cases, N.R.C. estimated that tens of thousands of people might be killed and even larger numbers injured. In addition, certain types of accidents could spread so much radioactive debris around the region that many people would have to be "relocated" and kept out of their homes for the next ten years; the contaminated area downwind of the plant could cover as much as 270 square miles. The astonishing economic losses from some of the potential accidents at Indian Point were estimated to run up to one hundred billion dollars or more.

The industry disputes the high probability estimates of the two A.C.R.S. experts, contending that many changes since Three Mile Island have improved plant safety. Given the number of plants in operation, and the high estimate of the accident risk per reactor-year, it will not take long to find out whether Okrent and Moeller or the industry spokesmen are correct. The cost of waiting for this experiment to be completed might be high.

The forecast accident, if it occurs, will very likely mean the prompt end of commercial nuclear power in the United States. It is doubtful that the American public will tolerate an unending series of such accidents which, even if they do not take lives, will result in the continuing trauma of thousands of people having to flee from their homes. Utility companies are also unlikely to want to invest in any more nuclear plants if the odds of having a billion-dollar facility destroyed by accidents are so very high.

There would seem to be some urgency to upgrading the safety of existing plants—and good cause, even, to curtail the operation of some of them, especially those with bad safety records and ones located in heavily populated areas. Unfortunately, some of the plants with the worst histories of safety violations—such as the Indian Point plant near New York City and the Zion plant north of Chicago—are also located at the worst sites. N.R.C. recognizes this fact, and has adopted what it calls its "Z.I.P. Action Plan" aimed at "imposing upgraded requirements in the quality assurance" at Zion and Indian Point. Like many of N.R.C.'s undertakings, "the program has since stalled and its implementation is now in doubt," according to a staff report by the President's Nuclear Oversight Committee last year, before President Reagan abolished the committee.

The continued warnings from government experts, the Three Mile Island accident, soaring construction costs and many other considerations suggest a needed retrenchment from the old goal of a large nuclear program. The utilities, because of the prohibitive building costs, have already turned away from nuclear power. The weight of common sense, however, has been unable to overcome the inertia behind the federal government's commitment to nuclear power.

A pulling back from the expansionist nuclear policies of the fifties and sixties is precisely what the Reagan Administration and N.R.C. are trying to avoid. While many in the general public, in the scientific community and at the electric utilities have lost faith in nuclear power, federal authorities adamantly refuse to moderate the government's long-standing optimism about it. To Glenn Seaborg, in 1964, economic nuclear power, which would make possible an age of abundance, was an "absolute certainty." To many of its proponents, it still is. Nuclear power remains, according to government policy, a key requirement for the country's long-run economic progress.

One can only hope that before the next nuclear accident, the authorities will finally recognize that when one is at the edge of a precipice, the only progressive move is a step backward.

NOTES

part one—High Priests

19
Late one Monday night . . .
Glenn T. Seaborg, *Nuclear Milestones, A Collection of Speeches by G. T. Seaborg* (W. H. Freeman, 1972), p. 6; see also, "Plutonium Revisited," remarks by G. T. Seaborg, Atomic Energy Commission press release S-34-70, October 8, 1970.

19
"It seems probable to me," . . .
Sir Isaac Newton, *Opticks,* quoted in H. A. Boorse and L. Metz, *The World of the Atom,* vol. I (Basic Books, 1955), p. 102.

19
In the early 1930s . . .
Edward Teller and Albert Latter, *Our Nuclear Future* (Criterion, 1958) pp. 58–59.

19
On the basis of theoretical calculations . . .
Ibid., p. 118.

20
"I recall that at first . . ."
Nuclear Milestones, op. cit., p. 6.

20
"It is impossible to describe . . ."
Ibid., p. 118.

20
As he paced the streets of Berkeley, . . .
Ibid., p. 6.

20
Glenn Theodore Seaborg . . .
Ibid., p. 5.

20
He had been born in . . .
Interview with Glenn T. Seaborg.

20
He was intent on . . .
Richard G. Hewlett and Francis Duncan, *A History of the United States Atomic Energy Commission,* vol. II, *Atomic Shield, 1947/1952* (Pennsylvania State University Press, 1969), p. 238.

20
Seaborg received his Ph.D. . . .
Interview with Glenn T. Seaborg.

21
"I read and reread every . . ."
Nuclear Milestones, op cit., p. 5.

21
"Since Ed McMillan and I . . ."
Ibid., p. 7.

21
On February 23, 1941 . . .
Ibid.

22
Burris Cunningham, who worked . . .
Ibid., p. 19.

22
Five weeks later, on March 28, 1941, . . .
"Plutonium Revisited," op. cit., p. 8.

22
shared the 1951 Nobel Prize . . .
Time, November 26, 1951, p. 102.

22
"He had a tremendous sense . . ."
Interview with John W. Gofman.

22
(Seaborg himself has gone . . .)
Glenn T. Seaborg, "Early History of Heavy Isotope Research at Berkeley," Lawrence Berkeley Laboratory, 1976.

23
"Seaborg was the granddaddy . . ."
Interview with Richard G. Hewlett.

23
The future of civilization, . . .
Glenn T. Seaborg and William Corliss, *Man and Atom: Building a New World Through Nuclear Technology* (Dutton, 1971).

23
"Seaborg was never . . ."
Interview with Richard G. Hewlett.

23
(In June 1945, Seaborg . . .)
Newsweek, October 16, 1961, p. 66.

23
According to his prospectus . . .
Man and Atom, op cit.

24
"each nuclear power plant surrounded . . ."
Ibid., p. 119.

24
"Where science fiction goes . . ."
Ibid., p. 232.

24
"My only fear is . . ."
U.S. News & World Report, September 2, 1968, p. 63.

24
"Scientists," according to the scientist-writer . . .
Time, January 2, 1961, p. 48.

24
"Their work shapes . . ."
Ibid.

24
Seaborg and other leaders of this secular religion . . .
Man and Atom, op. cit., p. 128.

25
"countless benefits" . . .
Ibid., p. 64.

25
Alvin Weinberg, the theoretical physicist . . .
Interview with Alvin Weinberg.

25
in travels that took him as . . .
Man and Atom, op. cit., p. 299.

25
No longer doing scientific work himself, . . .
Interview with Richard G. Hewlett.

25
By Seaborg's own description, . . .
"Peaceful Atom Sparks a War," *Life,* September 12, 1969, p. 31.

28
At 3:25 P.M. . . .
Interview with George Weil; see also "The First Pile," *Bulletin of the Atomic Scientists,* December 1962, pp. 19–24.

29
(Glenn Seaborg missed . . .)
Interview with Glenn T. Seaborg.

29
Toward the end of the war . . .
Oliver Townsend, "The Atomic Program in the United States," in *Atoms for Power* (The American Assembly, 1957), p. 46.

29
"The development of . . ."
Ibid.

30
Robert M. Hutchins, Chancellor . . .
Ralph E. Lapp, *The New Force* (Harper & Brothers, 1953), p. 137.

30
David E. Lilienthal, head . . .
David E. Lilienthal, "Science and Man's Fate," *The Nation,* July 13, 1946, p. 41.

30
George Gamow, the physicist and writer, . . .

George Gamow, *Atomic Energy and Human Life* (Macmillan, 1946), p. ix.

30
David Dietz, science editor . . .
David Dietz, *Atomic Energy in the Coming Era* (Dodd Mead, 1945) pp. 12–23.

31
Testimony before Congress . . .
James D. Nuse, *Legislative History of the Atomic Energy Act of 1946* (U.S. Atomic Energy Commission, 1955).

32
The A.E.C. was soon overwhelmed . . .
Hewlett and Duncan, *Atomic Shield,* op. cit., chapter 2.

32
The agency had inherited . . .
Ibid., p. 18.

32
The chairman of the new agency, . . .
Ibid., p. 48.

32
"There was nothing in the cupboard," . . .
Interview with Carroll Wilson.

32
"The power thing was pie in the sky, really," . . .
Ibid.

33
Lilienthal was flabbergasted . . .
Hewlett and Duncan, *Atomic Shield,* op. cit., p. 100.

33
"Had quite a blow today," . . .
David E. Lilienthal, *The Journals of David E. Lilienthal,* vol. 2, *The Atomic Energy Years 1945–1950* (Harper & Row, 1964).

33
Revising this draft a few months . . .
Hewlett and Duncan, *Atomic Shield,* op. cit., p. 116.

33
Physicist Eugene Wigner, . . .
Ibid., pp. 220–21.

33
Enrico Fermi, who had led . . .
Ibid., p. 209.

34
"We despair of progress . . ."
Ibid., p. 197.

34
The Commission had been under attack in Congress . . .
Ibid., chapter 1.

34
Commissioner Lewis L. Strauss . . .
Ibid., p. 100.

35
A.E.C. Commissioner Robert Bacher declared . . .
George T. Mazuzan and Roger R. Trask, *An Outline History of Nuclear Regulation and Licensing 1946–1979* (Historical Office, Office of the Secretary, Nuclear Regulatory Commission, April 1979), p. 10.

35
Chairman Lilienthal, on the other hand, . . .
Lapp, op. cit., p. 142.

35
"As to the military uses of nuclear . . ."
David Lilienthal, "We Must Grasp the Facts About the Atom," *The New York Times Magazine,* May 4, 1947, p. 7.

36
The years passed, Carroll Wilson observed, . . .
Interview with Carroll Wilson.

36
Surveying the reasons for the slow progress . . .
Mazuzan and Trask, op. cit., p. 14.

36
Dr. Kenneth Pitzer, who had been . . .
U.S. News & World Report, May 9, 1952, pp. 56–61.

37
The conventional subs used . . .
Richard G. Hewlett and Francis Duncan, *Nuclear Navy* (University of Chicago Press, 1974), p. 11.

37
In June 1946, with a delegation . . .
Ibid., p. 35.

37
By 1948, the program . . .
Ibid., p. 166.

37
From physicist Alvin Weinberg, . . .
Ibid., p. 56

38
The key to success, . . .
Ibid., p. 136; see also Norman Polmar and Thomas B. Allen, *Rickover: Controversy and Genius* (Simon and Schuster, 1982), p. 138.

38
an idea that Glenn Seaborg, . . .
Hewlett and Duncan, *Atomic Shield,* op. cit., p. 190.

39
The company was eager . . .
Hewlett and Duncan, *Nuclear Navy,* op. cit., p. 98.

39
An unprecedented contract . . .
Ibid., pp. 98–102.

39
According to the contract . . .
Ibid., p. 99.

39
So closely did the A.E.C. and the . . .
Congressional Record, Senate, August 13, 1974, p. 4134.

39
Aggressively, painstakingly . . .
Nuclear Navy, op. cit., pp. 102ff.

39
Within his own office, . . .
Ibid., p. 127.

40
He was not content to know . . .
Ibid., p. 172.

40
When it came to the actual building . . .
Ibid., p. 164.

41
Reacting speedily to the President's call, . . .
Madeleine W. Losee, *Legislative History of the Atomic Energy Act of 1954* (U.S. Atomic Energy Commission, 1955).

41
President Truman had considered . . .
Harry S. Truman, *Memoirs,* vol. 1 (Doubleday, 1955), p. 529.

41
Unleashing "the genius and enterprise . . ."
Lewis Strauss, "My Faith in the Atomic Future," *Reader's Digest,* August 1955, p. 17.

41
"There are about thirty-one references . . ."
Interview with Harold P. Green.

42
"Up to the present time, . . ."
Nucleonics, September 1953, in David Okrent, *On the History of the Evolution of Light Water Reactor Safety in the United States* (School of Engineering and Applied Science, University of California at Los Angeles, 1980), p. 1-61.

42
The "public hazard" . . .
Ibid.

43
In his briefing to committee members . . .
Ibid., p. 1-62.

43
To the contrary, he advised . . .
Ibid.

44
The authors of the Atomic Energy Act . . .
Interview with George T. Mazuzan.

44
Joint Committee Chairman Sterling Cole . . .
"Remarks of Representative Sterling Cole," Joint Committee on Atomic Energy press release, July 30, 1954.

44
[W]e cannot exclude the possibility . . .

Hearings Before the Joint Committee on Atomic Energy on Government Indemnity for Private Licensees and A.E.C. Contractors Against Reactor Hazards, 84th Congress, 2nd session 47 (1956), pp. 114–15, quoted in Harold P. Green, "Nuclear Power: Risk, Liability, and Indemnity," *Michigan Law Review,* January 1973, p. 484.

45
In the "worst case," . . .
"Theoretical Possibilities and Consequences of Major Accidents in Large Nuclear Power Plants," Atomic Energy Commission, 1957, p. viii.

45
"The study must be regarded . . ."
Ibid., p. vii.

46
The amount to be put into it . . .
Hearings Before the Joint Committee . . . , op. cit., p. 123.

46
The Joint Committee was concerned . . .
Interview with Harold P. Green.

46
The Price-Anderson Act was passed . . .
Green, "Nuclear Power: Risk, Liability, Indemnity," op. cit., pp. 486–87.

46
"faith in the atomic future," . . .
Strauss, "My Faith in the Atomic Future," op. cit., p. 17.

46
"to force-feed atomic development" . . .
Clinton P. Anderson, "Atoms for Peace: The Dream, the Reality," *The New York Times Magazine,* August 1, 1965, p. 13.

46
Intended to "open the way . . ."
Atomic Energy Commission press release 589, January 10, 1955.

47
So many possible types . . .
W. E. Hoehn, *The Economics of Nuclear Reactors for Power and Desalting* (The RAND Corporation, November 1957), p. 1.

48
The President lauded the effort . . .
Power Unlimited, from U.S. Atomic Energy Commission film series *The Magic of the Atom,* 1955.

48
Glenn Seaborg noted, . . .
Atomic Energy Commission press release S-18-170, May 25, 1970, p. 5.

49
"the sure hand of science . . ."
Power Unlimited, op. cit.

49
"Many safeguards are provided," . . .
Atomic Power Today: Service with Safety, Seneca Production for Atomic Industrial Forum, Inc., distributed by the Atomic Energy Commission Division of Public Information, 1966.

49
"A discussion of unknowns . . ."
C. Rogers McCullough, "Reactor Safety," *Nucleonics,* September 1957, p. 136.

50
"critical contact with the public," . . .
Lewis Strauss, remarks prepared for delivery at Founders' Day Dinner, National Association of Science Writers, New York City, September 16, 1954, p. 4.

50
"from five to fifteen years," . . .
Ibid., p. 9.

50
"Transmutation of the elements—" . . .
Ibid.

50
Strauss invited the science writers . . .
Ibid., p. 10.

50
Strauss feared that burdensome safety rules . . .
Strauss, "My Faith in the Atomic Future," op. cit., p. 17.

51
"will be killed aborning by unnecessary regulation."
Minutes of Atomic Energy Commission meeting, June 8, 1955.

51
"ridiculously cautious" . . .
U.S. News & World Report, May 9, 1952, p. 57.

51
"The Committee was about as popular— . . ."
Edward Teller and Allen Brown, *The Legacy of Hiroshima* (Greenwood, 1975), p. 102.

51
Given the additional assignment . . .
Minutes of Atomic Energy Commission meeting, April 18, 1955.

52
"basic regulations for the civilian atomic industry" . . .
"A.E.C. Announces Three Basic Regulations for Civilian Atomic Industry," Atomic Energy Commission press release 622, April 12, 1955.

52
"The A.E.C.'s objective . . ."
Ibid.

52
the governing principle behind A.E.C. . . .
Minutes of Atomic Energy Commission meeting, February 23, 1955.

53
A.E.C. regulations were not . . .
Atomic Energy Commission press release 622, op. cit., p. 1.

55
"Our main belief—I guess . . ."
Interview with Alvin Weinberg.

56
"The committee was perturbed," . . .
Memo from C. Rogers McCullough to K. E. Fields, July 29, 1965.

56
After a number of private meetings . . .
Memo from C. Rogers McCullough to K. E. Fields, June 6, 1956.

57
The Supreme Court ruled, . . .
Power Reactor Development Company v. International Union of Electrical, Radio and Machine Workers, AFL-CIO et al., 367 U.S. 396 (1961).

57
"When millions have been invested," . . .
Ibid.

58
"What has happened is . . ."
Howard Margolis, "Atomic Power: Cinderella Is Slipping Back into the Kitchen," *Science,* April 30, 1962, p. 244.

59
"Such competition is indeed formidable," . . .
Frank Pittman, "Nuclear Power Development in the United States," *Science,* May 19, 1961, p. 1566.

59
The atomic power program "has been quite a flop, . . ."
U.S. News & World Report, March 7, 1960, p. 88.

59
Given the widespread disillusionment . . .
Letter from Glenn T. Seaborg to President John F. Kennedy, November 20, 1962, p. 1.

60
Seaborg accepted the assignment . . .
Harold P. Green and Alan Rosenthal, *Government of the Atom* (Atherton, 1963), p. 264.

61
As long as you were talking about the future, . . .
Interview with Carroll Wilson.

61
Chairman Seaborg "was not a forceful, . . ."

Interview with Richard G. Hewlett.

62
His former associate at Berkeley, . . .
Interview with John W. Gofman.

62
The four power reactors . . .
The Nuclear Industry 1973 (U.S. Atomic Energy Commission, WASH-1174-73) p. 4.

63
"Back in '58,". . .
Fortune, September 1966, p. 132.

63
"an absolute certainty."
U.S. News & World Report, August 27, 1962, p. 67.

64
"I was involved very much . . ."
Interview with Alvin Weinberg.

65
"The reactor designer is responsive . . ."
Memo from Theos J. Thompson to Advisory Committee on Reactor Safeguards members, in Okrent, op. cit., pp. 2-114–15.

65
(Consolidated Edison, for example, . . .)
Ibid., p. 2-86A.

66
"The business grew at a phenomenal . . ."
Interview with Alvin Weinberg.

66
The A.E.C. did not impose such controls . . .
U.S. Atomic Energy Commission press release 5-21-71, p. 2.

67
The safety risk associated . . .
The study, never made public, is documented in some 2,100 pages of Atomic Energy Commission internal memos and draft reports.

67
The minutes of the early . . .
Memo from Albert P. Kenneke to Clifford K. Beck, August 24, 1964.

68
"A major reason for reconsidering . . ."
Memo from Albert P. Kenneke to steering committee, February 9, 1965, p. 4.

68
One member of the steering committee, . . .
Memo from Walter D. Claus to Kenneth W. Downes, August 11, 1964, p. 4.

68
"Great care should be exercised in any revision . . ."
Memo from S. Allan Lough to Clifford K. Beck, July 16, 1964.

69
"Dr. Beck asked if the computer . . ."
Minutes of steering committee on revision of WASH-740 at Brookhaven National Laboratory, October 21, 1964.

69
They had found that as many as 45,000 people . . .
Atomic Energy Commission press release, June 25, 1973.

69
According to the update, . . .
Memo from Stanley A. Szawlewicz to U. M. Staebler, Dec. 21, 1964, pp. 4–5.

69
By 1964, however, 1,000-megawatt . . .
Letter from C. Rogers McCullough, senior vice-president, Nuclear Utility Services, Inc., to Albert P. Kenneke, U.S. Atomic Energy Commission, March 9, 1965, p. 1.

69
"The possible size of the area of such a disaster . . ."
Memo from Albert P. Kenneke re minutes of steering committee on revision of WASH-740, January 28, 1965, February 12, 1965, p. 11.

70
The Brookhaven experts said no, . . .

"Draft #2" (re conclusions of post-WASH-740 study of damages resulting from major accident in a large nuclear reactor), January 18, 1965, p. 8.

70
In reexamining the details . . .
Unsigned draft on reexamination of calculations, March 31, 1965, p. 5.

70
Hoping for favorable results, . . .
Ibid., p. 6.

71
According to the minutes of subsequent meetings, . . .
Minutes of October 21, 1964, meeting op. cit., p. 12.

71
One member of the committee, . . .
Ibid., p. 11.

71
The minutes of one meeting included . . .
Ibid.

71
At another meeting, "there was considerable . . ."
Memo from Albert P. Kenneke to Clifford K. Beck, August 24, 1964, pp. 4–5.

72
"The matter of probability was brought up, . . ."
Ibid., pp. 9–10.

72
Nuclear plants, he wrote, in one of his drafts, . . .
Note from Clifford K. Beck to Messrs. Price, Lowenstein, Henderson, Mann, Doan, Western, and McBride attaching "Brookhaven report in its final tentative form," May 7, 1965, p. 14.

72
They did have various . . .
Memo from Clifford K. Beck to Atomic Energy Commission re draft report to Joint Committee on Atomic Energy on the 1965 restudy of WASH-740 ("Theoretical Possibilities and Consequences of Major Accidents in Large Nuclear Power Plants"), May 21, 1965, p. 19.

73
Totally unexpected abnormal . . .
Ibid., pp. 18, 19.

73
Beck concluded that the "most baffling . . ."
Ibid., pp. 8, 9.

73
Beck's various drafts were distributed . . .
Kenneke re minutes of steering committee on revision of WASH-740, op. cit., January 19, 1965, February 9, 1965, p. 19.

73
The attempt to find optimistic . . .
Ibid., p. 18.

73
The members of the steering . . .
Minutes of October 21, 1964, meeting, op. cit., p. 12.

73
According to the minutes of one meeting, . . .
Memo from Stanley A. Szawlewicz to U. M. Staebler on revision of WASH-740, November 27, 1964, p. 2.

73
The release of the results . . .
Memo from Stanley A. Szawlewicz to U. M. Staebler re steering committee meeting on the revision of WASH-740 December 16, 1964, December 21, 1964, pp. 4–5.

74
"As we look at the status . . ."
"Conference on Peaceful Uses of Atomic Energy Opens at Geneva," *Department of State Bulletin,* September 21, 1964, p. 408.

74
A few weeks later, in Vienna, . . .

Glenn T. Seaborg, "Nuclear Energy for the Benefit of Man," *Department of State Bulletin,* October 12, 1964, pp. 519–20.

76
"The only consensus . . ."
Steven Ebbin and Raphael Kasper, *Citizen Group Uses of Scientific and Technical Information in Nuclear Power Cases* (Program of Policy Studies in Science and Technology, Georgetown University, 1973), p. 246.

76
"Seaborg tended to have . . ."
Interview with Richard G. Hewlett.

76
According to the minutes of a January 1965 . . .
Kenneke re minutes of steering committee on revision of WASH-740, op. cit., January 19, 1965, February 9, 1965, p. 21.

76
Stanley Szawlewicz, . . .
Memo from Stanley A. Szawlewicz to U. M. Staebler re discussion with Brookhaven National Laboratory staff on revision of WASH-740, November 13, 1964, p. 1.

77
First, rebutting the study's . . .
Ibid.

77
Second, the public . . .
Ibid.

77
The Oyster Creek reactor, . . .
Memo from Howard G. Hembree re summary of discussions on WASH-740 rewrite, November 24, 1964, December 4, 1964, p. 4.

77
On January 28, 1965, . . .
Memo from Stanley A. Szawlewicz to U. M. Staebler, February 17, 1965.

78
"Considerable discussion . . ."
Ibid., p. 3.

78
Harold Price, the Director of Regulation, . . .
Memo from Harold L. Price "To the Files" on Brookhaven report—request from the American Public Power Association, March 12, 1965, p. 2.

78
On June 4, 1965, Seaborg . . .
Memo from W. B. McCool "To File" on submission of updated Brookhaven report to Joint Committee on Atomic Energy, June 8, 1965, p. 1.

78
Dr. Beck had advised the Commission . . .
Memo from Clifford K. Beck to Atomic Energy Commission on Brookhaven report "Theoretical Possibilities and Consequences of Major Accidents in Large Nuclear Power Plants" (WASH-740), March 17, 1965, p. 3.

79
Chairman Seaborg sent a brief letter, . . .
Letter from Glenn T. Seaborg to the Honorable Chet Holifield, chairman, Joint Committee on Atomic Energy, June 13, 1965.

79
Dr. David Okrent . . .
Kenneke re minutes of steering committee on revision of WASH-740, op cit., December 16, 1964, January 6, 1965, pp. 13, 14.

79
"technical job was essentially . . ."
Atomic Energy Commission chronology of 1964–65 WASH-740 reexamination (undated); see also Albert P. Kenneke memo of January 6, 1965, op. cit., p. 14.

79
(This was noted by Dr. Beck . . .)
Albert Kenneke re minutes of steer-

ing committee on revision of WASH-740, op. cit., January 19, 1965, February 9, 1965, p. 3.

80
In contrast to its public rationale ...
Note from Forrest Western to C. L. Henderson re point paper on WASH-740, August 27, 1969, p. 1.

80
W. B. McCool, the Secretary ...
Memo from W. B. McCool to the commissioners, March 29, 1971, pp. 14–15.

80
("AN ATOMIC BOMB IN THE LAND ...")
Fortune, September 1966, p. 132.

81
Actually, General Electric had once again ...
Philip Spoon, *Technology, Engineering, and Economics* (M.I.T. Press, 1969), p. 50.

81
"There are no secrets," ...
Atomic Power Today, op. cit.

82
He concluded that the next and ...
Glenn T. Seaborg, "Need We Fear Our Nuclear Future?" *Bulletin of the Atomic Scientists,* January 1968, p. 41.

part two—Heretics

85
Rittenhouse was born ...
Interview with Philip L. Rittenhouse.

86
When the research staff ...
Interview with David O. Hobson.

87
In April 1965 ...
Okrent, op. cit., p. 2-101.

87
The members of the A.E.C.'s ...
Ibid., p. 2-112.

88
The A.E.C.'s Director of Regulation, ...
Minutes of Advisory Committee on Reactor Safeguards meeting, August 7–9, 1969.

88
Industry representatives ...
Okrent, op. cit., p. 2-140.

88
When the Dresden, ...
Ibid., p. 2-284.

88
As the larger and more complex plants ...
Ibid., p. 2-285.

88
Dr. David Okrent, ...
Ibid., p. 2-135.

88
Indian Point, he believed, ...
Ibid., p. 2-143.

89
A.E.C. regulatory staff engineers ...
Interview with Robert D. Pollard.

89
the committee exerted "considerable pressure" ...
Memo from Clifford K. Beck "To Files," May 9, 1966, p. 5.

89
A.E.C. officials considered ...
Ibid., p. 2.

89
The minutes of that meeting ...
Minutes of Advisory Committee on Reactor Safeguards meeting, May 1966, p. 2.

89
Okrent, however, ...
Minutes of Advisory Committee on Reactor Safeguards Reactor Design and Operating Criteria Subcommittee, May 4, 1966, p. 2.

90
Theos J. Thompson, a Professor . . .
Thompson, in Okrent, op. cit., p. 2-105.

90
Another potential problem . . .
Okrent, op. cit., p. 4-36.

91
Cooperating with the official desire . . .
Ibid., p. 2-273.

92
The heads of the agency, . . .
Ibid., p. 2-96.

92
If reactors were not safe enough . . .
Ibid., p. 2-335.

92
Price told the A.C.R.S. . . .
Ibid., p. 2-94.

92
On this and numerous other occasions, . . .
Ibid., p. 2-337.

92
Glenn Seaborg, . . .
Interview with Glenn T. Seaborg.

92
Its public report to the Commission— . . .
Letter from David Okrent, chairman, Advisory Committee on Reactor Safeguards, to Glenn T. Seaborg, chairman, Atomic Energy Commission, August 16, 1966.

93
This second letter expressed . . .
Okrent, op. cit., p. 2-260.

93
Seaborg strongly objected to the letter . . .
Minutes of Advisory Committee on Reactor Safeguards meeting, September 8–10, 1966, in Okrent, op. cit., p. 2-267.

93
The A.C.R.S. itself could still . . .
Okrent, op. cit., p. 2-137.

93
Chairman Seaborg repeatedly told . . .
Ibid., p. 2-305.

94
James Ramey, the former staff director . . .
Minutes of Advisory Committee on Reactor Safeguards meeting, January 12–14, 1967, in Okrent, p. 3-115.

94
Complaining that the A.C.R.S. had become . . .
Address at Nuclear Safety Program Information Meeting, Oak Ridge National Laboratory, February 17, 1969, in Okrent, p. 2-412.

94
At one industry meeting . . .
Address at Joint Winter Meeting of American Nuclear Society and Atomic Industrial Forum, in Okrent, p. 2-410.

94
"Extreme care" would have to be taken . . .
Memo from W. K. Ergen to Advisory Committee on Reactor Safety, September 16, 1966.

95
The public report of Ergen's task force, . . .
W. K. Ergen et al., "Report of the Advisory Task Force on Power Reactor Emergency Cooling," Atomic Energy Commission, 1967.

95
The job that had been assigned . . .
Interview with Philip L. Rittenhouse.

96
They told Rittenhouse . . .
Letter from William B. Cottrell to Andrew Pressesky, June 30, 1970.

97
His team at Oak Ridge soon found . . .
William B. Cottrell, "ORNL Nuclear Safety Research and Development Program Annual Report for 1969," ORNL-4511.

97
"O.R.N.L. experiments ... demonstrated ..."
Cottrell to Pressesky, op. cit., p. 3.

98
"It was a demonstration for effect," ...
Interview with Philip L. Rittenhouse.

98
For years, Oak Ridge had published ...
Interview with William B. Cottrell.

98
The industry similarly objected ...
Letter from Philip L. Rittenhouse to J. E. Hench, General Electric Company, October 25, 1971.

98
Milton Shaw bluntly told laboratory officials ...
"In the Matter of Interim Acceptance Criteria for Emergency Core-Cooling Systems for Light-Water-Cooled Nuclear Power Plants," Atomic Energy Commission docket RM 50-1, transcript p. 7292 (hereinafter E.C.C.S. tr. p.).

99
"Water Reactor Safety Program Plan," which ...
"Water Reactor Safety Program Plan," Atomic Energy Commission, WASH-1146, February 1970.

100
According to the more detailed analyses ...
S. E. Jensen, "Oconee 100th Inlet Break Loss-of-Coolant Accident," Aerojet Nuclear Company Interim Report 2.2-1, February 1971.

101
During the winter of 1970–71, ...
Ian Forbes et al., "Nuclear Reactor Safety: An Evaluation of New Evidence," Union of Concerned Scientists, July 1971.

103
The plan was for the task force ...
Memo from Edson G. Case to Harold L. Price et al., March 5, 1971.

104
The Idaho experts concluded ...
George Brockett et al., interim report prepared for U.S. Atomic Energy Commission Division of Regulation, April 2, 1971, p. III 4.4-1.

106
"There are, as you know, a number of problems ...
Idaho Nuclear Corporation interoffice correspondence, J. W. McConnell to J. O. Zane, August 26, 1970, p. 1.

106
"The combination of poor data ..."
Ibid., p. 2.

106
"The 'why' of the situation ..."
Ibid., Roger Griebe to J. O. Zane, September 29, 1970, p. 5.

107
Test ZR-2, they concluded, ...
Ibid., George Brockett to J. O. Zane, May 8, 1970.

108
The joint Rosen-Colmar memo ...
M. Rosen and R. Colmar, "Comments and Recommendations to the Regulatory E.C.C.S. Task Force," June 1, 1971.

108
Seaborg and his colleagues, ...
Okrent, op. cit., p. 6-65.

109
Hanauer briefed the press ...
Edited transcript of press briefing on interim acceptance criteria, Atomic Energy Commission Office of Public Information, June 19, 1971.

109
The authors of the report ...
Notegram from S. E. Jensen to Distribution (undated page inserted in front of Brockett report).

109
(*Several months later, ...*)
E.C.C.S. tr. p. 2451.

109
No one on the Hanauer task force . . .
Interview with Philip L. Rittenhouse.

113
In one A.E.C. internal memo . . .
Memo from Milton Shaw to R. E. Hollingsworth, February 17, 1971.

114
A major internal report . . .
"Water Reactor Safety Augmentation Plan," Division of Reactor Development and Technology, November 1971.

114
"To summarize what follows herein," . . .
Letter from William Cottrell to L. Manning Muntzing, December 6, 1971.

115
Lawyers for the utility companies . . .
George C. Freeman, "The Emerging Role of Rulemaking in the A.E.C. Decisional Process," April 17, 1972, p. 3.

117
The committee's experts on E.C.C.S. privately . . .
Okrent, op. cit., p. 6-91.

118
They did so in order that . . .
Ibid., p. 6-79.

119
The A.E.C. witnesses were given a one-page . . .
"In the Matter of . . . ," op. cit., exhibit 1013.

121
The centerpiece of this supplementary . . .
Aerojet Nuclear Company, "Loss of Coolant/Emergency Core Cooling Augmented Program Plan," August 1971.

123
He had told A.E.C. lawyers privately, . . .
Interview with Philip L. Rittenhouse.

123
At the outset of his testimony, . . .
E.C.C.S. tr. pp. 4714ff.

123
Asked to comment more specifically . . .
Ibid., pp. 4721–57.

124
Pressed to explain the basis . . .
Ibid., pp. 4910–21.

124
"I have decided that the kindest . . ."
Interview with Philip L. Rittenhouse.

125
"Are you having trouble remembering . . ."
E.C.C.S. tr. pp. 5318ff.

126
"A.E.C. EXPERTS SHARE DOUBTS OVER . . ."
The New York Times, March 12, 1972.

127
The following morning he slowly read . . .
E.C.C.S. tr. p. 5344.

127
While the hearing was still in progress . . .
Edward Cowan, "A.E.C. Aide Foresees Some Changes in Safety Criteria for Nuclear Power Reactors," *The New York Times,* July 17, 1972.

128
At a congressional hearing some . . .
House Committee on Appropriations, *Hearings on Second Supplemental Appropriations Bill, Investigation of Atomic Electric Power,* 84th Congress, 2nd session, June 25–July 3, 1956, pp. 174–75.

128
His disclosure was just one more indication . . .
Clinton Anderson, *Outsider in the Senate* (World Publishing, 1970), p. 159.

128
"The recent article in The New York Times . . ."
Letter from Edward J. Bauser to L. Manning Muntzing, July 18, 1972.
129
A decade after the E.C.C.S. . . .
Interview with Philip L. Rittenhouse.
130
"Phil got blackballed," . . .
Interview with Patricia Rittenhouse.

part three–The Bible

134
The Commission's "crabbed interpretation" . . .
Calvert Cliffs Coordinating Committee v. A.E.C., 449 F.2d 1109 (1971).
134
A few weeks later, in a widely publicized . . .
Remarks of James R. Schlesinger at the all-conference banquet of the Atomic Industrial Forum–American Nuclear Society Annual Meeting, October 10, 1971, Atomic Energy Commission press release, 5-21-71.
136
The chance of a catastrophic reactor accident, . . .
Man and Atom, op. cit., p. 81.
136
In the hearings on emergency cooling systems, . . .
Daniel Ford and Henry W. Kendall, *An Assessment of the Emergency Core Cooling Systems Rulemaking Hearings* (Union of Concerned Scientists, 1973), chapter 3.
137
A study had already . . .
Letter from Manson Benedict to James R. Schlesinger, March 17, 1982, p. 1.
137
"Associating technically defensible . . ."
Peter Morris, "Federal Agency Comments on Accident Analysis," U.S. Atomic Energy Commission internal memo, April 1972.
137
Earlier attempts by the A.E.C. . . .
That is, the 1964–65 update of WASH-740.
137
There is one chance in . . .
Walter Gibson, *Poker's the Name of the Game* (Harper & Row, 1974), p. 8.
138
"Do we dare undertake such a study . . ."
Stephen H. Hanauer, "Notes on M.I.T. Study Proposal," March 22, 1972.
139
Accordingly, Schlesinger asked . . .
Letter from Benedict to Schlesinger, op. cit., p. 1.
139
Benedict referred to Rasmussen . . .
Ibid.
139
Like Benedict, Rasmussen has had . . .
"Norman C. Rasmussen, Resume" (received from Dr. Rasmussen's office, 1977).
140
"If I'd had a good chemistry teacher, . . .
Interview with Norman C. Rasmussen.
140
Rasmussen, in fact, had never . . .
Rasmussen résumé, op. cit.

140
"At the time, . . .
Norman C. Rasmussen, "Nuclear Reactor Risk Analysis—Some Thoughts and Observations," April 27, 1978 (paper presented in Sweden).

140
His limited involvement . . .
Rasmussen résumé, op. cit.

141
They told the A.E.C. . . .
Letter from Norman C. Rasmussen and Manson Benedict to Stephen H. Hanauer, March 17, 1972 (with copies to James R. Schlesinger and I. [sic] Manning Muntzing).

142
Jerome Saltzman of the A.E.C. staff . . .
Memo from Jerome Saltzman to Lyall Johnson, April 11, 1972.

143
The subtle work of developing . . .
Morris, op. cit.

143
Rasmussen and Benedict concluded, . . .
Rasmussen and Benedict to Hanauer, op. cit., p. 2.

145
Despite their extensive fault-tree study, . . .
Henry W. Kendall et al., *The Risks of Nuclear Power Reactors: A Review of the N.R.C. Reactor Safety Study* (Union of Concerned Scientists, August 1977), pp. 10–13.

146
Hanauer himself, . . .
Letter from Stephen H. Hanauer to Norman Roberts, July 29, 1971, p. 2.

147
(The A.E.C. had so little specific . . .)
Interview with Robert D. Pollard.

147
At the outset of the study, . . .
Meeting with industry representatives, October 12, 1972.

147
The internal memos written . . .
J. A. Murphy, "Telecon with D. Paddleford 1/16/73"; "Outstanding Questions to 10/10/73 (BWR)."

148
The industry regards them . . .
Memo from J. A. Murphy to Saul Levine, July 24, 1973.

148
Stone & Webster, the designers . . .
Memo from J. A. Murphy to Saul Levine, September 17, 1973.

148
They concluded, in an October 1973 . . .
Malcolm Ernst et al., "Task Force Report: Study of the Reactor Licensing Process," Atomic Energy Commission, October 1973.

150
Quality assurance has been called . . .
Science, July 7, 1972.

151
Chairman Schlesinger had already gently . . .
Schlesinger, op. cit.

151
On October 12, 1973, they held . . .
Memo from Edward Gilbert to Saul Levine, T. Cole, John Bewick, "Q-A/Q-C Portion of Design Adequacy Task; Options and Recommendations," October 23, 1973.

151
Gilbert noted the two "approaches" . . .
Ibid., p. 1.

153
Gilbert himself has subsequently explained . . .
Harold W. Lewis et al., "Risk Assessment Review Group Report to the N.R.C.," September 1978, p. 42.

154
A twelve-member review group . . .
Letter from Harold Etherington to Norman C. Rasmussen, June 1974.

154
According to the letter . . .
Ibid.

154
"There are many ways . . ."
Daniel Kleitman, undated comments prepared for June 1974 review group.

155
"Common-mode failures can have a . . ."
Stephen H. Hanauer, "Consideration of Common-mode Failure in the Reactor Safety Study," December 26, 1973, p. 1.

155
He was also a member of the June . . .
Stephen H. Hanauer, "Reactor Safety Study and Appendices IV, V, and IX," June 20, 1974.

155
"The discussion of common-mode failures . . ."
R. DeYoung, "Reactor Safety Study and Appendices I, II (vols. 1 & 2), VIII, IX, X," undated.

157
Chairman Ray, as she preferred . . .
Remarks delivered by Dixy Lee Ray at the National Press Club, January 21, 1974, pp. 8–9.

159
"In the interim the Commission . . ."
Weekly Energy Report, August 26, 1974, p. 3.

160
"Campaigners Against Nuclear Power . . ."
The Guardian, August 21, 1974.

161
A few months later, on March 22, 1975, . . .
Daniel Ford et al., "Browns Ferry: The Regulatory Failure," Union of Concerned Scientists, 1976.

162
Hanauer's handwritten record . . .
Stephen H. Hanauer, handwritten note, "Telecon Rasmussen 12/5/74."

162
Even before the objections . . .
Interview with Norman Rasmussen.

163
The American Physical Society, . . .
Harold W. Lewis et al., "Report to the American Physical Society by the Study Group on Light-Water-Reactor Safety," *Reviews of Modern Physics,* vol. 47, suppl. no. 1, summer 1975.

163
"I presented this proposal . . ."
Interview with Frank Von Hippel.

167
"The Rasmussen study was done . . ."
Testimony of William Anders before the Joint Committee on Atomic Energy, February 5, 1975.

167
Moreover, instead of insisting . . .
Subcommittee on Energy and the Environment, Committee on Interior and Insular Affairs, "Observations on the Reactor Safety Study," January 1977, pp. 2–7.

167
Fearing a "standstill" . . .
Ibid., p. 3.

167
Since the study dealt with the key . . .
Edward Halman, "Statement of Findings re N.R.C. Contract in Support of the Reactor Safety Study," Nuclear Regulatory Commission memo, Oct. 3, 1975.

168
"The regulatory staff had . . ."
Memo from Brian Grimes to H. R. Denton, September 3, 1975.

168
N.R.C. Chairman William Anders . . .
Nuclear Regulatory Commission press release, October 30, 1975.

168
Joint Committee Chairman Price, . . .

Subcommittee on Energy and the Environment, op. cit., p. 4.

168
Rasmussen himself, briefing Congress . . .
Frank Von Hippel, "Looking Back on the Rasmussen Report," *Bulletin of the Atomic Scientists,* February 1977, p. 46.

169
The technical appendix on this subject . . .
Kendall et al., op. cit., p. 105.

170
Von Hippel noted that . . .
Von Hippel, "Looking Back . . ." op. cit., p. 44.

171
"I personally believe that . . ."
Frank Von Hippel, "The Emperor's New Clothes—1981," *Physics Today,* July 1981, pp. 36–37.

171
"Many of the calculations . . ."
Lewis et al., "Risk Assessment Review Group . . . ," op. cit.

172
In January 1979, . . .
"N.R.C. Statement on Risk Assessment and the Reactor Safety Study Report (WASH-1400) in Light of the 'Risk Assessment Review Group Report,' " January 18, 1979, p. 3.

172
Hendrie testified that N.R.C. . . .
Oversight Hearings Before the Subcommittee on Energy and the Environment of the Committee on Insular Affairs, 96th Congress, 226 1st session, February 26, 1979, pp. 9–10.

173
"What are we going to do . . ."
Hanauer, "Notes on M.I.T. Study Proposal," op. cit., p. 2.

part four–Loss of Faith

178
"I hired Steve because his father . . ."
Interview with Alvin Weinberg.

181
In 1976, N.R.C.'s inspector general, . . .
Report from Thomas J. McTiernan to Chairman Marcus Rowden et al., July 23, 1976.

181
"Requirements established for licensing . . ."
Ibid., p. 217.

181
Government safety policy, . . .
Ibid., p. 196.

181
"It's not a question of overregulating . . ."
Ibid., p. 235.

182
"We should recall that . . ."
Remarks of Victor Gilinsky, Nuclear Regulatory Commission press release 5-6-81, November 5, 1981.

184
"How paper our tigers are!" . . .
Note from Stephen H. Hanauer to Frank Kreusi and John F. O'Leary, February 6, 1973.

184
Instead of submitting detailed designs, . . .
Memo from Stephen H. Hanauer to Victor Gilinsky et al., March 13, 1975, attachment 2, p. 1.

184
Hanauer noted in a 1972 internal . . .
Memo from Stephen H. Hanauer to Joseph M. Hendrie, August 23, 1972.

185
When asked to justify A.E.C. . . .

Hanauer, "Notes on M.I.T. Study Proposal," op. cit., p. 2.

185
Case explained that "judgment . . ."
Interoffice memo, Joint Committee on Atomic Energy, from Seymour Shwiller to E. J. Bauser, July 8, 1969.

186
They were not always very specific, . . .
Memo from Stephen H. Hanauer to Edson G. Case, March 28, 1972.

186
The "implementation" section . . .
Memo from Stephen H. Hanauer to Guy Arlotto, September 29, 1975.

187
"I cannot find a single redeeming feature . . ."
Letter from Stephen H. Hanauer to Jay Forster, July 21, 1971.

187
The A.E.C. licensed the plants . . .
Note from Stephen H. Hanauer to E. J. Bloch, January 15, 1973; note from Stephen H. Hanauer to Edson G. Case, January 12, 1973.

188
The task force wanted . . .
"Task Force Review, Fermi 2 C.P., " January 27, 1971, p. 1.

188
Apprised that one of the basic . . .
Ibid., p. 2.

189
The A.E.C. staff informed . . .
Ibid., p. 1.

189
There was also a "potential . . ."
Ibid.

190
"It is likely that erecting . . ."
Memo from L. C. Shao to D. Eisenhut, October 1, 1976.

190
"Turbine missiles," Hanauer told . . .
Memo from Hanauer to Gilinsky et al., op. cit., attachment 2, p. 1.

190
The "decision" column . . .
"Task Force . . . Fermi," op. cit., p. 1.

191
"We have licensed many . . ."
Note from Stephen H. Hanauer to J. A. Norberg, March 8, 1973.

191
Instead, the A.E.C. had . . .
Note from Stephen H. Hanauer to Joseph M. Hendrie, October 18, 1972.

191
The E.C.C.S. problem remained . . .
Note from Stephen H. Hanauer to E. J. Bloch, January 15, 1973; note from Stephen H. Hanauer to Edson G. Case, January 12, 1973.

191
A "real improvement in E.C.C.S." . . .
Memo from Stephen H. Hanauer to John F. O'Leary et al., August 10, 1973.

191
The E.C.C.S. issue was "about . . ."
Memo from Hanauer to Gilinsky, op. cit., attachment 1, p. 3.

191
The A.E.C. staff, Hanauer noted . . .
Note from Stephen H. Hanauer to R. G. Smith and J. A. Norberg, May 23, 1972.

192
Hanauer's views on needed safety . . .
Memo from Stephen H. Hanauer to D. F. Ross, May 7, 1974.

193
"G.E. wants us and A.C.R.S. . . ."
"Task Force Review, Bypass Effects in G.E. Pressure Suppression Containments," Atomic Energy Commission, December 3, 1971, p. 3.

193
"Here's an idea to kick around," . . .
Memo from Stephen H. Hanauer to John F. O'Leary et al., September 20, 1972.

194
"Steve's idea to ban . . ."
Note to John F. O'Leary from Joseph M. Hendrie, September 25, 1972.

195
Robert Pollard, a former A.E.C. . . .
Interview with Robert D. Pollard.

196
"I know of no present safety-system . . ."
Memo from Stephen H. Hanauer to D. F. Ross, May 7, 1974.

196
His advice: "eliminate" . . .
Memo from Stephen H. Hanauer to John F. O'Leary et al., August 10, 1973.

197
Hanauer dismissed this as "nonsense" . . .
Memo from Stephen H. Hanauer to Joseph M. Hendrie, August 29, 1973.

197
"No further discussion on this case," . . .
"Task Force . . . Fermi," op. cit., p. 2.

198
"If a person mentions a safety problem," . . .
McTiernan, op. cit., p. 49.

198
Don Lasher, who was also . . .
Ibid., p. 200.

198
Raymond Scholl, another . . .
Ibid., p. 189.

199
At Florida Power Corporation's Crystal . . .
Emerson Consultants, "Florida Power Company Crystal River #3 Organization Study," 1977.

200
"Not a day goes by without . . ."
Memo from Stephen H. Hanauer to Peter A. Morris, September 13, 1971.

200
At an unidentified reactor— . . .
Robert D. Pollard, editor, *The Nugget File* (Union of Concerned Scientists, 1979), pp. 8–9.

202
Certain key parts of valves . . .
Note from Stephen H. Hanauer to Peter A. Morris et al., June 26, 1972.

202
"If only valves could read!" . . .
Memo from Stephen H. Hanauer to Brian Grimes, April 18, 1973.

203
Hanauer sent a copy . . .
Memo from Stephen H. Hanauer to Tom Ippolito, July 10, 1973.

203
Among the omens of possible . . .
"The SL-1 Accident," *Nuclear Safety*, March 1962.

203
According to the subsequent . . .
"SL-1 Final Report," *Nuclear Safety*, March 1963.

204
The "accident," Hanauer noted, . . .
Memo from Stephen H. Hanauer to C. D. W. Thornton, September 10, 1971.

204
No such screening is attempted, . . .
General Accounting Office, EMD-77-32, April 7, 1977.

205
A "special management review" . . .
Remarks of L. Manning Muntzing, Quality Assurance Conference for Operating Power Reactors, November 26–29, 1973, p. 6.

206
The A.E.C. management took . . .
John W. Gofman and Arthur Tamplin, *Poisoned Power* (Rodale Press, 1971).

207
The reluctance of the A.E.C. . . .
Remarks of L. Manning Muntzing, op. cit., p. 6.

207
Instead, A.E.C. officials . . .
Remarks of W. C. Seidle, Regional Quality Assurance Conference, November 26–29, 1973.

208
A 1974 study by the General . . .
Daniel Ford, "Nuclear Power: Some Basic Economic Issues," Union of Concerned Scientists, April 28, 1975, pp. 15–16.

209
"We did not . . . anticipate . . ."
Donald Brand, testimony before the California Public Utilities Commission, June 6, 1979, pp. 17–18, quoted in Charles Komanoff, *Power Plant Cost Escalation* (Komanoff Energy Associates, 1981), p. 78.

212
In an internal memo entitled . . .
Memo from Edwin G. Triner to L. Manning Muntzing, May 16, 1974, p. 2.

213
"Quite frankly, our performance . . ."
Ibid., p. 3.

214
"Faster is better" . . .
Ibid., p. 6.

214
The new agency's highest priority . . .
McTiernan, op. cit., p. 188.

214
"N.R.C. exists to license safe plants, . . ."
Ibid., p. 222.

214
José Calvo told the inspector general . . .
Ibid., p. 66.

218
Among other things, the management . . .
"Changes, Tests, and Experiments," Atomic Energy Commission regulation 10 C.F.R. 50.59.

219
Browns Ferry "had lost so much . . ."
Hearings Before the Joint Committee on Atomic Energy on the Browns Ferry Fire, 96th Congress, 1st session, September 16, 1975, p. 138.

220
Lester Rogers, the A.E.C.'s Director . . .
Letter from Lester Rogers to John C. Russ, May 31, 1973.

221
A.E.C. officials told the company . . .
Seidle, op. cit.

221
In 1969, F. U. Bower, an A.E.C. . . .
Memo from F. U. Bower to John G. Davis, July 3, 1969.

221
"T.V.A. lacked an organized and documented . . ."
E. M. Howard et al., "Report of Inspection, Browns Ferry Units 1, 2, 3," Atomic Energy Commission, January 19–23, 1970, p. 3.

222
Following a discussion of Browns Ferry's . . .
Summary report, meeting of Ad Hoc Working Group on Fire Protection, Atomic Energy Commission, January 19, 1973, p. 9.

225
"There is an apparent management . . ."
McTiernan, op. cit., p. 189.

229
In one set of experiments, . . .
Memo from R. Feit to L. S. Tong, August 5, 1977.

230
"I said, 'Ho, hum, I've . . .' "
Interview with Harold Denton.

232
Before it went out of business, . . .
Letter from Bruce Babbitt et al. to President Jimmy Carter, September 26, 1980.

232
"Immediately following the accident . . ."

James Cummings, "Report to the Commission: N.R.C.'s Implementation of the Three Mile Island Action Plan," June 1981.

233
"Little has been done to develop . . ."
Report of the Reactor Safety Research Review Group to the President's Nuclear Safety Oversight Committee, September 1981, pp. 1–4.

233
The priority that N.R.C. . . .
"Action Plan Developed as a Result of the T.M.I. Accident," Nuclear Regulatory Commission, table B.1, "Priority Ranking System."

234
"Some day we all will wake up," . . .
Note from Stephen H. Hanauer to Tom Ippolito, July 10, 1973.

236
"Nuclear power proponents . . ."
Interview with Carroll Wilson.

236
Peter Bradford, a member of the N.R.C. . . .
"Testimony Before the Subcommittee on Energy and the Environment of the House Committee on Insular and Interior Affairs, May 22, 1978," Nuclear Regulatory Commission, p. 10.

237
"People can foresee the future . . ."
Sonia Orwell and Ian Argus, eds., *The Collected Essays, Journalism, and Letters of George Orwell,* vol. III (Harcourt Brace Jovanovich, 1968), p. 297.

238
"Core damage is credible," . . .
Note from Stephen H. Hanauer to Guy Arlotto, et al., April 6, 1979.

238
Two members of N.R.C.'s Advisory Committee . . .
Annual Review of Energy, 1981, pp. 43–88.

239
N.R.C. recognizes this fact, and has . . .
Memo to N.R.C. assessment file from Steven Blush, August 17, 1981.

INDEX

ABOUT THE AUTHOR

DANIEL FORD is an economist and writer specializing in nuclear-policy questions. A graduate of Harvard College, and former executive director of the Union of Concerned Scientists, he has worked on a variety of studies related to nuclear-power-plant safety. His most recent work is *Three Mile Island: Thirty Minutes to Meltdown* (Penguin, 1982). He is also the co-author of six technical volumes on nuclear power and national energy policy, including *Energy Strategies* (with Henry Kendall and Steven Nadis), which was named one of the best energy books of 1980 by *Library Journal.* Mr. Ford also writes for *The New Yorker.* He lives in Cambridge, Massachusetts.